"This unique and useful collectio
logians from across the world, ar
ence in South Africa. The theme o. ....
them, building on and enriching recent insights from what has been
termed *missional hermeneutics and theology*. The authors commend
this comprehensive missional impulse while bringing it into conversation with the riches of Reformed theology. Yet they demonstrate
that Reformed distinctives are no addendum. Their Potchefstroom
Missions Declaration begins with the bold statement, "The Reformed
faith is missional, or it is not Reformed." This collection does more
than enlarge on the missional component of core theological themes.
The authors also make application to the heart of those engaged
in missions, to the outward-focused identity that the church must
embrace, and to new missional realities in the world."
　　—Rob Edwards, Assistant Professor of Pastoral Theology,
　　Westminster Theological Seminary

"*A Covenantal Vision for Global Mission* is a treasure trove of mature
theological reflections on how Reformed covenantal theology inter-
sects with various aspects of global missions. The renowned scholars
who have written for this significant work should be commended
for their insights and contribution to Reformed missiology for this
generation and generations to come."
　　—Lloyd Kim, Coordinator, Mission to the World, PCA

"This book is the outcome of a missions conference held at the
Potchefstroom campus of North-West University in South Africa in
July 2015. While the contributors are from around the globe, and
their points of view reflect various Reformed traditions, the book
has a cohesiveness: a covenantal vision for the global mission. This
is reflected in the Missions Declaration that was formulated at the
conference's conclusion. For Reformed theology, the covenant is the
source and well of world mission. The *pactum salutis*, the pretemporal,
intra-Trinitarian covenant of redemption, provides the center of gravity for Reformed thinking. It is followed by the covenant of works/
creation, which because of Adam's sin would invite the covenant of

grace, and the other covenants up to the covenantal structure of the Great Commission. If theologians and missiologists are still debating the merits and problems of *missio Dei* theology, Reformed theology with its Christ-centered focus, rooted in the biblical redemptive history of promise and fulfillment, provides an antidote to certain of its dangers. The book is recommended reading for all those who want to familiarize themselves with good biblically based Reformed mission theology."

    —**Hannes Wiher**, Associate Professor of Missiology, Faculté libre de théologie évangélique, Vaux-sur-Seine, Faculté Jean Calvin, Aix-en-Provence, France

A
COVENANTAL
VISION
for
GLOBAL
MISSION

**EDITED BY PAUL WELLS,
PETER A. LILLBACK, AND HENK STOKER**

WSP✤ WESTMINSTER
SEMINARY PRESS

P&R
PUBLISHING
P.O. BOX 817 • PHILLIPSBURG • NEW JERSEY 08865-0817

Italics within Scripture quotations indicate emphasis added.

Printed in the United States of America

Library of Congress Cataloging-in-Publication Data

Names: Wells, Paul Ronald, editor. | Lillback, Peter A., editor. | Stoker, Henk, editor.
Title: A covenantal vision for global mission / edited by Paul Wells, Peter A. Lillback, and Henk Stoker.
Description: Phillipsburg, New Jersey : P&R Publishing, [2020] | Includes bibliographical references and indexes. | Summary: "An international group of scholars from five continents show how Christian missions are grounded in the classic biblical and historic Reformed theological understanding of God's covenantal relationship with mankind"-- Provided by publisher.
Identifiers: LCCN 2019034922 | ISBN 9781629957302 (trade paperback) | ISBN 9781629957319 (epub) | ISBN 9781629957326 (mobi)
Subjects: LCSH: Missions--Theory. | Reformed Church--Missions. | Reformed Church--Doctrines. | Mission of the church.
Classification: LCC BV2063 .C68 2020 | DDC 266--dc23
LC record available at https://lccn.loc.gov/2019034922

To the multitude of Reformed and Presbyterian
missionaries who replied to Christ's call to foreign missions
throughout our history since the Reformation

Contents

Foreword

This book brings together contributors from Africa, Asia, North and South America, and Europe. It is the outcome of a missions conference held at the Potchefstroom Campus of North-West University in South Africa in July 2015, and the majority of the contributions were presented there. It is my privilege, on behalf to the editors, to thank the organizers at Potchefstroom and the Educational Commission of South Africa for making this meeting possible.

We herein seek to celebrate the Christian church's mission concern and the global vision and international scope of the gospel of Christ. Indeed, the church's worldwide missionary task embraces the biblical claim that the good news of Christ's death and resurrection is to be preached for the salvation of mankind. More specifically, these articles reflect the reality that the Reformed tradition has long been an active participant in the proclamation of the gospel of Christ to the four corners of the earth.

The reason for our conference and these studies, however, is not merely to reaffirm the global Reformed mission. We have sought to reemphasize it, but we do so with a specific aim in mind. As Reformed confessional Christians, we assert that the practice of missions must be pursued with a simultaneous commitment to a missional theology that is grounded in the biblical-theological teaching of Scripture. In other words, our Reformed missional practice and our Reformed missional doctrine should be viewed as being inseparably connected. As the apostle Paul admonished the church in Ephesus, "Speak the truth in love" (Eph. 4:15).

Thus, the weighty subject of missions is presented here, not only as a vital practical concern of the church, but also as a theological and academic enterprise that requires deep thought and careful research. It is the conviction of the editors and the contributors to this volume that the union of the task of missions with the theology of the covenant is the best paradigm for developing Christ's global mission. Discussions concerning the mission of the church are too often conducted with insufficient engagement with the great theological truths of the biblical covenants—of redemption, of creation, and of grace.

These articles seek to ground the growing interest in the missional character of Christian outreach in the classic biblical and historic Reformed theological understanding of God's covenantal relationship with mankind. It is our sincere hope that these essays will inspire further reflection on these important concerns of the church, so as to motivate greater practical and theological means for advancing Christian witness throughout the world.

And finally, let me note that in the editing of the papers, we have employed blind peer review as an integral part of the process. Moreover, the writers have made fresh contributions that advance their previous interests in the covenant and global mission. Further, this collection is the culmination of scholarly research, reflecting various academic emphases and differing theological traditions. While the contributors come from around the globe, and their insights and points of view reflect various Reformed traditions, there is a cohesiveness to the message—a biblically based, covenantal vision for the global mission of the Reformed tradition. This coherent vision is reflected in the Missions Declaration that was formulated at the conclusion of the conference in Potchefstroom in 2015 and refined at a meeting in Jakarta the following year.

May our Lord's kingdom mission hereby be advanced. May his missionary mandate be encouraged. And may the growing collaboration of Reformed scholars worldwide continue to expand and deepen on an global scale. *Soli Deo gloria.*

Finally, we express our sincere gratitude to the respective organizations represented by each of the contributors to this book, with special gratitude to North-West University, Westminster Theological

Seminary, and the ministry of the international journal *Unio cum Christo* in conjunction with the Reformed Evangelical Seminary in Jakarta. We also express our gratitude to the World Reformed Fellowship for bringing us together in São Paulo, Brazil, where the writing of this book was first proposed.

Peter A. Lillback
Convener and Editor

A Missions Declaration

1. The Reformed faith is missional, or it is not Reformed. [Isaiah 6:1–7; John 3:16; Romans 1:16–17]
2. Mission has its origin in God's eternal being and plan: it has its content in the good news that God is Lord of creation and its Savior in Christ; it has as its goal the glory of God in his kingly rule. [Psalm 110; Hebrews 2:10–18; Revelation 21:1–8]
3. Mission is good news: the Father is known in the Son, the one mediator, in his person, life, death, and resurrection; the Son sends witnesses as ambassadors with his word; the Spirit applies the truth in newness of life. [Psalm 87; Matthew 28:19–20; 2 Corinthians 5:17–21; Colossians 1:24–29]
4. The Reformed faith announces the renewal of broken covenants: God restores fallen creation, he regenerates sinful people, he renews communities in reconciled life. Mission proclaims and results in God's *shalom*, peace in all spheres of life. [Jeremiah 33:14–26; John 17; Romans 5:12–20; Revelation 21:1–4]
5. Mission is covenantal activity: God reaches out to lost sinners in the universal gospel call; believers are God's elect people united in *koinonia* (fellowship) in Christ and receive the signs of God's covenant; they worship God in spirit and in truth in the *ecclesia* (church) and proclaim redemption in all of life. Their worship is also a witness to the majestic presence of God among them. [Jeremiah 31:31–37; Acts 2:37–41; 1 Peter 2:4–12; 1 John 3:1–3; 1 Corinthians 14:23–25]

Baakwards

6. The church in her mission reaches out to the suffering with the compassion of Christ in faith, love, and hope, assisted by the transforming power of his Spirit. [Psalm 103; Job 29:11–17; Isaiah 53; Matthew 5:16; Mark 6:34; Colossians 3]

7. In her mission, the church heralds the new creation to be revealed at Christ's *parousia* (return), when God's glory and man's freedom will be completely manifested. [Psalm 96; Isaiah 11:1–10; 1 Corinthians 15:20–28; 2 Corinthians 5; Revelation 21:5–8]

8. The Reformed faith always seeks ways of expressing its global mission in the multicultural, multiethnic contexts of the present world in which believers are called to live and witness. [1 Corinthians 1:18–2:5; 9:19–23; Galatians 3:27–29; James 2:1–13; 1 John 2:7–11]

9. The churches of the Reformation from the earliest times have been mindful of their mission, and examples of self-sacrificial witness abound. Nevertheless, they have not always maintained mission as a priority. By failing to heed the call of Christ, they have often fallen into self-satisfaction, indifference to the lost, coldness to the needy of the world, unnecessary love of possessions, and internal conflicts. We pray that the Lord would deliver us from self-centered worldliness and help us to increasingly become all things to all people for the sake of the gospel. [Romans 1:17; 1 Corinthians 9:19–23]

Potchefstroom, July 31, 2015
Jakarta, March 11, 2016

Introduction

This book is an approach to Christian mission from the covenantal perspective of Reformed theology, with contributions coming from five continents. It is the outcome of a conference held on the Potchefstroom Campus of North-West University in South Africa at the end of July 2015. It seeks to lay the foundations for Christian mission from the perspective of the Reformed tradition, considering what missional calling and practice are, and what a global vision for missions in a covenantal context might look like. This context is both biblical and theologically pivotal, for Jesus Christ is the head of God's covenant dealings with creation and human beings.

There is no greater challenge to the Christian church today than the one posed by mission to a shrinking and rapidly changing world, one that is incredibly diverse with its ethnic, religious, cultural, social, and political conflicts, plus the major fracture between poverty and affluence. What is mission, what is its vision and motivation, and how can it be done effectively?

Reformed theology and mission are two subjects that might seem to be strange bedfellows, because they are sometimes wrongly assumed to be incompatible. In this case, however, first taste does not tell, because contrary to received ideas, the structural lines of Reformed theology are missional and press outward in kingdom-oriented action. This thrust is energized by the "in Christ" focus of Reformational thinking: Christ is the key because he is the electing divine actor who is central in history, the incarnate missionary, the visionary sender of the apostolate, and the coming Lord who will roll up the heavens and earth, bringing in the eternal kingdom of reconciliation in a new creation of love, righteous justice, and peace.

If the jury is still out, deliberating on the merits and imbalances of late-twentieth-century *missio Dei* theology, then Reformed theology, with its focus on Christ, rooted in the Bible's redemptive history of promise and fulfillment, the already and the not yet, provides an antidote to certain of its dangers. It is not more active theology or more social strategy that is needed in global missional reflection, but more of Christ and his word, and, with him, more love, more faith, and more hope, with a warmth of heart that he alone gives to those he sends. It is his comforting and consoling presence that is longed for by the church suffering oppression under the cross in many places today, and it is his humility and meekness that are needed to model attitudes in other places, where Christians have become rich, prosperous, and sadly indifferent. So if this book is about Reformed theology and mission, it is always and ever about the coming of Christ's reign into a shadowy, gray world. All the contributions in the three parts of this book point in that one direction: theology, missional calling to action, and global vision.

Mission work itself is a form of mediation. Missionary witnesses stand with the truth, *for* God and *before* men. Put this way, we can see that mission must always be accomplished "in Christ" as he, *par excellence*, is the one who stands for God and before men in his unique incarnate work of mediation: "There is one mediator between God and men, the man Christ Jesus" (1 Tim. 2:5). In this respect, it can be said that the purpose and work of God is mission to a world gone wrong, that Christ is a missionary, and also that all mission work is accomplished in Christ. This is the spirit that animates this book.

The words "in Christ" express the whole of God's mission to and in the world: *from* eternity, *to* time, *to* eternity—including secret election, incarnation, redemption accomplished and applied, justification, sanctified life, and finally glorification. But how is this mission carried out? What is the status of Christ, and how does he act as missional agent? These questions can only be answered theologically—by reference to Christ's divinity and humanity. Karl Barth's so-called Christocentrism, which makes Christ simultaneously the elect and the reprobate one, is not biblically grounded. Following Calvin, it is more appropriate to speak of Christ as the one mediator in his divine and human natures, pointing to the historical person and work of the God-man and the fulfillment of the covenant promise in him.

When we speak of the person of the mediator, we cannot forget the Chalcedonian formulation concerning the eternal person of the Son. The act of mediation is "in Christ," and Christ is at once the electing God and the elect man. As God, Christ himself, considered in his divinity, contains all the essence of the Godhead. In election, he it is who eternally designates himself as mediator, in communion with the Father, and he it is also who subordinates himself to the Father in the economy of incarnation. As the second person of the Trinity, Christ has the *jus eligendi*, the right to choose, and as Son he accepts the office of mediator, involving incarnation, humiliation, suffering, and salvation, as we have it in Philippians 2. In his High Priestly Prayer, Jesus witnesses to the success of his mission accomplished: "I glorified you on earth, having accomplished the work that you gave me to do" (John 17:4). In his divinity and humanity, Christ the mediator is the electing God and the elected man. Divine transcendence and aseity are the fount of Christ's humanity, and his mediation in the flesh is eloquently witnessed to in the letter to the Hebrews (Heb. 9:15; 12:24).

This perspective is a good way of relating the two aspects of election in Reformed theology that people stumble over, because they think it blocks missions; the *vertical* and *horizontal* perspectives are united in the person of the mediator. As Calvin put it, "The decree was eternal and unchangeable, but must be carried into effect by *Christ Jesus our Lord*, because in him it was made."[1] But how is this done? As elect man, Christ comes into the world to accomplish active and passive obedience as the second and final Adam, the perfect covenant servant. Can the well-known expression that Christ is the "mirror of election" be endorsed? It seems necessary to be more precise than

---

1. John Calvin, *Commentaries on the Epistles of Paul to the Galatians and Ephesians*, trans. William Pringle, Calvin's Commentaries (repr., Grand Rapids: Baker Book House, 1979), 256 (comm. on Eph. 3:11).

this, and in a biblical sense.[2] As mediator of the divine and human natures, Christ stands as prophet, priest, and king, to use Calvin's *munus triplex*. In his unique divine and human person, he fulfilled the offices in suffering and glory. In his humanity, Jesus stands as the rejected prophet, the sacrificed priest, and the king on the cross. In his divinity, he is the Logos, the efficacious sacrifice of infinite value, and the king of glory. The mission of Christ has as its content the three offices. It is through these that election is accomplished on the horizontal plane and is recognized by the many sons whom Christ will bring to glory (Heb. 2:10–18).

The mediation of the resurrected Christ in his glorification is concretized in his heavenly intercession. His work of salvation in the expiation of sin has infinite value and is universally sufficient for all. This is the foundation of the worldwide mission of the church and of the Great Commission of Matthew 28:20—the horizontal task of the free offer of the gospel. Yet in his divine, vertical intercession, Christ represents his own, the elect, chosen according to grace. Reconciliation, actual redemption, and propitiation are particular, personal, and efficacious because of the precise nature of Christ's intercession for his own. Christ *will* save, through the preaching of the good news, those for whom he died; none of his children will be snatched from his hand (John 10:28). The fact that Christ continues his mediatorial work in heaven is the foundation of mission work and the assurance of its success.

Union with Christ, being a new creation "in Christ," implies union with him as risen Lord in his mission of salvation. The privilege of the people of God is to be a witnessing people, partaking in the *munus triplex* of the mediator: "You are a chosen race, a royal priesthood, a holy nation, a people for his own possession, that you may proclaim the excellencies of him who called you out of darkness into his marvelous light" (1 Peter 2:9). The prophetic, priestly, and kingly offices of the mediator become incarnate once again, in a new and

---

2. Richard A. Muller, *Christ and the Decree: Christology and Predestination in Reformed Theology from Calvin to Perkins* (Grand Rapids: Baker Book House, 1986), 17–38.

surprising way, in the humanity of Christ's people. Their missional calling and responsibility is to shed abroad the light, as those whose identity is bound up with the Light of the world. Because they have received mercy, they can do no other than be messengers of mercy.

So the horizontal end of the golden chain that began in divine election, with Christ as the elect One, God and man, comes into view with him as the prophet, priest, and king in his suffering and glory. The mission that Adam failed to accomplish in creation as prophet, priest, and king is fully and finally realized in Christ. The new people of God are called to bear witness in mission to the new creation, already begun here and now in and through the work of the mediator. As a people with prophetic, priestly, and kingly functions, they are called to ministry of the word, to priestly demonstrations of mercy, and to kingly victory in trampling under their feet the powers of darkness, sin, and evil. The messianic community, in Christ, exists for mission, not for institution or human ambition.

The mission of the church is not expressed by attributes of divine glory, but in the strangely contrary way of divine choosing, which is the path of humility and suffering. Its calling reflects in content and form the ministry of the mediator. Treasure there is, but the treasure is in earthen vessels. As the medieval mystic John Tauler said, commenting on "Learn from me, for I am gentle and lowly in heart" (Matt. 11:29): "We must give our minds with willing industry to read it over and over again attentively, and practise it in our life, ever looking to the admirable model of the divine humanity of Christ, whose whole life was not only meek and humble, but whose words, ways, walk, and all that ever He did, are simply the illustration of this doctrine."[3] The way of election is that of mission in self-emptying and meekness. Jesus also suffered outside the city gate to make the people holy through his own blood: "Therefore let us go to him outside the camp and bear the reproach he endured. For here we have no lasting city, but we seek the city that is to come" (Heb. 13:13–14).

---

3. John Tauler, "Sermon for the Sixth Sunday after Epiphany," in *The History and Life of the Reverend Doctor John Tauler of Strasbourg, with Twenty-Five of His Sermons*, trans. Susanna Winkworth (London: H. R. Allenson, 1905), 109.

As the body of Christ, the church is a ministry of mission. This constitutes the calling of the whole body, as all are one in Christ and one with him. This must be so, and we must strive for it to be so, in terms of the church as both organism and as organization. Organizations that do not exist for this goal inevitably fade away into sociological forms of human bureaucracy. Mission must always keep the threefold office in the forefront of its policies as determinative of its vision, so that the service of God in a lost world finds expression in the service of our fellow human beings.

The contributors to this volume follow their efforts with the earnest prayer that they will stimulate missions to the glory of God—Father, Son, and Holy Spirit—and that many will confess with Peter, "To whom shall we go? You have the words of eternal life, and we have believed, and have come to know, that you are the Holy One of God" (John 6:68–69).

Paul Wells, Peter A. Lillback, Henk Stoker
Editors

PART 1

THE COVENANT
THEOLOGY OF MISSION

1

The Source of Mission in the Covenant of Redemption

Davi Charles Gomes

Abstract

In the first chapter of this book intended to contribute to a missional Reformed vision by placing it in the context of a covenantal approach to theology, the challenge is to set the rhythm and the framework. Other contributions will develop the connection with covenant theology and relate it to the implied missions, church life, and the world. God's revelation in Scripture gives us a metanarrative of history as redemptive history, beginning in Trinitarian acts in eternity past, embracing time, and culminating in a new history, the history of the new creation in Christ. Mission is not simply one aspect of theology or a sideshow in this history, but the substance of the story: the whole Bible is a missional phenomenon, with the amazing grace of God as its heartbeat. In this perspective, the Great Commission is not an epiphenomenon of the church's historical existence, but the summary of a program for the fulfillment of an even deeper and eternal purpose that implicates the being of God himself.

Introduction

"Behold, the dwelling place of God is with man. He will dwell with them, and they will be his people, and God himself will be with them as their God. He will wipe away every tear from their eyes, and death shall be no more, neither shall there be mourning, nor crying, nor pain anymore, for the former things have passed away" (Rev. 21:3–4).

Only a person who is dead inside would not be moved by this picture painted in the book of Revelation. Here we find one final gift of scripturally revealed grace, as God brings to a close his verbal self-disclosure with a glimpse at the end of the book, an insight that serves as a fixed point, a provisional conclusion, to the first step in the fulfillment of a plan God set out for himself. Its provisional character will be considered later, but for the present the main point is that this vision serves as the closing bracket, the final quotation mark, of the great metanarrative of human history. What then is the starting point, the opening mark? Before getting into how theology has sought to answer that question, it is important to make the connection between this metanarrative and the fulfillment of the Great Commission.

Christopher Wright describes how this became clear for him as a young theologian troubled by the lack of connection he observed between theology and missions: "Theology was all about God. . . . Mission was about us."[1] He continues: "Mission is about what we do." That was the assumption, supported of course by clear biblical commands. "Jesus sends me, this I know, for the Bible tells me so." Many years later, after a time when Wright taught theology as a missionary in India, he found himself giving a module entitled "The Biblical Basis of Mission" at All Nations Christian College, an international mission training and graduate school in southeast England. The module title itself embodied the same assumption. "Mission" is a noun, the given reality. It is something we do, and we basically know what it is. "Biblical" is an adjective, which we use to justify what we already know we should be doing. The reason why we should be doing missions—the basis, foundation, or ground on which we justify it—must be found in the Bible.[2] Wright recognized this to be a "mild caricature," yet his concern with this disconnect created in

---

1. Christopher J. H. Wright, *The Mission of God: Unlocking the Bible's Grand Narrative* (Nottingham: Inter-Varsity Press, 2006), 21.
2. Wright, *Mission of God*, 21–22.

him a desire to show students that the Bible does not simply contain passages that justify the mission endeavor, but rather "that the whole Bible is itself a 'missional' phenomenon":

> The Bible renders to us the story of God's mission through God's people in their engagement with God's world for the sake of the whole of God's creation. The Bible is the drama of this God of purpose engaged in the mission of achieving that purpose universally, embracing past, present and future, Israel and the nations, "life, the universe and everything," and with its center, focus, climax, and completion in Jesus Christ.[3]

So what is the difference? Is not finding in the Scriptures a basis for doing missions the same thing as seeing the Scriptures from a missional perspective? Not really! What makes the difference is the depth of purpose, understanding that Jesus' mandate to the church summarized in the Great Commission is not simply an epiphenomenon in the church's historical existence, but in fact the summary of a program for the fulfillment in the church of a deeper and eternal purpose that has to do with the being of God himself (Eph. 1:3–23). Brazilian theologian Wadislau Martins Gomes speaks of that: "The purpose of God, in this case, is to instill his holiness (his glory, his grace, his character) in us, as members of his body; ours is to reflect the glory of his character, by grace through faith."[4] The connection is clear: the mission of the church (*missio ecclesiae*) derives from the mission of God (*missio Dei*), and the latter is the manifestation of God's purposes rooted in his own being!

At this point, I will offer the plan for this essay. So far, I have dealt with the connection between "doing missions" and the grand purpose of God himself. Revelation 21 offers a marvelous glimpse of the fulfillment of that grand design, but other passages are just as

---

3. Wright, *Mission of God*, 22.

4. Wadislau Martins Gomes, *Sal da Terra em Terras dos Brasis: Como Vemos e Somos Vistos na Cultura Brasileira* [Salt of the earth in Brazilian lands: How we see and are seen in Brazilian culture] (Brasília: Monergismo, 2014), 29.

exciting. Its universality, for example, is pictured in the words of the prophet Habakkuk: "For the earth will be filled with the knowledge of the glory of the LORD as the waters cover the sea" (Hab. 2:14). The next step is to offer a perspective on the source and origin of God's plan. Then I will turn to some missional implications of this perspective. Finally, I will return briefly to the eternity of God's plan, as the "beyond" hinted at in the very fulfillment of the eschatological hopes expressed in Revelation 21 and Habakkuk 2.

The Covenant of Redemption

A perspective on the plan of salvation that wishes to avoid synergism will of necessity gravitate toward a covenantal viewpoint. Princeton theologian Charles Hodge put it succinctly: "The plan of salvation is presented under the form of a covenant." This is evident, he continues, "proved not only from the signification and usage of the words . . . [but] more decisively from the fact that the elements of a covenant are included in this plan," such as parties, mutual promises or stipulations, and conditions.[5]

The first obvious aspect of a covenantal approach to the plan of salvation is the relationship that God establishes with those who will become the objects of his grace through Christ. In Reformed theology, this is traditionally called the covenant of grace. However, there is something else that is implicit in the existence of such a covenant, as Augustine recognized:

> Behold, then, why the Son of God was sent; nay, rather behold what it is for the Son of God to be sent. Whatever things they were which were wrought in time, with a view to produce faith, whereby we might be cleansed so as to contemplate truth, in things that have a beginning, which have been put forth from eternity, and are referred back to eternity: these were either testimonies of this mission, or they were the mission itself of the Son of God.[6]

5. Charles Hodge, *Systematic Theology* (Grand Rapids: Eerdmans, 1995), 2:354.
6. Augustine, *On the Trinity*, IV.19 (25).

Two things are remarkable about this passage from *De Trinitate*. First, it is here that we begin to find references to the mission of the Godhead (the *missio Dei*). Second, Augustine makes a distinction between the aspects of this mission that unfold within time and the aspects that "are referred back to eternity."

In sixteenth-century thought, not only was the idea of a covenant of grace between God and his people present, but in many ways the idea that this would be rooted in a transaction within the Godhead was also there. Some have argued that it was first in the theology of Cocceius (1603–69) that a more explicit concept of an intra-Trinitarian pact at the root of the covenant of grace makes its appearance. Geerhardus Vos, however, shows how this idea was present before Cocceius, in such writers as Caspar Olevianus (1536–87), William Ames (1576–1633), and others.[7] Richard Muller defines the concept of a covenant of redemption, or *pactum salutis*, in its developed form:

> In Reformed federalism, the pretemporal, intratrinitarian agreement of the Father and the Son concerning the covenant of grace and its ratification in and through the work of the Son incarnate. The Son covenants with the Father, in the unity of the Godhead, to be the temporal *sponsor* of the Father's *testamentum* (q.v.) in and through the work of the Mediator. In that work, the Son fulfills his *sponsio* (q.v.) or *fideiussio* (q.v.), i.e., his guarantee of payment of the debt of sin in ratification of the Father's *testamentum*.[8]

Muller goes on to make an interesting analogy, arguing that even if for some the idea of a *pactum salutis* may seem speculative, it has an

---

7. See Richard A. Muller, *Dictionary of Latin and Greek Theological Terms: Drawn Principally from Protestant Scholastic Theology* (Grand Rapids: Baker Books, 1985), 217 ("pactum salutis"); Geerhardus Vos, "The Doctrine of the Covenant in Reformed Theology," in *Redemptive History and Biblical Interpretation: The Shorter Writings of Geerhardus Vos*, ed. Richard B. Gaffin, Jr. (Phillipsburg, NJ: Presbyterian & Reformed, 1980). Peter A. Lillback points to passages in Zwingli and especially in Calvin that adumbrate the idea of a pretemporal intra-Trinitarian covenant (*The Binding of God* [Grand Rapids: Baker Book House, 2001], 101, 212–13). Cf. John V. Fesko, *The Trinity and the Covenant of Redemption* (Fearn, UK: Christian Focus, 2016).

8. Muller, *Dictionary of Latin and Greek Theological Terms*, 217.

important role in accentuating "the eternal, inviolable, and trinitarian foundation of the temporal *foedus gratiae*, much in the way that the eternal decree underlies and guarantees the *ordo salutis*."[9] However, some, including Karl Barth, have looked upon the idea of this covenant of redemption as less than biblical, or at best as lacking explicit scriptural support. For Vos, this criticism is mistaken:

> It was not taken from the Scriptures ready and completed, but grew out of them. The federal theologians after Cocceius sometimes painted too human a picture. It has not always been defended too happily exegetically either. But, as far as its core is concerned, it lies so firmly in the principles of Reformed theology that it has endured every attack and, despite its transcendent character, has assured itself of a permanent place in the minds of believers.[10]

Before we proceed, however, and especially because of our interest in the connection between the covenant of redemption and a missional vision, it may be good to attempt a description (rather than a definition) of that compact. With "poetic license" and at the inevitable risk of anthropomorphism that is always present when we describe aspects of intra-Trinitarian relations, I propose the following description: The covenant of redemption (*pactum salutis*) refers to the "event" outside time and space, sometimes called a "counsel of peace," in which Father, Son, and Holy Spirit, in an overflow of love in the Godhead, agreed upon and committed to create a people as an object of love and grace, so that they would be brought into a familial relationship with God himself. This is expressed in God's own promise: "I will put my law within them, and I will write it on their hearts. And I will be their God, and they shall be my people" (Jer. 31:33). This intra-Trinitarian covenant is, for Reformed theology, the starting point in the metanarrative of human history. God himself purposes to become the sender, the sent, and the enabler in a mission

9. Muller, *Dictionary of Latin and Greek Theological Terms*, 217.

10. Vos, "Doctrine of the Covenant in Reformed Theology," 335; Hodge, *Systematic Theology*, 2:360; cf. Ps. 40; Rom. 5:12–21; Heb. 10:10.

of redemptive purpose, in order to establish, outside his own being, unique objects of his grace and glory!

Contours of the Intra-Trinitarian Covenant

One way to delineate the basic contours of the covenant of redemption is to see it in contrast to the covenant of grace in three of the basic aspects of each covenant: the parties, the promises, and the conditions.[11]

First, as to *the parties* of the covenants, the covenant of grace is made between God and the elect. Christ appears in this covenant with a double role, for he is the mediator of the covenant and at the same time, as a person of the Godhead, its initiator. Yet, in the covenant of redemption, it is the Father who covenants with the Son and the Spirit concerning this plan. Hodge discusses the common confusion between the two covenants as follows:

> This confusion is avoided by distinguishing between the covenant of redemption between the Father and the Son, and the covenant of grace between God and his people. The latter supposes the former, and is founded upon it. The two, however, ought not to be confounded, as both are clearly revealed in Scripture, and moreover they differ as to the parties, as to the promises, and as to the conditions.[12]

Second, *the promises* involved in the two covenants are also distinct. In the covenant of grace, God promises to reconcile to himself, through Christ's complete work, those whom he has called. His gracious offer of salvation is received by the faith produced in the believer by his Holy Spirit. The same Spirit so unites believers to Christ that they become partakers of the merits of Christ and are progressively conformed to his perfect image. This transaction has the

---

11. Hodge, *Systematic Theology*, 2:358–59.
12. Hodge, *Systematic Theology*, 2:358–59. Hodge also makes an important distinction between an Augustinian view that considers the elect as the human party to the covenant and the Pelagian, semi-Pelagian, Arminian, and Lutheran views that would take all of fallen humankind to be the party of the covenant.

Trinity on one side, Christ as mediator, and the elect on the other side as recipients of the promises. Yet, once more, it presupposes that other transaction, in which promises are made within the persons of the Godhead. These promises involve the creation of a special people, their redemption through Christ to the praise of his glorious grace, and the establishment of a union by the Holy Spirit that enables this people to enjoy permanent and intimate communion with God.[13]

Third, *the conditions* presented in these two covenants are different. The covenant of grace demands that Christ offer up himself as a sacrifice on behalf of those who will be God's people, and it also demands that through the action of the Holy Spirit they will receive by faith the grace dispensed in Christ. In the covenant of redemption, the Father, in order to fulfill his purpose of creating for himself a people, assigns a task to the Son and to the Holy Spirit, a task they commit to accomplish in order to secure the realization of the eternal purposes of the Trinity:

> That a multitude whom no man can number should thus be made partakers of his redemption, and that ultimately the kingdom of the Messiah should embrace all the nations of the earth.[14]

The Source of History and Time

All three covenantal aspects described above involve the idea that the covenant of grace presupposes the covenant of redemption. Perhaps we can explain their relationship in a way that will highlight the importance of the pretemporal nature of the covenant of redemption: if the covenant of grace unfolds through created time, then the covenant of redemption has as its backdrop timeless eternity itself,

---

13. Morton H. Smith, *Systematic Theology* (Greenville, SC: Greenville Seminary Press, 1994), 1:329: "Hoeksema has a very helpful treatment of the whole subject. He makes the point that the idea of a covenant in the Bible is not that of a pact or agreement. 'It is the relation of the most intimate communion of friendship in which God reflects his own covenant life in his relation to the creature, gives to that creature life, and causes him to taste and acknowledge the highest good and the overflowing fountain of all good.'"

14. Hodge, *Systematic Theology*, 2:362.

with only God's own being "back of it." That is why it becomes, in turn, the condition of the unfolding of the covenant of grace.

By analogy, if the covenant of redemption implies that God set himself a mission that precedes all of created reality (the *missio Dei*), then the purposes of that created reality, as the temporal unfolding of a timeless purpose, are, *sub specie aeternitatis*, the creaturely analogue of the Creator's mission. The *missio ecclesiae* then traces its roots to the *missio Dei*. Time and history are the stage for the unfolding of a glorious plan in which Christ by the Spirit attracts to himself those whom the Father gave him. This divine plan places them together as a body of which he is the head, a body indwelt by his Spirit, that becomes the instrument whereby redemption is proclaimed and experienced. Before time itself, as the very source of history, stands a counsel of peace, a pretemporal disposition and compact of a gracious God, established with none other than himself. Herman Hoeksema adds further color to this image:

> This covenant is not conceived as a means to an end, as a way unto salvation, but as the very end itself, as the very highest that can ever be reached by the creature; not as a way to life, but as the highest form of life itself; not as a condition, but as the very essence of religion; not as a means unto salvation, but as the highest bliss itself. . . . In that case the counsel of peace is presented as the decree which dominates all other decrees of God concerning the ultimate end of all things as God has conceived it in His counsel. Instead of a decree concerning the means, the counsel of peace is the decree concerning the end of all things.[15]

The glory of such a plan lies in the fact that this eternal arrangement roots all our experiences and collective histories, the whole of history itself, in a grace-giving movement of the glorious and eternal Trinity. At the same time, the missional character of this perspective becomes so clear that I cannot help but recall the words that a Brazilian poet and songwriter used to describe the vision of a final

---

15. Herman Hoeksema, *Reformed Dogmatics* (Grand Rapids: Reformed Free Publishing Association, 1985), 318.

moment of eschatological revelation, although his own pantheistic hopes for the eschaton completely missed the point:

> And what, at that moment, shall be revealed to all people, will surprise everyone, not for being exotic, but for the fact that it could have remained hidden, when it was always so obvious![16]

Implications of a Covenantal Missional Perspective

In the beginning, I referred to the picture painted in Revelation 21 as a provisional end point of the biblical metanarrative. If the previous section provided some help in grasping the import of the eternal source of that beautiful story of the mission of God, it will be useful to complete the picture with a further aspect. This missional approach opens up an array of other horizons—beautiful strands of this narrative, such as its gracious nature and its gracious manifestation through the church, as well as the all-encompassing reach of the plan that unfolds through created reality.

The Gracious Nature of the *Missio Dei*

The eternal covenant made within the Trinity determines a temporal missional goal for the whole work of Christ and of his Spirit, namely the creation of a people, a "multitude that no man can number," made up of every language, nation and tribe, so that "the kingdom of the Messiah should embrace all the nations of the earth."[17] Hodge emphasizes that even within the covenant of redemption there is interplay between the universality of the redemptive mission and its particular goal:

> In virtue of what the Son of God covenanted to perform, and what in the fullness of time He actually accomplished, agreeably to the

16. Caetano Veloso, "Um Índio," in *Bicho* (Studio Album, PolyGram, Universal Music, 1977), track 5 (my translation): "E aquilo que nesse momento se revelará aos povos / Surpreenderá a todos não por ser exótico / Mas pelo fato de poder ter sempre estado oculto / Quando terá sido o óbvio."
17. Hodge, *Systematic Theology*, 2:362.

stipulations of the compact with the Father, two things follow. First, salvation is offered to all men on the condition of faith in Christ. Our Lord commanded his disciples to go into all the world and preach the gospel to every creature. . . . It follows, secondly, from the nature of the covenant between the Father and the Son, that the covenant of grace has also special reference to the elect.[18]

God has determined in himself a mission that includes Christ's lordship over all creation, the proclamation of salvation in Christ to all people, to be received by faith, and that this gracious offer of salvation that makes us willing partakers of Messiah's kingdom will be effective in those given by the Father to the Son from the beginning. Both determinations of this mission, including all of creation and applying particularly to the elect, are overtly and essentially gracious. They flow from the grace and love that are inherent in the very being of God. The eternal and glorious Trinity moves outward in a gracious expression that has as its purpose the reflection of his glory in the objects of his grace!

The first implication of this gracious movement of God is that its recognition should cause wonder and awe. Martyn Lloyd-Jones highlights one aspect of this when he says, "Here we come to something that is the source of the deepest assurance and consolation that any Christian person can ever know in this world of time." He then adds, "What could be more comforting and reassuring than the fact that there is nothing contingent about this salvation, nothing accidental, nothing that needs modification?"[19] Yet this aspect of personal reassurance, based upon the gracious nature of the *missio Dei*, can be complemented by another implication that Lloyd-Jones also pointed out: "Salvation has originated in the mind of God—it is God's own purpose." This means that "even the Lord Jesus Christ does not have to placate God" in the sense that it might be thought that there was reluctance on the part of God with regard to the elect. He continues:

18. Hodge, *Systematic Theology*, 2:362–63.

19. D. Martyn Lloyd-Jones, *Saved in Eternity: God's Plan of Salvation* (Wheaton, IL: Crossway Books, 1988), 55.

Sometimes our hymns can be rather dangerous, and there are certain of them that would lead us to the conclusion that the Son of God has to plead with the Father to have mercy and pity upon us. But that is a gross misunderstanding of the term "Advocate," it is something that is absolutely foreign to biblical teaching. Rather, the Bible teaches that "God was in Christ, reconciling the world unto himself, not imputing their trespasses unto them" (2 Cor. 5:19); "God so loved the world, that he gave his only begotten Son . . ." (John 3:16). It is all from God. So this idea that the Lord Jesus Christ is at great pains to persuade God the Father to forgive and accept us is utterly unscriptural and entirely false; the source and origin of salvation is the great and eternal heart of God.[20]

So this vision of God's mission, as a pure manifestation of a gracious disposition toward his creatures, places us on a belvedere from which we can view the whole story, the whole narrative. From this perspective, we realize that everything about our lives, our own personal histories, our institutional histories, indeed all of human history—all these things are not actually central plots or main narratives, but subplots of a greater narrative. Everything that happens in time and space consists of perfect strands, flawlessly adjusted subplots, that fit together in the fulfillment of one narrative that starts with God, ends with him, and is all about him—a wonderful expression of God's gracious decision to elect and create adequate objects of his grace and love.

The Gracious Manifestation in the Mission of the Church

Once the gracious nature of the covenant of redemption and the mission of God is grasped—keeping in mind that from that first covenant flows the covenant of grace, in which salvation and participation in the kingdom of Christ are offered to the elect—then that grace is seen as manifested in time through the mission of God's people. Flip Buys says, "I believe that a revitalization of our understanding of

20. Lloyd-Jones, *Saved in Eternity*, 55.

the concepts of the covenant of redemption (*pactum salutis*) . . . and the covenant of grace is vital for developing a Reformed approach to global missions and understanding the true calling of the church in the world." He goes on to say that this should clarify an understanding that:

> (1) The church as the covenant community of the King, is the instrument of God's Mission (cf. Matt. 9:37–38; John 13:20; 15:16; 17:18; Eph. 3:8–10). The church is not the end of God's mission, but the instrument of it—God's tool in the outworking of his plan to usher in his kingdom. But (2) the church is also the goal of mission (cf. Rev. 5:9–10; 7:9–12). This is not to say that the church is somehow secondary to the mission: on the contrary, the multitude of the redeemed worshipping the Lord through Christ in the New World is the church of God, the new humanity in Christ, the church (as assembly) of Christ. We need to refresh our vision of the church called to be the covenant community of the King.[21]

In summary, what is the mission of the church, if not the temporal manifestation of the graciousness of the rule of Christ? Does this instrument of God's glorious grace make music only for its own sake? If its mission is rooted in the very movement of the Trinity outside himself, it is only natural that it must also be a movement that expresses the beautiful music of grace to all of creation, for the sake of the glory of the King. Hence, the mission of the church has to do with the hope of seeing the "multitude that no one can count" singing in one voice the great hymn that celebrates the glorious grace of the King. It is about expressing outwardly the grace that has created, gathered, and prepared a wonderful symphony of joy for those who perform it and of beauty for all to see and delight in!

This implies that the mission of the church is rooted in grace and must be gracious in every aspect. It also means that it expresses outwardly moving beauty. Finally, this mission is permeated by a sense of

---

21. P. J. Buys, "The Church as Part of God's Mission in the Light of God's Eternal Covenant of Redemption." Unpublished class notes for Biblical Foundations of Missions, Mukhanyo Theological College (quoted with the author's permission).

otherness conjoined with participation, in which we realize the beauty of being able to speak at once of "I," of "thou," and of "we"—which is found in perfect form only within the unity and diversity of the triune God himself. This establishes the Trinity as the archetype for relational movements, of which the church must be an ectype. This makes the church obligated to her Lord, to her own, and also to those outside her—obligated and obliged to become what she is intended to be, compelled to be a well-adjusted body in which each part fulfills its calling under the head, duty-bound to express its true nature and its calling in engagement with all of creation.

Three overarching implications follow: First, the church must be a canvas on which God paints a beautiful and colorful display of his grace. Second, the church has a mission to sound clearly the glorious music of the gospel to the ears of the listening world, since the same creator of the melody creates the instruments of his sound and the ears that receive it. Finally, the church must understand that its mission includes being an instrument to gather in the whole number of those given to the King, and also being the ever more perfect expression of the realization of the covenant of redemption for the whole of creation. This is how Christopher Wright summarizes it:

> God calls his people to share his mission. The church from all nations stands in continuity through the Messiah Jesus with God's people in the Old Testament. With them we have been called through Abraham and commissioned to be a blessing and light to the nations. With them, we are to be shaped and taught through the law and the prophets to be a community of holiness, compassion and justice in a world of sin and suffering. We have been redeemed through the cross and resurrection of Jesus Christ, and empowered by the Holy Spirit to bear witness to what God has done in Christ. The church exists to worship and glorify God for all eternity and to participate in the transforming mission of God within history.[22]

---

22. Christopher J. H. Wright, "What Do We Mean by 'Missional'?" Foreword to *Reformed Means Missional*, ed. Samuel T. Logan (Greensboro, SC: New Growth Press, 2013), xii–xiii. In this book, different authors deal with the practical implications of

The Radical Reach of a Missional Approach

Having dealt theologically with the source and origin of missions in God's own covenant with himself, the next step is to consider the consequences. In an endorsement for the multiauthor book *Reformed Means Missional*, I commented: "At a time when some people are asking how to be Reformed and missional at the same time, this book comes to show that being Reformed *is* to be *intrinsically* missional."

We need to apply the implications of a Reformed perspective that should be intrinsically missional. In the afterword to the same book, Frank James sounded a warning about using the word *missional* as an empty buzzword, "the latest fad, or the lingo of trendy Christianity." He continued:

> To be missional takes courage. It requires a revision of what it means to live out the gospel in this messy postmodern world. It obliges us to contemplate the Trinity in deeper ways, understanding that the mission begins there, with the intratrinitarian "sending" from which the church is analogously "sent" into a redemptive mission. . . . To be missional is to accept the challenge and responsibility to be his agents in advancing his mission.[23]

Indeed, the church needs to be constantly reminded, not only of her missional nature, but also of the roots of this identity, in order to speak effectively to and in the postmodern world, and to continue speaking until the kingdom comes. Wright, once more, helps us grasp how radical this can be:

> Now such an understanding of the mission of God as the very heartbeat of all reality, all creation, all history and all that yet lies

---

a Reformed missional outlook: ecclesiology (Martin Allen), belief and behavior (Samuel T. Logan), theology (Thomas Schirrmacher), social justice (Flip Buys), the city (Timothy Keller, Susan M. Post), responses to violence and abuse (Diane Langberg, Basyle Tchividjian), migration (Elias Medeiros), secularism, Islam, "hidden believers," homosexuality (Robert Calvert, John Leonard, John Nichols, John Freeman).

23. Frank James, afterword to *Reformed Means Missional*, ed. Logan, 253.

ahead of us generates a distinctive worldview that is radically and transformingly God-centered. . . . This worldview, constituted by putting the mission of God at the very center of all existence, is disturbingly subversive and it uncomfortably relativizes one's own place in the great scheme of things.[24]

Wright goes on to illustrate some of the shifts that this understanding should cause: Instead of asking "Where does God fit in the story of my life?" we begin to wonder where we fit in his story. Instead of seeking for an individually tailored purpose for our lives, we ask how we can be "wrapped up in the great mission of God for the whole of creation." Furthermore, instead of seeking to apply the Bible to our lives, we should see the Bible as the reality to which our lives should conform. Instead of wondering how to make the gospel relevant to the world, we should see that God is "transforming the world to fit the shape of the gospel." Rather than trying to see if our care of creation and nature "might fit into our concept and practice of mission," we should make sure we are aligned with God's purpose for all of creation and the anticipation of a new heaven and new earth. Finally, instead of asking "What can legitimately be included in the mission God expects from the church," we should ask what kind of church God expects for his mission. In summary, "I may wonder what kind of mission God has for me, when I should ask what kind of me God wants for his mission."[25]

Conclusion: Eternity and Beyond

There is, however, one final issue, as previously indicated: to explain why the vision pictured in Revelation 21 is only a provisional conclusion to the great narrative that opens with the *pactum salutis*.

Just as the covenant of redemption is pretemporal, so its fulfillment, in an absolute sense, is eternal. Yet the metanarrative of created reality does come to a conclusion, which is the eschatological hope

24. Wright, *Mission of God*, 533–34.
25. Wright, *Mission of God*, 533–34.

that should motivate and move the church toward a fixed consummation. The great wedding feast of the Lamb, the perfectly personal and yet universal moment when Christ himself wipes away all tears and puts an end to death, is the conclusion: Behold, God is now making his permanent tabernacle with his people! Behold, he has written his will in their hearts! Behold, "the former things have passed away" (Rev. 21:3–4)!

However, in another sense this is only the end of the first things, the fulfillment of the covenant of grace and the history of redemption as we know it, as revealed. Is this the end of the whole story? I think not, for there we also find the promise: "Behold, I am making all things new"!

Might we not consider that, in another sense, this is simply the beginning? Could it be that the covenant of grace, as the temporal subspecies of the covenant of redemption, implies that the eternal mission of God will go on, as that wonderful assembly of the redeemed is enveloped in the eternal song of worship in the new heaven and the new earth? God has not revealed what lies beyond, so perhaps we do well not to speculate. One thing, however, is sure: knowing that the whole human *épopée* is rooted in eternity and standing in amazement of what lies between creation and consummation, directs the church to wait in the holy, joyous expectation that is wonderfully captured in the verse borrowed from the African-American churches by Harriet Beecher Stowe (1811–96) and added to John Newton's (1725–1807) hymn "Amazing Grace":[26]

> When we've been there ten thousand years,
> Bright shining as the sun,
> We've no less days to sing God's praise,
> Than when we first begun.

This expectation for eternity and beyond should jolt us to action, to act now!

---

26. Jonathan Aitken, *John Newton: From Disgrace to Amazing Grace* (Wheaton, IL: Crossway Books, 2007), 235.

2

Covenant of Creation, Cultural Mandate, and Mission

Pierre Berthoud

Abstract

The supernatural creation and absolute beginning expressed in the prologue of Genesis stand in stark contrast to contemporary naturalism. God freely chose to create the universe and human beings by the power of his word. The infinite, personal God is the ultimate reality, the Creator who exists independently of creation and who is not to be confused with matter or energy. God is the warrant for the objective existence of reality and truth. The correlation of human knowledge and the structure of reality witnesses to divine intelligence, providence, and intervention in time and space. The theology of creation and covenant accounts for man in the universe, the moral nature of evil, and revelation that progressively sheds light on redemption accomplished in Christ. Man's call and mission is an integral part of creation, carried out through the cultural mandate in communion with the Creator. Salvation not only concerns human individuals or communities, but also embraces all creation and transfigures all things in heaven and on earth.[1]

---

1. This is an adaptation of sections from my French monograph: Pierre E. Berthoud, *En quête des origines: Les premières étapes de l'histoire de la révélation: Genèse 1–11* (Cléon d'Andran: Excelsis; Aix-en-Provence: Kerygma, 2008).

Introduction

It might seem strange to bring together mission and the covenant of creation, and even more covenant and creation. Nevertheless, for a proper understanding of the theology of mission, it is important to start with Genesis and the key concept of covenant. The first chapters of Genesis help us to grasp a world-and-life view that is foundational to global mission. The notion of the covenant of creation sets the stage for an appraisal of the mission that God has given to his creatures, on both creational and redemptive levels. This requires that we address the questions of being, the cultural mandate, evil in this world, and salvation.

The Origin of Being in Contemporary Context

Contemporary thought argues for the existence of being rather than nonbeing. The question of "Why is there something rather than nothing?" reflects on the origin and the meaning of reality. In the words inscribed on a painting by Paul Gauguin, "Where do we come from? What are we? Where are we going?" Gaugin was asking about the origin of human destiny, the meaning and finality of existence.[2] If something exists, what is its nature? Humanist and materialist perspectives presuppose that ultimate reality is infinite and impersonal, defined in terms of matter and energy. But how can this account for the highly complex universe and the unique character of man, qualitatively distinct from other living beings? On the other hand, the biblical perspective proposes that ultimate reality is personal and infinite. This starting point is essential to a philosophy based on the content of Scripture and a global outlook that answers the question

2. Gauguin's painting is in the Boston Art Museum. It was his last major work, in which he expressed his despair, for his humanist philosophy didn't allow him to find the ultimate reality that would have brought meaning and serenity. Cf. Francis A. Schaeffer, *The God Who Is There*, in *The Complete Works of Francis A. Schaeffer* (Westchester, IL: Crossway Books, 1982), 1:28; Hans R. Rookmaaker, *Art, Artists and Gauguin*, vol. 1 of *The Complete Works of Hans R. Rookmaaker*, ed. Marleen Hengelaar-Rookmaaker (Carlisle: Piquant, 2000), 191–97.

of origins. It takes into account the unity and diversity of reality and highlights a unique anthropological concept in its psychological, social, and cultural aspects.

As the infinite and personal being, God took the initiative to create all things *ex nihilo* solely by the power of his word.[3] This key notion is expressed in the first chapter of Genesis. The verb "to create" (*bara*), used only with God as subject, describes a uniquely creative activity.[4] The Hebrew root is used in three contexts in chapter 1: in relation to the creation of the universe, of aquatic and flying beings, and of human beings: man and woman (Gen. 1:1–2, 20–21, 27–28). God's specific intervention is apparent with respect to physics, biology, and anthropology. The last divine act underscores the unique character of humans as created in the image of God. Consequently, the answers given to these questions bear on the way in which the universe and the destiny of man are understood.

Renewed Interest in the Theology of Creation

The infinite, personal Creator of the universe has an objective existence that is distinct from his creation, and is not a figment of the imagination, a projection of the mind, or the expression of an ideal. The Creator, man's ultimate counterpart, is truly there. This is important because much contemporary theology of creation emphasizes the existential and subjective, without answering the question of being.

Robert Martin-Achard, for example, says that "to speak about the creation of the world corresponds, for the Old Testament tradition, to a triple preoccupation": doxological, polemical, and soteriological. In other words, creation texts invite the believer to praise the unique God, reject idols, and welcome salvation offered by the Lord.[5] In order to avoid ambiguity, the Swiss theologian recognizes that "the theme of creation does not appear as the natural conclusion of the research of the scientist, but belongs to a liturgical act by which

3. The Latin expression means "out of nothing," implying no preexisting matter.

4. It is important to note here that *bara'* does not usually express the idea of a creation *ex nihilo*, as we will see later.

5. Passages referring to the Creator and to creation, such as Isaiah 40, Job 38, and Genesis 1, must be interpreted accordingly.

the community proclaims its faith and glorifies its God."[6] The discourses of faith and of science, he says, belong to different realms and can hardly be harmonized. It is imperative to resist the temptation of concordism, but what is the meaning of a faith that is not grounded upon "true" truth and that avoids the question of being? Claus Westermann likewise argues that the creation accounts do not answer the question of origins. At best, they shed light on the fragile condition of humans who live in a dangerous environment. In the midst of the threats that people encounter, the stories of creation are comforting and reassuring. The intellectual aspect is sidestepped, so as to lay the emphasis on its existential nature.[7]

This approach accounts for one aspect of biblical revelation, but why separate the ontological and the existential dimensions? The validity of this solution is undermined by a divided field of knowledge. To confess one's faith in a Creator-God is meaningful only if the biblical perspective is intellectually true and trustworthy. The answer to the question of being bears necessarily upon that of meaning. To believe in the Creator and in creation implies that God has taken the initiative to create the universe, and that this work is of an objective nature. The first chapters of Genesis are not to be compared to a scientific treatise, but when the biblical narrative bears witness to the activity of God in our world, it speaks in truth. God is also the Lord of science.[8]

An Unexpected Contribution

While the contemporary theology of creation avoids the question of origins, astrophysicists, curiously, have made a significant

6. Robert Martin-Achard, *Et Dieu crée le ciel et la terre* (Genève: Labor et Fides, 1979), 22–23.

7. Claus Westermann, *Genesis 1–11: A Commentary* (London: SPCK, 1984), 11; Samuel Amsler, *Le secret de nos origines* (Poliez-le-Grand: Editions du Moulin, 1997), 8–9. The same dichotomy is found in Ralph H. Elliott, "A Word about Controversy: Science and Religion," *Review and Expositor* 103 (2006): 303–4. The author distinguishes between "material facts" and "existential facts," thereby building his argument on a divided field of knowledge.

8. For a more detailed presentation of the contemporary understanding of the doctrine of creation, see Berthoud, *En quête*, 179–83.

contribution. Their discoveries have led them to reconsider the question of being and the origin of the universe. They have had to face the challenge of the "zero moment" of the universe, with all its implications. In 1978, Robert Jastrow, an agnostic, wrote *God and the Astronomers*, not only to describe the Big Bang theory, according to which the universe began about 15 to 20 billion years ago, but also because the embarrassed reactions of his colleagues to its creational implications fascinated him. Scientists who maintained the eternity of matter or energy have been forced to reconsider the origin of the universe. To argue that the universe has a beginning brings the question of a Creator into view—which was thought to have been definitely excluded. Jastrow understood this when he humorously remarked:

> The scientist's pursuit of the past ends in the moment of creation. . . . It is not matter of another year, another decade of work, another measurement or another theory; at the moment it seems as though science will never be able to raise the curtain on the mystery of creation. For the scientist who has lived by his faith in the power of reason, the story ends like a bad dream. He has scaled the mountains of ignorance, he is about to conquer the highest peak; as he pulls himself over the final rock, he is greeted by a band of theologians who have been sitting there for centuries.[9]

Many scientists refuse to enter this debate, but others, such as Trinh Xuan Thuan, accept the challenge:

> The recent discoveries of cosmology have shed a new light on the most fundamental and oldest of questions. And it matters that any serious reflection on the existence of God take this new evidence into account. After all, the questions asked by the cosmologist are strikingly close to those that concern the theologian: How was the

9. Robert Jastrow, *God and the Astronomers* (1978; repr., New York, London: W. W. Norton, 1992), 115–16. Jastrow was the founder and director of NASA's Goddard Institute for Space Studies, professor of astronomy at the University of Columbia, and professor of earth sciences at Dartmouth University (USA).

universe created? Is there a beginning to time and space? Will the universe have an end? Where does it come from and where is it going? The sphere of God is that of mystery and of the invisible, that of the infinitely small and of the infinitely large. This sphere no longer belongs exclusively to the theologian, it also belongs to the scientists; science is there, it adds up discoveries and disrupts preconceptions. The theologian has no right to remain indifferent.[10]

Theologians should not ignore the debate on the question of origins among astrophysicists, but nor should the latter seek, in the name of science, to escape the question of God and the autonomy of human existence and knowledge. The ultimate issue is not the encounter between God and modern cosmology, but the Davidic statement that "the heavens declare the glory of God, and the sky above proclaims his handiwork" (Ps. 19:1).

The Biblical Perspective: Creation *Ex Nihilo*

The concept of creation *ex nihilo* is central to the biblical perspective. The major arguments in favor of this foundational notion are: the unique character of the biblical account of creation in the context of ancient Near Eastern cosmogonies, the interpretation of Genesis 1:1–3, and the meaning of the Hebrew verb *bara'*, "to create."

A Unique Concept in the Ancient Near East

The differences between the Babylonian story of creation, *Enuma Elish*, and the Genesis narrative are mainly due to incompatible philosophical/religious perspectives, and discrepancies in the way they perceive reality and the human condition.[11] On the one hand, in the

---

10. Trinh Xuan Thuan, *La mélodie secrète* (Paris: Gallimard, 1991), 296–97. The author advocates the Big Bang theory and does not believe in chance and necessity. Cf. John J. Davis, *The Frontiers of Science and Faith* (Downers Grove, IL: IVP, 2002), 11–36. For interesting input on the contribution of physics and mathematics to the debate, see Igor and Grichka Bogdanov, *La pensée de Dieu* (Paris: Grasset, 2012), 9–39, 337–51.

11. For a detailed discussion of this point, see Berthoud, *En quête*, 186–92.

Babylonian epic, Apsû and Ti'âmat represent the uncreated living matter that contains all the elements necessary to the birth of the gods and the universe. The divine spirit and matter form a unity, coexist, and are eternal. As Alexander Heidel says, it follows that "the universe has its origin in the generation of numerous gods and goddesses personifying cosmic spaces or forces of nature, and in orderly and purposeful arrangement of pre-existent matter."[12] The act of creation is similar to the process by which an artisan gives form to raw material. On the other hand, in Genesis there is one God who "creates matter out of nothing and exists independently of all cosmic matter and remains one God to the end."[13] The creating act depends on the sovereign will and powerful word of the Lord, without any resort to external means. The accounts belong to two different traditions; their similarities can be accounted for by a shared cultural environment and a common subject.

The vision of the world presented in divine revelation is so new and unique in the context of antiquity that it has a polemical dimension. The Genesis creation story is a radical challenge to the worldview of the polytheistic paganism that was a deadly temptation for Israel throughout her history. God creates by the power of his word of wisdom (Gen. 1:3–4) and not by means of magical formulas.[14] Gordon Wenham comments that Genesis 1 "is not merely the demythologization of oriental creation myths, whether Babylonian or Egyptian, rather it is a polemical repudiation of such myths."[15]

Genesis 1:1–3[16]

The first verse of Genesis is usually translated: "In the beginning, God created the heavens and the earth" (NIV, ESV). However, several

12. Alexander Heidel, *The Babylonian Genesis* (Chicago: University of Chicago Press, 1972), 139, 89, 96.

13. Heidel, 140.

14. See Gerhard F. Hasel, "The Significance of the Cosmology in Genesis 1 in Relation to Ancient Near Eastern Parallels," *Andrews University Seminary Studies* 10 (1972): 1–20; Hasel, "The Polemic Nature of the Genesis Cosmology," *Evangelical Quarterly* 46 (1974): 81–102.

15. Gordon J. Wenham, *Genesis 1–15*, WBC (Waco, TX: Word Books, 1987), 9.

16. For more comprehensive presentations of the different interpretations of Genesis 1:1–3, see Berthoud, *En quête*, 211–16; Wenham, *Genesis 1–15*, 11–13;

modern translations link the first two verses like this: "In the beginning of creation, when God made heaven and earth, the earth was without form and void, with darkness over the face of the abyss, and a mighty wind that swept over the surface of the waters" (NEB). Exegetes who suggest this translation maintain that verse 2 contains the main clause, rather than the first verse. However, these readings are questionable on grammatical as well as on literary grounds, as they do not account for the final form of the text. Nor is it difficult to recognize the important theological consequences of such readings, because they imply the preexistence of matter or energy and therefore its eternity. A careful study of the Scriptures reveals that such a view is contrary to the biblical understanding of God and creation.

Some scholars consider verse 1 as the main clause, but take it to be a title.[17] Again, for both literary and theological reasons, this option cannot be retained. Commenting on the final form of the prologue, Wenham argues that the synchronic analysis of the creation narrative favors the traditional reading. Verse 1 is a main clause that describes the first of the divine acts of creation, while verses 2 and 3 refer to later phases of the Creator's work. The ancient versions are also in favor of this interpretation.[18] The phases of this synchronic reading can be summarized as follows: verse 1, the first act of creation; verse 2, a description of the consequences of that act; verse 3, the first explicit creative word.

The traditional reading of the first three verses of Genesis gives the best account of the syntax of this passage, while integrating the literary form of the first account of creation. It highlights the unique

---

Edward J. Young, "The Relation of the First Verse of Genesis One to Verses Two and Three," in *Studies in Genesis One* (Philadelphia: Presbyterian and Reformed, 1964), 1–14.

17. John H. Walton, *The Lost World of Genesis* (Downers Grove, IL: IVP, 2009), 45, speaks of a "literary introduction." Against Walton, and with Wenham, Young, and Heidel, *bereshit* indicates a "point in time" rather than a "period of time" in Genesis 1:1.

18. From the third century B.C. (the Septuagint) to the tenth century A.D. (the Masoretic Text). Among the modern scholars who hold this view: J. Wellhausen, A. Heidel, D. Kidner, N. H. Ridderbos, E. J. Young, B. S. Childs, G. F. Hasel, and W. H. Gispen.

and original contribution of the creation account, while challenging the idea of the eternity of matter or energy, and asserts an absolute beginning and a creation *ex nihilo*.

The Meaning of the Root *Bara'*, "to Create"[19]

The root *bara'* is used six times in the prologue (1:1, 21, 27; 2:3) and eleven times in the book of Genesis. In the Hebrew Bible, it is used forty-nine times to describe a unique creative act that has God as its subject. It is not used to describe the activity of pagan gods. It describes the cosmic activity of the Creator: the creation of particular beings, individuals, or animals; the divine activity which unfolds within history; and the conditions set up by God allowing salvation and justice to shine forth.

It underscores the exclusive and new nature of the creative act, the extraordinary consequences of which surpass human imagination. The direct object of the verb expresses that which is created, but the material used is not specified. The verb is not reserved for *ex nihilo* creation, but it nevertheless carries the idea of an absolute creation. Karl-Heinz Bernhardt captures the uniqueness of this term: "As a specific theological term, *bara'* is used to express clearly the incomparability of the creative work of God in contrast to all secondary products and likenesses made from already existing material by man."[20] So, even if the root *bara'* does not itself explicitly refer to creation *ex nihilo*, it conveys the idea of a free, sovereign act without constraint.[21]

The prologue of Genesis sheds light on the question of the ultimate origin of things by emphasizing that the infinite and personal God is the ultimate being who created the whole universe. This is a

---

19. For a further study of this notion, see Berthoud, *En quête*, 216–18, and especially G. Johannes Botterweck and Helmer Ringgren, eds., *Theological Dictionary of the Old Testament*, vol. 2 (Grand Rapids: Eerdmans, 1977), 242–49.

20. Karl-Heinz Bernhardt, *TDOT*, 2:246. We disagree with John Walton, who argues that the verb *bārā* expresses "a function-giving activity" and not "a material activity" (*The Lost World*, 38–46).

21. The idea of creation *ex nihilo* is evident in other texts of the Old Testament, which declare that God created by his word (Ps. 148:5; Prov. 8:22–27). The verb *bara'* is also used with other verbs that describe divine creative acts.

pillar of the global biblical perspective, and it gives significance to the functional, existential, and environmental aspects of the creation narrative. To ignore it or to limit its scope means giving up one of the most original and important aspects of divine revelation.

Creation and Covenant

In answering the question of being, the first chapters of Genesis elaborate a theology of creation structured around the covenant as the foundation of a biblical perspective on the world and human existence.[22] In what follows, the covenant of life and the creation of man in the image of God are discussed.

The Divine Work of Creation or the Covenant of Life[23]

A covenant is a treaty that God the suzerain has concluded with man the vassal, which implies that man is not autonomous and has no ultimate reference point other than the Creator. The creature is responsible to the one who "himself gives to all mankind life and breath and everything" (Acts 17:25).

This concept is shared by all the biblical writers. The book of Amos is a good example, and although it does not use the notion of covenant explicitly, it underlies the whole. Its oracles reveal the double dimension of the covenant, both creational and redemptive. The evidence in favor of the covenant of creation is significant:

- Into oracles of doom, the prophet introduces doxologies that praise the Creator: "For behold, he who forms the mountains

---

22. The theology of the covenant has received special attention in the Reformed tradition. See Mark W. Karlberg, "The Original State of Adam: Tensions within Reformed Theology," *Evangelical Quarterly* 87 (1987): 291–96.

23. On the relationship between the notion of covenant and the theology of creation, see Henri Blocher, *Révélation des origines*, 2nd ed. (Lausanne: PBU, 1988), 52–129; Rowland S. Ward, *God and Adam: Reformed Theology and the Creation Covenant* (Wantima: New Melbourne Press, 2003); O. Palmer Robertson, *The Christ of the Covenants* (Grand Rapids: Baker Book House, 1980), 67–87; William J. Dumbrell, *Covenant and Creation* (Carlisle: Paternoster, 1997 [1984]).

and creates the wind, and declares to man what is his thought, who makes the morning darkness, and treads on the heights of the earth—the LORD, the God of hosts, is his name!" (4:13).[24]

- When God brings an action against Samaria, he invites the forts of Philistia and Egypt to be the witnesses of the confusion and the violence that is "in her midst" (3:9).
- Speaking of the future of the people of God, Amos foresees the universal scope of the restoration that the Messiah is going to accomplish (9:11–12).[25]
- Amos does not restrict his prophecy to Israel and Judah. His first oracles include the neighboring nations, also accountable to the Creator, the Lord of the universe (1:3–2:3).

The theology of creation underlies the oracles of Amos, and it is important for understanding his social message: the cause of the political, social, and legal disorders and injustices in Israel is spiritual, namely the rejection of God and his covenant stipulations. Without repentance and conversion, the worst is to be feared.

The Covenant of Life Renewed

The covenant of life established by God with man in creation is renewed, in a world under the consequences of sin, in the treaty concluded with Noah (Gen. 9:8–17).[26] This is fundamental for understanding the depth, power, and relevance of the Word of God that men have transmitted, sometimes at the risk of their own lives.

The word *covenant* does not appear at the beginning of Genesis. However, these chapters contain some of the characteristics of a treaty, and several later biblical texts confirm this, more or less explicitly:

24. See also Amos 5:8; 9:5–6.

25. For the translation of verse 12 we follow the Septuagint, confirmed by the New Testament (Acts 15:16–18): "so that the remnant of men, all the nations that bear my name, may seek the Lord."

26. Genesis 1 also speaks of the covenant of works. See Pierre Berthoud, "The Covenant and the Social Message of Amos," *European Journal of Theology* 14.2 (2005): 99–109, and "L'alliance, le cadre du message social et politique du prophète Amos," *Revue réformée* 58.2–3 (2007): 1–40.

- *Biblical references*: Speaking of Israel's refusal to repent, Hosea says: "Like Adam, they have broken the covenant" (Hos. 6:7 NIV). This allusion to Adam is one of the numerous references to the ancient history of the people of Israel in Hosea (2:8, 14; 9:10; 11:8; 12:4). Also, when Job recalls his past integrity, he seems to refer to the fall in Eden when he asks "if I have concealed my sin as Adam did" (Job 31:33).[27] Another possible reference is in Psalm 82:7, which could be understood as "Nevertheless, like Adam you shall die, and fall like the first of princes" (Ps. 82:7). These three passages imply that their authors understood the primeval events as a covenantal relationship, judicial and personal. They recognized that the first chapters of Genesis present elements of a covenant.

- *The covenant parties*: The Lord is the initiator of the covenant of life. By his creating act, he reveals himself as the God of the heavens and the earth, the universe. Although infinite and invisible, God is a personal being. He thinks and communicates; he loves without forsaking justice, and acts in freedom. Although transcendent, he is close to his good creation (Gen. 1:2). Indeed, the latter is a source of joys and delights (Prov. 8:30).

- *All things depend on the Lord*: The Creator-creature motif specifies the relationship of man to God and to the interdependent world around him.[28] God gives a *law* reminding man that he is not the ultimate source of wisdom. *Sanctions* are pronounced: blessing and life are promised to those who respect the commandments; curse and death await those who despise and reject the divine word (Gen. 2:15–17). Finally, the Sabbath is *the token* of this treaty. It seals the lordship of the Creator over the whole of creation, including human beings.

---

27. In a footnote, the NIV suggests the reading "as Adam did" instead of "as men do," which corresponds with the Hebrew text.

28. In an article dealing with the theology of creation and ethics, Heidi Hadsell indicates the recurring interest in the present debate for two key concepts: (1) creation understood in its totality as universe and cosmos, and (2) nature having

The Westminster Larger Catechism offers a synthesis of this covenantal perspective: "What was the providence of God toward man in the estate in which he was created?" Answer: "The providence of God toward man in the estate in which he was created, was the placing him in paradise, appointing him to dress it, giving him liberty to eat of the fruit of the earth; putting the creatures under his dominion, and ordaining marriage for his help; . . . entering into a covenant of life with him, upon condition of personal, perfect, and perpetual obedience, of which the tree of life was a pledge; and forbidding to eat of the tree of the knowledge of good and evil, upon the pain of death."[29]

The Creator is the initiator of a covenant of universal scope: active obedience to God enables man to know fullness of life. This covenant is concluded by God with Adam, the head of the human race (Rom. 5:12–21). A creature dependent upon the Creator is a personal being created in the image of his ultimate counterpart. Placed in the garden of Eden, Adam received a specific task, the cultural mandate: dwelling in the garden in fellowship with the living God, his calling was to manage creation in a spirit of gratitude.

Man Created in the Image of God

The nonautonomous human creature is a unique being defined by a relationship with the Lord. The personal nature of communion is not a mystical fusion between God and man. The image of God in man and the cultural mandate have their meaning within the framework of the covenant of life. Genesis speaks of man being created "in the image of God" (Gen. 1:27), and the psalmist expresses the same thought: "You have made him a little lower than the heavenly beings and crowned him with glory and honor. You have given him dominion over the works of your hands; you have put all things under his feet" (Ps. 8:5–6). These passages underscore two ideas, the nature or essence of man, and his function or mandate in creation.

---

intrinsic worth apart from humanity as God's good creation ("Creation, Theology and the Doing of Ethics," *Horizons in Biblical Theology* 14 [1992]: 93–94).

29. Westminster Larger Catechism, 20.

1. The Nature or Essence of Man

Henri Blocher says the word *image* means: "effigy, idol, representation" (1 Sam. 6:5; 2 Kings 11:18; Ezek. 23:14). For the ancients, an image was lifelike, partaking of the qualities of the object or person depicted. Man is defined in relation to God, and being like God, is a personal being: he thinks and communicates, loves without forsaking justice, and acts in freedom. The relationship of personal intimacy between God and the creature is real. The idea of filiation is found in Jesus' genealogy, where Adam is called "the son of God" (Luke 3:38), and the apostle Paul conveys the same thought: "We are indeed his offspring" (Acts 17:28).[30]

Since the mid-twentieth century, studies in biblical anthropology have emphasized the psychosomatic unity of man, questioning the duality of nineteenth-century idealism: man doesn't have a body; he is body. This biblical perspective avoids the immortality of the soul of animism or Platonic thought. A pitfall, however, is to be avoided: the modern paradigm reduces the human being to a horizontal dimension, its biochemical or neuropsychological components, whereas a balance between the unity and the duality of human nature is present in the Genesis account. "Created in the image of God" underscores the specificity of the human being (Gen. 1:27). No doubt man is "of the earth," related to the living beings, but he is also distinct. The breath that animates man is vital and personal (Gen. 2:7). The words and the concepts for this are not always used in a precise manner. Alfred Vacant remarked, many years ago, that the spiritual identity of man that transcends death is called by different terms with diverse meanings in Hebrew: soul (*nefesh, neshamah*, the life of the body), spirit (*ruah*, man endowed with power), heart (*lev*, man endowed with reason).[31] When "spirit" is not "breath," it refers only to God or man. The metaphor "heart" is not used of animals. On the other hand, the biblical authors speak of the "heart of God," the place of his watchfulness and deliberation, his will for justice and goodness. The biblical view also emphasizes

---

30. Blocher, *Révélation*, 72.

31. Alfred Vacant, "L'âme," in *Dictionnaire de la Bible*, ed. E. Vigouroux (Paris: Letouzey et Ané, 1895–1912), 1:453–73.

the vertical dimension of man, a spiritual being capable of a conscious relationship with God that transcends the body. Blocher rightly says that "the spirit of man is earthly" and "the body of man is the expression of his spirit."[32] John Cooper speaks of "holistic duality,"[33] while Gerald Bray affirms that "we are to think of the image as something given and immutable, an ontological reality in the human being."[34]

2. *The Function of the Cultural Mandate*

The calling of man in the image of God is to exercise dominion over the earth. To accent the dignity of man, Psalm 8 uses enthronement language and reiterates the creational mandate: "Let them have dominion over the fish of the sea and over the birds of the heavens and over the livestock and over all the earth and over every creeping thing that creeps on the earth" (Gen. 1:26). The first chapter of Genesis emphasizes the subjection of creation: man has an extraordinary destiny to exercise authority in the name of God over all of creation. The terms used convey the idea of the subjection of creation and the development of the resources of the earth. The first verb, *radah*, means "to dominate, govern, subject." A second term, *kabash*, means "to subject, to subjugate, and to maintain under influence." Man is to exercise this responsibility before God with his blessing. He can only be a faithful steward if he recognizes God and receives from him the grace indispensable to a proper use of talents and gifts: "The blessing of the LORD brings wealth, and toil does not add to it" (Prov. 10:22). The second chapter of Genesis gives "the translation, in another language, of the mandate to submit the earth presented in the first."[35] However, it brings a slightly different emphasis, as if to anticipate practical abuses: rather than ruthless plunder of creation, man's action should be service.[36] The

32. Blocher, *Révélation*, 82.

33. John W. Cooper, *Body, Soul, and Life Everlasting* (Grand Rapids: Eerdmans, 1989), 36–80.

34. Gerald Bray, "The Significance of God's Image in Man," *Tyndale Bulletin* 42 (1991): 223–24.

35. Blocher, *Révélation*, 115.

36. *'Avad*: to work, cultivate, serve, to serve in the temple, to adore God (Ex. 5:18; 21:6; 2 Kings 21:3; Ex. 3:12).

verb *'avad* (Gen. 2:15a) means "to serve" ritually in the temple, and by extension to worship God. When man rules creation in the presence of God, he takes care of what God has entrusted in worship and service, through daily tasks. Domination is qualified as service. Furthermore, the verb *shamar*, "to keep" (2:15b),[37] indicates that God intends Adam to be in charge of the garden. He empowers him with an authority exercised with wisdom and goodness. Man is part of creation and in its service. By taking care of the garden in Eden, man looks after its well-being and protects it. By calling man to "keep" the garden, God means Adam to be responsible for it, an intendant, steward, or assistant-governor, under the Lord. "Not only will man command over nature by obeying its laws" (Francis Bacon), "but he will do so for the good of creation itself, so that it fulfills its "calling" to glorify God.[38] Dominion expresses the same solicitude that God the Father manifests toward his handiwork (Job 38:39–41; Ps. 104:11–30). Will not the whole of creation benefit from the priceless redemption acquired by Jesus Christ (Rom. 8:18–22)?

The human calling implies a high and positive view of work, in contrast to the ancient Near Eastern outlook suggesting that man was created to relieve the gods from their burdensome and exhausting tasks![39] Numerical and economic growth is implicit in the injunction of Genesis: "God blessed them. And God said to them, 'Be fruitful and multiply and fill the earth and subdue it'" (Gen. 1:28). This suggests that property and possession of material goods are legitimate, but with the recognition that everything belongs to God.

Man, in the image of God, is to administer God's creation with care. The faithful fulfillment of man's work-service honors God, and his position on earth is that of a manager. He is accountable for the way he carries out the cultural mandate and how he uses and enhances the resources of the earth and its products and goods. His

---

37. *Shamar*: to keep, watch over, protect, save (1 Sam. 17:20; Ps. 121; Gen. 41:35).
38. Blocher, *Révélation*, 115.
39. Atrahasis, Tablet I, in *Les religions du Proche-Orient asiatique*, ed. René Labat et al. (Paris: Fayard/Denoël, 1970), 26. In Genesis, work is not degrading for God. The creative activity of the Lord offers him both satisfaction and joy. The centrality of the Sabbath confirms this point: Gen. 2:2–3 (cf. Prov. 8).

duty is to promote the lordship of God in all spheres of existence and to meet his responsibilities. Such is the creational mission of the descendants of Adam, of mankind.

The Unique Contribution of Genesis on Evil

The aim of the second section of Genesis (2:4–3:24) is to separate the origin of good from the origin of evil. In the ancient Near Eastern context, in Babylonian theogonic myth, "evil is incorporated into the cosmos as one of the main ingredients of reality. Man is therefore inclined to evil from the very beginning." In tragic myth, evil "is a property of being," and in the myth of the exiled soul, evil pertains to "the metaphysical structure of humanity." Myth integrates evil into the ultimate reality, as an ontological etiology, offering a model that is timeless and "allergic to history."[40]

However, if evil were intrinsic, man would be excusable, since he faces an "invincible fate." Paul Ricoeur says that "evil becomes scandalous at the same time as it becomes historical."[41] To distinguish between the "origin of the goodness of creation" and "the wickedness of history" is a significant contribution of divine revelation in Genesis. Adam is not only a mirror, but also an efficient cause of the present human condition. Situated in time at the beginning of humanity, he is the head of the covenant of life contracted with humankind, when God created the visible and invisible universe.[42]

Evil is intolerable because it "proceeds from the historical use of freedom": it is not metaphysical, but moral. According to Blocher, "the biblical concept of sin . . . confirms this unique emphasis."[43] It is a "disorder that nothing justifies." Man as a creature is accountable for his choices, guilt is central in human experience, and a personal and

---

40. Blocher, *Genesis*, 156–58; Berthoud, *En quête*, 150–53.

41. Blocher, *Genesis*, 157. In his study (chap. 7, "La Rupture," 130–67), Blocher presents Ricoeur's thought and offers a balanced, critical evaluation. Ricoeur refuses to distinguish between the origin of being and of evil, having recognized it in the first chapters of Genesis.

42. Blocher, *Genesis*, 163–64, 158.

43. Blocher, *Genesis*, 163.

collective consciousness of the tragic horror of sin is a reality. Finitude and guilt are different. Man's misfortune is not that he is a creature, finite and imperfect. His problem is the consequence of moral rebellion against God's word of wisdom and life.[44] The tree of the knowledge of good and evil, representing the principle of probation, confirms this point. As Adam and Eve succumb to temptation, they desire to become their own reference point for deciding what is right and wrong (Gen. 2:9; 24:50; 31:24, 29; Num. 24:14).[45] As John R. R. Tolkien said:

> I do not now feel either ashamed or dubious on the Eden "myth". It has not, of course, historicity of the same kind as the New Testament, which are virtually contemporary documents, while Genesis is separated by we do not know how many sad exiled generations from the Fall, but certainly there was an Eden on this very unhappy earth.[46]

The Cultural Mandate in a Broken World

The Progression of Civilization

The line of Adam through Cain accounts for the progression of civilization as an expression of the cultural mandate, involving a diversity of human activities. Cain builds a town, a permanent dwelling place without reference to its size, and gives it the name of Enoch, his son (Gen. 4:17). Further on in the genealogy of Cain, we are told that Lamech's son, Jabal, is the father of seminomadic farming. He is "the father of those who dwell in tents and have livestock" (4:20).[47] Such activities were already mentioned in verse 2: Abel is "a keeper of sheep" and Cain is "a worker of the ground." The curse that strikes

---

44. Blocher, *Genesis*, 165.

45. See Berthoud, *En quête*, 234–37, for a discussion of the meaning of "the tree of the knowledge of good and evil."

46. John R. R. Tolkien, *Letters* (London: Harper Collins, 1995), 109–10. Cf. Clive S. Lewis, "Myth Become Fact," in *God in the Dock* (Grand Rapids: Eerdmans, 1976), 63–67.

47. The Septuagint reads: "the tent of the livestock" (*'ahole miqneh*). The same expression is found in 2 Chron. 14:15; Gen. 46:32; 47:6.

Adam—"By the sweat of your face you shall eat bread" (3:19)—implies man's hard labor and, consequently, the creational calling to cultivate and keep the garden of Eden (2:15). Man's dominion spreads over all of creation, and that includes breeding of domesticated animals. With Jabal, seminomadic farming is organized. Jubal, his brother, is the father of musicians and of culture: "of all those who play the lyre and pipe" (4:21). Tubal-cain, the half-brother of both Jabal and Jubal, is the father of technology and industry: "the forger of all instruments of bronze and iron" (4:22). Naamah is to be linked to Jubal, father of musicians, as the meaning of her name seems to be related to music and singing.[48]

These narrative details, illustrative of Near Eastern literary practice, provide information about the development of civilization. If it is true that Cain was "a wanderer on the earth" and that cultivated ground did not yield its crops to him (Gen. 4:12), then his descendants settled in permanent towns and laid the foundations of civilization: agriculture, industry, technology, culture, and the arts. Israel's neighbors credited the organization of civilization to the gods.[49] Without denying divine inspiration, the Torah states that civilization is the action of ordinary mortals.[50] The dignity and the value of human beings is brought to the forefront. Endowed with ingenuity, wisdom, and imagination, the sons of Adam express creativity in a diversity of ways. That these activities developed in the lineage of Cain is not without significance, nor are they reprehensible.[51] Adam and Eve's rebellion introduced ambiguity into human thought and action as

---

48. U. Cassuto, *A Commentary on the Book of Genesis*, trans. I. Abrahams (Jerusalem: Magnes Press, 1961, 1964), 1:238.

49. In Ugarit, for example, the technique and the art of the blacksmith were imputed to the god *ktr wḥss*. See Cassuto, 1:230.

50. In his providence, God equipped Bezalel to create what he planned for the tabernacle (Ex. 31:2–4).

51. John L. McKenzie, "Reflections on Wisdom," *Journal of Biblical Literature* 86 (1967): 1–9. Cf. Mircea Eliade, *Histoire des croyances et des idées religieuses* (Paris: Payot, 1976–83), 1:64ff., 80. McKenzie reads the biblical text from a modern viewpoint, whereas Eliade considers Genesis 4:17–22 in the Near Eastern context without highlighting its biblical specificity. Biblical revelation, even in the case of genealogies and narrative details, is to be appreciated within a monotheistic, not a mythological, framework.

to the meaning of civilization when men became their own reference point and final authority. Do not these enterprises nourish interests and desire for autonomy and become the cause of bitterness and disillusionment? The book of Ecclesiastes explains that the problem lies not in the imagination or the inventiveness of human beings, but rather in their arrogance and hubris.[52] The choice of the first couple in favor of autonomy, over against God and his law, had tragic repercussions for the whole of creation. Robert R. Ellis sees in this choice a negative use of God-given human responsibility. By seeking to take the place of God, Adam and Eve rejected limitations shared with other creatures and opposed the Creator's intention.[53] Neither the ability nor the competence of human beings is the cause of anguish and misery, but rather the human desire for emancipation from God's wisdom and guidance.

The Noachic Covenant and the Dignity of Man[54]

In the Noachic covenant, God in his patience prescribes ordinances that contribute to the realization of his design (Gen. 9:1–17). The emphasis is on the propagation, preservation, and protection of life in an aggressive environment, the threat coming from both animals and humans. After the flood and the destruction of the earth and its inhabitants, the Lord decided in his sovereignty to conclude a universal covenant with Noah (Gen. 10:13–14).

1. The Presence of Evil and the Noachic Covenant

In a fallen world, where evil and sin are at work, where does man stand in relation to God and with regard to his earthly calling? The covenant concluded with Noah and his sons gives an answer. It introduces a time of patience, allowing God to accomplish his plan

---

52. Pierre Berthoud, "Gilgamesh et l'Ecclésiaste, deux sages en quête de bonheur," in *L'amour de la sagesse: Hommage à Henri Blocher*, ed. Alain Nisus (Vaux-sur-Seine: Edifac; Cléon d'Andran: Excelsis, 2012), 75–102.

53. Robert R. Ellis, "Divine Gift and Human Response: An Old Testament Model for Stewardship," *Southwestern Journal of Theology* 37 (1995): 4–6.

54. Mark D. Van der Hart, in spite of the new context after the flood, sees in the covenant concluded with Noah an allusion to the cultural mandate that God gave to man at creation, in a redemptive-historical perspective ("Creation and Covenant," *Mid-America Journal of Theology* 6.1 [1990]: 9–13).

of redemption (Gen. 3:15; 8:21b; Rom. 3:25). This covenant is made on God's sole initiative: it is universal and is concluded with Noah, his descendants, and the creatures and the earth (9:9–13)—as well as being unconditional and eternal, "while the earth remains" (8:22). The rainbow signifies universal scope (Isa. 54:1–10) and certifies that God in his faithfulness has chosen to withhold judgment. God renews man's earthly mandate in a world where evil is a dynamic reality. Human institutions, in particular judicial institutions, limit the development of evil and punish wrongdoers (Gen. 9:5–6). André Neher highlights three aspects of the Noachic covenant:[55]

- It aims at pacifying the forces of nature; the rainbow guarantees cosmic stability (9:8–19).
- It is concluded with Noah and his sons as the ancestors of the whole human race (9:1): "all races and nations are related."
- The "Noachic code" (9:1–7) is made up of practical, moral articles: it affirms the inherent value of the human person (v. 5) and links criminal law to metaphysical and theological considerations (v. 6).[56] A criminal act is an offence against the dignity of man and the honor of God. An old Jewish tradition speaks of Noah's seven commandments, forbidding idolatry, contempt for the name of God, bloodshed, adultery, theft, and the consumption of blood with the flesh of animals, with the provision for the institution of civil authority (b. Sanh. 105a).[57]

2. A Renewed Covenant of Life

Man thought to free himself from God, but after the fall the Creator-creature motif remains, as man is accountable (Acts 17:31). Although evil and misery have become part of human existence, the

---

55. André Neher, *Amos: Contribution à l'étude du prophétisme* (Paris: J. Vrin, 1950), 65.

56. The uniqueness of the human being created in the image of God justifies the possibility of capital punishment in the case of deliberate homicide. See James E. Priest, "Genesis 9:6: A Comparative Study of Bloodshed in Bible and Talmud," *Evangelical Theological Society* 31 (1988): 145–51.

57. Raphaël Drai, *La Thora: La législation de Dieu* (Paris: Michalon, 2000), 36.

children of Adam do not lose their unique identity. They live in the shadow of death, but still bear the image of God. Man has become fragile, threatened by his natural environment and fellow creatures, but in his goodness God protects him. The world may have become a dangerous and violent place, but this is not the end of the story. The covenant of creation is renewed in a world where evil, hatred, and violence have free reign. God adapts, but does not resign himself, committing himself to his creation and paving the way for his plan of salvation for the whole of creation: "In the frame of Hebrew theology, which is based on creation, the unconditionality of the Abrahamic and Davidic covenants must have a 'cosmic' foundation of the kind provided by the universal Noachic covenant."[58]

The Divine Initiative and the Promise of Redemption

The Protoevangelium (Genesis 3:15)

A number of scholars have argued convincingly for the continuity between the narratives of primeval history and the history of the patriarchs.[59] This emphasis is a prerequisite when dealing with the antecedents of the promises made to Abraham (Gen. 12:1–3). Generations before, God expressed his intent to save lost humanity. During that period, the threads that would crystallize in the call of Abraham were woven together. The roots of the patriarchal promise are found in the sentence pronounced in Eden on the serpent: "I will put enmity between you and the woman, and between your offspring and her offspring; he shall bruise your head, and you shall bruise his heel" (Gen. 3:15). If the history of revelation requires that we not immediately introduce a Christological reading of this text, it hardly follows that there are no redemptive overtones to this passage.

58. Joze Krasovec, "Two Types of Unconditional Covenants," *Horizons in Biblical Theology* 18 (1996): 67.

59. Cf. Albert de Pury, "La tour de Babel et la vocation d'Abraham," *Etudes théologiques et religieuses* 1953 (1978): 80–97; "Genèse 12–36," in *Introduction à l'Ancien Testament*, by Thomas Römer et al. (Genève: Labor et Fides, 2004), 134–35, 143, 154–55; David J. A. Clines, *The Theme of the Pentateuch*, JSOTSup, 10 (Sheffield: University of Sheffield, 1978), 61–79.

Although we should proceed carefully in the exegesis of this text,[60] it is difficult not to see with Franck Michaeli "an allusion to the fight that man must constantly engage against temptation and the power of evil, with the hope of conquering them one day by the grace of God."[61] If "offspring" usually has a collective meaning, a reference here to an individual is also possible, a reading adopted by the Septuagint: "He will aim for your head and you will aim at his heel." A battle will take place between Satan and an individual "representing humanity that will not go without suffering for the latter." Blocher speaks of "the prophecy of reciprocal bruising through the crushing of the evil one."[62] The fulfillment of the promise in the coming of Jesus of Nazareth, the Messiah, unveils the full scope of this text, shedding light on what remained obscure. For this reason, John Calvin, with the church fathers, emphasized that humankind has access only to the final victory in Abraham's offspring, Christ (Eph. 2:11–22).[63] This victory, at such a great price, will be fully manifested only when Christ returns: "The God of peace will soon crush Satan under your feet" (Rom. 16:20). Paul refers to Genesis 3, underlining its prophetic and eschatological dimensions.[64]

From a human perspective, this text represents the beginning of the history of revelation and God's redemptive initiative. It contains in a nutshell what the history of revelation will progressively unveil.

The Line of the Promise

This primeval promise contains the hope of a line that will carry God's answer to man's insane rebellion. It begins with Seth, whom God gave in place of Abel (Gen. 4:25). Some significant names

60. For a discussion of the interpretation of Genesis 3:15, see Berthoud, *En quête*, 137–39.

61. Frank Michaeli, *La Genèse* (Neuchâtel: Delachaux et Niestlé, 1957), 55.

62. Blocher, *Révélation*, 192; Cf. in particular 1 John 3:8; Heb. 2:14; Gal. 4:4.

63. John Calvin, *Commentaries on the First Book of Moses Called Genesis*, trans. John King, Calvin's Commentaries, 2 vols. (repr., Grand Rapids: Baker Book House, 1979), 1:171 (comm. on Gen. 3:15).

64. Blocher notes that Eve, in naming her son Seth (Gen. 4:25), relates him to the verb *shat* ("put, place, designate, institute") in 3:15: "Seth and his descendants will maintain enmity with the Serpent" (*Révélation*, 205).

belonging to this line may be mentioned. It was in Enosh's day that "people began to call again upon the name of the LORD" (4:26). In the midst of depraved humanity, the Lord had an authentic witness who was the foundation of true worship: Enoch "walked with God" (5:22)—or, in the words of the Septuagint, "was pleasing to God." The patriarch's intimacy with the Creator was such that he alone with Elijah was taken up by the Lord without knowing death. As for Noah, his father Lamech said: "He will comfort us in the labor and painful toil of our hands caused by the ground the LORD has cursed" (5:29 NIV). "Noah found favor in the eyes of the LORD. . . . He was a righteous man, blameless in his generation" (6:8–9). Through him, God spared and restored creation and humanity by the renewal of the covenant of creation in a world marred by the fall, and he had a positive impact on his family and the whole creation (8:20–22).[65] Noah was the father of Shem, on whom God pronounced a blessing for the history of salvation (9:26–27): he would reveal himself fully as YHWH, the Lord of the covenant, in and through the family of Shem. The covenantal name emphasizes the divine nature of God in his work of redemption, and is itself a blessing. The Lord commits himself to Shem as the God who fulfills the promise and enacts salvation. Shem's genealogy is important because it is the link between primeval and patriarchal history. During the first stage of protohistory, God wove together the threads of the redemption that he would reveal to Israel and the nations. It is therefore possible to speak of the antecedents of the redemptive work of God during the primeval history of humanity.

The call of Abraham represents the beginning of a new stage in the history of redemption, but it is also the result of God's often imperceptible activity, which began with the protoevangelium. Brevard Childs's understanding of Genesis in its final form accounts for the creative and redemptive aspects of the narrative:

> The canonical role of Genesis 1–11 testifies to the priority of creation. The divine relation to the world stems from God's initial creative purpose for the universe, not for Israel alone. Yet Israel's

65. Cf. Heb. 11:7; 1 Peter 3:20–21.

redemptive role in the reconciliation of the nations was purposed from the beginning and subsumed within the eschatological framework of the book.[66]

From Eden to Abraham, light is shed on the divine purpose of salvation in the promise made to the son of Terah. The Hebrew Bible progressively reveals the mission that the Lord entrusted to the seed of the woman and to the covenant community: to glorify and enjoy God, to be the bearer of his oracles in view of the redemption of the people of Israel and the nations, and to manifest in a broken world an authentic witness to the living Lord, in which loving-kindness, justice, and peace "kiss each other" (Ps. 85:10).

The Bearings of the Cultural Mandate on the Mission of the Church

A few concluding remarks may be made on the relationship of the cultural mandate as presented in the covenant of creation and the mission of the church in the New Testament. The unity of divine revelation calls for it, and the authors of the New Testament are unanimous in emphasizing that the promises of redemption contained in the Old Testament were fulfilled in Jesus of Nazareth, the anticipated Messiah.

A Divine Institution

The church, like the universe, is created by the Lord. Being both a human and a divine institution, it came into being by a supernatural act. It is the covenant community that is sealed in Jesus Christ. We can therefore say with the Heidelberg Catechism "that the Son of God from the beginning to the end of the world, gathers, defends, and preserves to himself by his Spirit and word, out of the whole human

---

66. Brevard S. Childs, *Introduction to the Old Testament as Scripture* (London: SCM, 1979), 155. Victor P. Hamilton separates Genesis 1–2 from Genesis 3–11 and fails to draw the consequences for creation from the reconciliation that God initiates in the promise made to Abraham and his descendants (*The Book of Genesis: Chapters 1–17*, NICOT [Grand Rapids: Eerdmans, 1991], 52).

race, a church chosen to everlasting life, agreeing in true faith."[67] By the church, "the communion of the saints," we understand "first, that all and everyone who believes, being members of Christ, are in common partakers of him, and of all his riches and gifts; secondly, that everyone must know it to be his duty readily and cheerfully to employ his gifts, for the advantage and salvation of other members."[68]

The supernatural character of the church determines its mission, but with the advent of the Messiah and the outpouring of the Holy Spirit at Pentecost, it takes on a new profile: the covenant community is distinct from Israel, it emphasizes the priesthood of all believers and its calling is to proclaim the gospel of reconciliation to the ends of the earth, to both Jews and Gentiles.

Creation, Fall, and Redemption

The whole of God's good creation suffered the consequences of the primeval rebellion and fall, and redemption acquired in Jesus Christ has a cosmic dimension, including the renewal and transformation of all things in heaven and on earth (Rom. 8:19–23).[69]

A proper understanding of the Lord's saving design requires an understanding of the origin of evil. Adam chose to turn away from his ultimate reference point, and the dilemma is moral and not metaphysical. The basic biblical motif of creation, rebellion and fall, and redemption, to which sanctification and glorification could be added, has profound significance. God is good and there is hope for a solution. It is also possible to fight evil and to act according to moral absolutes and ethical values as "sojourners and exiles in the world" (1 Peter 2:11).

A Renewed Vision of the Cultural Mandate

The cultural mandate reminds us that human beings are unique creatures with a special calling to take care of the earth and to develop

---

67. Heidelberg Catechism, 54.
68. Heidelberg Catechism, 55.
69. This hope is already anticipated in the book of Isaiah (65:17; 66:22), is reaffirmed by Peter (2 Peter 3:13), and is further developed by John (Rev. 21:1).

its resources. The Creator bestowed upon humans many talents, a creative mind, and a spirit of enterprise to fulfill this task. The dramatic events of Eden did not erase the dignity of man, his gifts and special mandate, but because of the dynamic reality of evil, his enterprises and goals remain ambiguous, bearing witness to estrangement from God, creation, and neighbor. Man lives in a real sense under "the shadow of death" (Ps. 23:4). But when believers are reconciled with their heavenly Father, they become a "new creation. The old has passed away; behold, the new has come." Existence is reoriented to the source of life. Paul adds, "All this is from God, who through Christ reconciled us to himself and gave us the ministry of reconciliation" (2 Cor. 5:17–18). The teaching and edification of believers includes the proclamation of the gospel, so that they may become mature and responsible disciples, as well as credible witnesses in the city of men.

The gospel of Jesus Christ provides renewed understanding of the cultural mandate, which promotes a corresponding lifestyle. We are not "of the world," but are called to be "the salt of the earth." With the talents God has given, the gifts of the Holy Spirit and the power of the Word, we are called to participate actively in the divine work of reformation and transformation. As J. Gresham Machen said, "Human institutions are really to be molded, not by Christian principles accepted by the unsaved, but by Christian men; the true transformation of society will come by the influence of those who have themselves been redeemed."[70] We are not working to implement utopia or an ideal human society, whatever its ideology, but to further the kingdom of God that will only be fully manifested when Jesus, the Messiah, returns in glory. Being faithful stewards in our daily undertakings is a foreshadowing of the city we anticipate in hope. The apostle Paul exhorts us:

> I urge, then, first of all, that requests, prayers, intercession and thanksgiving be made for everyone—for kings and all those in

---

70. J. Gresham Machen, *Christianity and Liberalism* (Grand Rapids: Eerdmans, 1923), 158.

authority, that we may live peaceful and quiet lives in all godliness and holiness. This is good, and pleases God our Savior, who
wants all men to be saved and to come to a knowledge of the truth.
(1 Tim. 2:1–4 NIV)

3

The Covenant of Grace as the Paradigm for Mission

Peter A. Lillback

Abstract

The covenant of grace is the theological launching pad for global mission, in terms of both theology and practice. The implications of the covenant of grace for mission are far-reaching. *Covenant theology* means:

- God makes the first move to establish a covenant relationship with his people.
- God has entered into a covenant relationship with the whole world—one that all have broken.
- God is reaching out to the whole world. His global intention is seen in his covenant call in the gospel.
- Christ's saving grace restores the broken covenant relationship between God and man and thereby brings divine power for healing cultures through believers who are marked by God's signs of the covenant.
- The Scriptures are a covenantal book providing us with the message of justifying grace for our sins and sanctifying wisdom for our lives.
- Global evangelization advances through the proclamation of the gospel by the powerful, regenerating witness of the Holy Spirit, the promised gift of the new covenant of grace.

Reformed missions labor to preach the gospel to each person as created in God's image, but also as covenant breakers in Adam's fall. The gospel alone restores union with God and repairs broken relationships, whether in family, church, state, or culture. Ultimately, a gospel-saturated culture enables each of these covenant realities to thrive. People in such an environment repent of their covenant breaking, and as covenant keepers they move their culture toward God, reflecting truth, peace, justice, and liberty of conscience, governed by the Golden Rule.

Introduction

The Global Reformed Mission

What is the motive for missions? Johannes H. Bavinck explains:

> To establish the proper basis of missions, it is necessary to reflect upon the motivation behind the missionary enterprise and to ascertain the true scriptural motive of missions. Is it to be found in the sympathy we feel for those who do not know Christ? Or is it simply in obedience to God's commands that we send missionaries? The history of missions shows a great diversity in motivation. Some missionaries were motivated by an ascetic view of life, and chose missions as a form of self-denial; others were stimulated by a desire to hasten the return of Christ; and frequently missionary work has been connected with a tendency to spread Western culture, regarded as far superior to all other forms of life. At times missionary activity became a part of colonialism, a task of the government more than of the church. History certainly presents a medley of motives and ideas. But which ones are authorized in Scripture?[1]

There have been various motives for missionary activity, such as humanitarian aid, cultural improvement, geopolitical stabilization,

---

1. J. H. Bavinck, *An Introduction to the Science of Missions*, trans. David H. Freeman (Philadelphia: Presbyterian and Reformed, 1960), 3.

the dignity of the human being, and compassion for the suffering. *But the Reformed motive for global mission has always emphasized obedience to Scripture.* The Great Commission of our Lord Jesus Christ comes with the full authority of the resurrected Lord:

> And Jesus came and said to them, "All authority in heaven and on earth has been given to me. Go therefore and make disciples of all nations, baptizing them in the name of the Father and of the Son and of the Holy Spirit, teaching them to observe all that I have commanded you. And behold, I am with you always, to the end of the age." (Matt. 28:18–20)

This is the heart of the modern missionary movement and the continuing missionary efforts made by Reformed Christians today. Indeed, Jesus prayed to the Father for us, saying, "As you sent me into the world, so I have sent them into the world" (John 17:18).

The Great Commission is buttressed by Scripture's teaching of the lost state of the world.[2] Moreover, the world into which Jesus was sent by the Father's love (John 3:16) is the world that Jesus in turn has sent us into: "As you sent me into the world, so I have sent them into the world" (John 17:18). Similarly, John 20:21–22 records the risen Lord's words to his disciples, "'Peace be with you. As the Father has sent me, even so I am sending you.' And when he had said this, he breathed on them and said to them, 'Receive the Holy Spirit.'"

Accordingly, effective global mission initiatives have emanated from Reformed ministries in the Presbyterian churches of Scotland in the nineteenth century and from American and Korean Presbyterian churches in the twentieth and twenty-first centuries. Parachurch ministries such as Campus Crusade for Christ, Evangelism Explosion, and many forms of gospel media have reached around the world. Reformed individuals have participated in these efforts. Today, as much as ever, the Reformed motive for global mission is obedience to Scripture.

---

2. Luke 15:4–7; 19:10; John 3:19, 36; 17:14; 2 Cor. 4:4; Gal. 1:3–4; 1 John 5:19.

The Twenty-First Century

Our moment in time affords us a fascinating tapestry of inter-woven forces propelling mission activities around the world. Some of the significant realities of missions in the twenty-first century are:

- As unprecedented travel opportunities and global communication technologies are harnessed for the kingdom of God, the reality of a global missionary effort becomes ever more possible for mission-minded Christians.
- This is aided by the new global lingua franca, the English language.
- Multiculturalism and postmodernity can sometimes oppose historic Christian evangelism; nevertheless, they have also made many more aware of the urgent opportunities for global cross-cultural missions.
- So global missions is becoming a reality, given ever-increasing global interconnectivity.
- This has occurred while the decline of Christianity in the West has become apparent.
- Thus, global Christian missions and witness are no longer directed primarily from the West to Asia and the global South. Instead, these once spiritually impoverished mission fields, from a past Western perspective, have become the center of Christianity.
- The Korean churches have undertaken missions with great earnestness and are now one of the largest sending nations in the world.[3]
- The languages and dialects of the world have been mapped and identified, and plans have been made for biblical translation into each of the remaining unreached linguistic groups in the coming years, aided in great measure by the advances in computer technology.
- The twenty-first century has seen the dawning of a global Christian witness.

3. Melissa Steffan, "The Surprising Countries Most Missionaries Are Sent From and Go To," *Gleanings*, July 25, 2013, http://www.christianitytoday.com/gleanings

Indisputably, we live in an unparalleled epoch for evangelism and global missions. With such potential to fulfill our Lord's missionary mandate, let us strive to increase our global missionary momentum and focus our efforts for greater effectiveness to seize these God-given opportunities.

What Does Covenant Theology Have to Do with Missions?

Let us then consider the impact of covenantal thought on Reformed global missions. As Reformed believers in missions, we must reach the world through a keen understanding of the covenant of grace that undergirds the Great Commission.

To start, we understand that the covenant of grace is the heart of God's sovereign plan for his people throughout the world. By this covenant of grace, those who are chosen in Christ in eternity are in time redeemed in him from their sin through saving faith in Christ's life, death, and resurrection. Thus, mission flows from the eternal, electing purpose of God that is realized in time by God's establishment of a covenant with his people. Jesus partly unveils the divine intentions for redemption in John 17:2, 6, praying to his Father, "You have given him [the Son] authority over all flesh, to give eternal life to all whom you have given him. . . . I have manifested your name to the people whom you gave me out of the world. Yours they were, and you gave them to me."

Bavinck explains the connection between missions and the covenant in this way:

> The work of missions is possible only within the concept of a covenant. Pagan religions have room for conquest and tyrannical coercion; the gods of the conquerors are forced upon the conquered. . . . A nation can discover that its gods are identical with those worshiped by another nation under a different name. But what is impossible within pagan religion is a sincere effort to convert another nation to faith in one's own god by bearing a spiritual

/2013/july/missionaries-countries-sent-received-csgc-gordon-conwell.html.

witness. The latter is possible only within the framework of a covenant. If Jehovah is the God of Israel because he has made a covenant with Israel, it is conceivable that other nations will also some day be included in that covenant. For Israel has no individual and peculiar claim upon God; its privileged position is due solely to God's electing grace.[4]

This perspective is manifest in the teachings of Scripture. The covenant of grace emerges from within the Trinity as God's saving decree (John 17:1–3; Eph. 1:3–6; 2:8–10; 2 Tim. 1:9) and flows into time and space through the church's missions mandate (Matt. 28:18–20; John 17:18; 20:21–22; Acts 1:8). God's decree of election is realized in time through the covenant of grace with his chosen people, both in the Old Testament[5] and in the New Testament.[6]

Accordingly, sovereign election is balanced with the gospel invitation in Jesus' words in Matthew 11:25–30:

> I thank you, Father, Lord of heaven and earth, that you have hidden these things from the wise and understanding and revealed them to little children; yes, Father, for such was your gracious will. All things have been handed over to me by my Father, and no one knows the Son except the Father, and no one knows the Father except the Son and anyone to whom the Son chooses to reveal him. Come to me, all who labor and are heavy laden, and I will give you rest. Take my yoke upon you, and learn from me, for I am gentle and lowly in heart, and you will find rest for your souls. For my yoke is easy, and my burden is light.

In the Scriptures, God's sovereign act of choosing a particular people (Gen. 12:1–2) is coupled with his global vision (12:3). The redeemed

4. Bavinck, *Missions*, 14.
5. Gen. 17:7; Lev. 26:12; Ps. 105:7–11; Isa. 42:6; 59:21; Jer. 31:31–24; Ezek. 37:26; Dan. 9:4; Hos. 2:18; Mal. 2:4–5; 3:1.
6. Matt. 26:27–28; Luke 1:72; Acts 3:25; Rom. 11:27; 1 Cor. 11:25; 2 Cor. 3:4–6; 7:16–18; Gal. 3:15; Eph. 2:12; Heb. 8:6–13; 9:1; 10:16, 29; 12:24; 13:20; Rev. 21:3.

in the covenant of grace are from "every tribe and language and people and nation" (Rev. 5:9).

Divine Initiative

God makes the first move to establish a covenant relationship with his people. Divine initiative in the salvation of the sinner is seen in the words "I will be your God, and you will be my people." This phrase has been called the *formula of the covenant*. By these words, God adopts a people for himself. "I will be your God, and you will be my people" underscores God's one-sided or unilateral promise of saving grace. "For it is by grace you have been saved, through faith—and this not from yourselves, it is the gift of God—not by works, so that no one can boast" (Eph. 2:8–9 NIV). Sometimes theologians describe this unilateral divine initiative as monergism, or the unique working of God in salvation. The formula of the covenant asserts that the salvation of the sinner is unilateral in initiation, and sovereignly accomplished by God, who is the Lord of this relationship of salvation. Indeed, it is God who is seeking worshipers to worship him in Spirit and truth (John 4:23–24).

But God's sovereign initiative in salvation is not severed from his global vision of grace. This means that missions in the world will also reflect that the redeemed in the covenant of grace come from "every tribe and language and people and nation." No nation can be construed to be outside of God's mission mandate. So we must fulfill our duty and seize the opportunities to bring the good news of Christ to the world.

We do not go alone to evangelize. We do not create a people for God. Rather, God has already known his people, and has deigned to use our witness as a means of fulfilling his own divine initiative and sovereign purpose in redeeming his people throughout the world.

A Universal Broken Covenant

God has entered into a covenant relationship with the whole world, a covenant that all have broken. While the covenant begins with the "I" of divine initiative, the formula of the covenant shows that it is mutual in realization. The "I" who is God speaks to a people that he calls "*you*," indeed "*your* God," assuring them that "*you* will be my people." Thus, God's formula of the covenant expresses that those he seeks to be his can be personally addressed with the mutually obligating promise, "You will be my people."

The elements of a covenant show that a close interpersonal relationship is intended between God and man in the covenant. A list of the various aspects of the covenant often includes:

- *Parties*—two or more individuals or groups are entering into the covenant.
- *Promise/Oath*—those making covenant, whether God or man, give an oath to the other that is to be relied upon or trusted.
- *Conditions*—the covenant relationship demands that certain duties or requirements be fulfilled, whether by God, man, or both.
- *Stipulations*—these identified conditions are to be fulfilled as requirements to the other and are enforced by benefits flowing from the covenant, as well as penalties that will be experienced if the covenant is violated.
- *Blessings and Curses*—since oaths make covenants binding, the covenants' conditions are required and enforced by stipulations. This means covenants have the potential for wonderful benefits or grave consequences, which are appropriately called blessings and curses.
- *Sacrifices*—the shedding of blood by a sacrifice is part of a covenant. The sacrifice may be a sign of warning for failure to keep the covenant as well as a sacrament pointing to the very cost required so the covenant is sure and will be realized. The blood of the covenant sacrifice seals the bond or covenant between the parties. Hence, sacrifices emphasize the sanctity of the stipulations, and guarantee and symbolize the reality of the covenant's blessings and curses.[7]

7. John H. Walton, *Ancient Israelite Literature in Its Cultural Context: A Survey of Parallels between Biblical and Ancient Near Eastern Texts* (Grand Rapids: Zondervan,

From this overview it is evident that a covenant is inherently a mutual relationship. When applied to missions, the covenant means that God is overcoming the barriers of sin to be joined with believers. The covenant means that God is binding himself to his people in Christ. It also implies that in our Christian experience we are to bind ourselves together as believers whatever our ethnicities. Since we affirm the saving work of our Lord, we are to strive to be truly a church of all nations.

The Covenantal Gospel Call

God's intention in reaching out to the whole world is seen in his gracious covenant call in the gospel. All stand in Adam by creation and fall (Gen. 1–3; Rom. 5:12–21; 1 Cor. 15:42–49). There is a universal connection of all men to God's original relationship with Adam in his creation in the *imago Dei*, in the promises, blessings, and curses of the stipulation of the creation order, and in the tragic consequences of Adam's rebellion and judgment. As human beings of all nations simply by being born and having descended from Adam, we stand in a broken covenant relationship. The Creator/creature distinction of Eden is now the Creator/sinner separation by the breach of the covenant of creation. This Augustinian and Reformed theology has historically been called the covenant of works, established between God and Adam as the head of the human race in Eden. Thus, God originally established a covenant relationship with all mankind, with Adam as the federal head. The account of Adam in Genesis 2–3 reflects the elements of a covenant identified above.

Similarly, all stand in Noah's covenant (Gen. 6:18; 9:8–17), since his covenant after the judgment of the flood was a restatement of man's creation duties and a wonderful affirmation of God's common grace for sinners (8:20–9:7). Even the sacrifices imply the hope of salvation to be offered to all who would descend from Noah (7:1–5; 8:20–22).

Nevertheless, as the history of the covenant continues, not all

---

1989), 95–107; Meredith G. Kline, *The Structure of Biblical Authority*, rev. ed. (Grand Rapids: Eerdmans, 1972), 27–38.

stand in Abraham's covenant of special redeeming grace. The covenant and election are more closely linked in the Abrahamic covenant.[8] Genesis shows God's election of Abraham and his descendants. The Lord says to him in Genesis 17:7–8:

> And I will establish my covenant between me and you and your offspring after you throughout their generations for an everlasting covenant, to be God to you and to your offspring after you. And I will give to you and to your offspring after you the land of your sojournings, all the land of Canaan, for an everlasting possession, and I will be their God.

Nevertheless, the promise made to Abram when God first called him included "all the families of the earth"—namely, the nations! Genesis 12:1–3 states:

> Now the LORD said to Abram, "Go from your country and your kindred and your father's house to the land that I will show you. And I will make of you a great nation, and I will bless you and make your name great, so that you will be a blessing. I will bless those who bless you, and him who dishonors you I will curse, and in you all the families of the earth shall be blessed."

This means that from the beginning of God's redemptive work, whether with Adam, Noah, or Abraham, God's plan was for his grace to reach his people in whatever nation they might be.

But there is a foundational problem for evangelism and mission in this world. Jesus declares that the world hates the message of the Son of God: "If the world hates you, know that it has hated me before it hated you. If you were of the world, the world would love you as its own; but because you are not of the world, but I chose you out of the world, therefore the world hates you" (John 15:18–19). The dire straits of the world in rebellion against God is declared in Jesus' verdict against even his own national people, those who wrongly

---

8. Gen. 12:1–3; 15:6, 17–21; 17:1–22.

claimed that Abraham's covenant was theirs due to their descent from the patriarch of Israel:

> Why do you not understand what I say? It is because you cannot bear to hear my word. You are of your father the devil, and your will is to do your father's desires. He was a murderer from the beginning, and does not stand in the truth, because there is no truth in him. When he lies, he speaks out of his own character, for he is a liar and the father of lies. But because I tell the truth, you do not believe me. (John 8:43–45)

The free offer of the gospel (Isa. 55:1; Matt. 11:28–30) is to be preached to all, as this is the task of those who share in God's covenant of grace. But believers reach out to covenant breakers, who on their own cannot come to Christ due to their human inability in the spiritual realm.[9] Apart from the application of the covenant of grace, the unbeliever exists in a state of utter spiritual helplessness. This is true of the lost in every nation of the world. The covenant blessings and promises are to be proclaimed globally, recognizing that the restoration of the broken covenant relationship rests with God's sovereign application of the covenant in his grace. As Jesus said, "Many are called, but few are chosen" (Matt. 22:14). The good news of the covenant of grace is that God raises the dead to new life in Christ (John 5:24–27; Eph. 2:1–7).

Restoration of the Covenant of Grace in Christ

Christ's grace restores the covenant relationship between God and man, bringing healing to individuals around the globe. Clearly, covenant theology warrants a global vision. It insists that missions should seek to reach every person in every land since every human bears the image of God (Gen. 1:26–28; 9:6), and each as a sinner is also under the divine judgment of death due to their standing in Adam's broken covenant with God.[10]

---

9. John 3:3; 6:44; 8:43; 14:17; 15:4–5.
10. Gen. 2:17; Ezek. 18:20–21; Rom. 6:23; 5:12, 18.

Consequently, each individual needs salvation through redemption in Christ. And when personal salvation is received, the grace imparted has the potential to impact all that person's relationships and ultimately every institution as he becomes the salt of the earth and the light of the world in Christ (Matt. 5:13–16). The redeemed are to live confidently and expectantly in light of the power of their obedience to the Lord, for "the Lord will reward everyone for whatever good he does, whether he is slave or free" (Eph. 6:8 NIV). The New England Puritan Cotton Mather put it this way:

> Though our Savior has furnished us with a perfect and spotless righteousness, when his obedience to the law is placed unto our account; yet it is a sin for us at all to fall short in our own obedience to the law. We must always loathe and judge ourselves for the sin. We are not under the law as a *covenant of works*: our own exactness in doing of good works, is not now the condition of our entering into life. Woe unto us if it were! But still, the *covenant of grace* holds us to it as our duty; and if we are in the covenant of grace, we shall make it our study to do those good works which once were the terms of our entering into life.[11]

Thus, the gospel is to be freely offered to the individual, to "whoever" (John 3:16; Acts 2:21), since each person bears the image of God. The need of the individual is the need of all, since each and every person is a covenant breaker in Adam. We are to "go into all the world and proclaim the gospel to the whole creation," so that "whoever believes and is baptized will be saved" (Mark 16:15–16). The gospel is to be preached to every living person.

Covenantal Healing for Culture

Christ's grace restores the covenant relationship between God and man, bringing healing to cultures worldwide. The gospel impacts

---

11. Cotton Mather, *An Essay upon the Good That Is to Be Devised and Designed by Those Who Desire to Answer the Great End of Life, and to Do Good While They Live*

the world through individuals who ultimately impact their cultures. Individuals impact their families. Family impact the church. The church impacts the state. As these spheres of family, church, and state are brought into a gospel context, the culture is redefined. Thus, in God's sovereign purposes, cultures are capable of being transformed from a covenant-breaking culture to a covenant-keeping culture. Let us review the biblical understandings of culture, family, church, and state.

What Is Culture?

Human culture is pervasive in influence. It permeates the individual, the family, religion, the state, and all that emerges from these. As the connection between "cult" and "culture" shows, there is an intimate connection between culture and religion. Culture can be viewed as a people's inner religion turned outward to the community and the public square. A covenantal understanding of Scripture will fortify the impact that missions will make on world cultures.

Culture may function with a redemptive spirit of obedience or a rebellious spirit of unbelief. A culture will be characterized by its attitudes regarding justice, mercy, and forgiveness. A culture ultimately will be marked by capriciousness and tyranny that swallow up the rule of law, or by order that seeks to manifest equity and human dignity. What does covenant theology mean for the impact of missions on global cultures? It provides a deep confidence in God's power to make a difference through the faith of believers, even if we seem small (Zech. 4:10), because of God's incomparable power at work in his people (Matt. 17:20; Eph. 1:18–23; 3:20–21). The Messiah is the one who blesses his people with the new covenant of grace.

Isaiah 42:6–9 describes the sweeping influence of the Messiah here identified as the very "covenant" of God:[12]

> I am the LORD; I have called you in righteousness; I will take you
> by the hand and keep you; I will give you as a covenant for the

(Boston: Massachusetts Sabbath School Society, 1845), 53–54.

12. Christopher J. H. Wright, *Knowing Jesus through the Old Testament* (Downers Grove, IL: InterVarsity Press, 1992), 153–80, esp. 179–80.

people, a light for the nations, to open the eyes that are blind, to bring out the prisoners from the dungeon, from the prison those who sit in darkness. I am the LORD; that is my name; my glory I give to no other, nor my praise to carved idols. Behold, the former things have come to pass, and new things I now declare; before they spring forth I tell you of them.

The Messiah is the "covenant," and he is "the messenger of the covenant" (Mal. 3:1), bringing the new covenant (Jer. 31:31–34) that can renew all things through the gospel.[13] This means that the covenant message of missions begins by declaring, "Therefore, if anyone is in Christ, he is a new creation" (2 Cor. 5:17). The broken covenant of creation can be restored. The preaching of the gospel comes with the full authority of the risen Christ, even though it may not be welcomed in closed countries. The gospel of the covenant of grace thus ultimately impacts both individuals and cultures, since cultures are made up of individuals. The covenant of grace will be reflected in the family, the church, and the state as the covenant with the Creator is restored in Christ and others come to faith.

Recent presentations of covenantal theology have also emphasized the "creation-centered" nature of God's mission in the world. Biblical eco-theology focuses on the importance of keeping the earth in a state of wholeness to reflect the beauty of the work of the Creator. Biblically, this also can be seen as an implication of the divine covenant with Noah. Thus, Christopher Wright argues that "environmental action is therefore a legitimate and integral dimension of Biblical mission."[14]

13. Ps. 96:1; Isa. 65:17; Ezek. 36:26; Matt. 9:17; John 13:34; 2 Cor. 5:17; Eph. 2:15; Col. 3:10; Heb. 10:20; Rev. 2:17; 21:5.

14. Christopher J. H. Wright, *The Mission of God: Unlocking the Bible's Grand Narrative* (Downers Grove, IL: InterVarsity Press, 2006), 210–24. For more on the relationship between covenant and creation, see O. Palmer Robertson, *The Christ of the Covenants* (Phillipsburg, NJ: Presbyterian and Reformed, 1980), 67–68; William J. Dumbrell, *Covenant and Creation: A Theology of Old Testament Covenants* (Carlisle: Paternoster, 1984); "Integral Mission," Lausanne III:13.

Family, Church, and State

Each *family*, whether it knows it or not, is based on the covenant bond of marriage ordained at the beginning by God.[15] Ultimately, marriage and the family are to reflect God's redemption in Christ (Rev. 19:6–10; 21:1–4). The gospel of the covenant of grace will begin to build healthy covenant Christian families that emulate the gospel work of Christ.

The *church*, the body of Christ (1 Cor. 12:12–27; Eph. 5:22–33), is the arena of God's great program of salvation in history (Matt. 16:18; John 10:15–16; Eph. 1:21–23). The religions of mankind, however, are aberrations of God's truth. As manufactured by human creativity, they are idolatrous substitutes put in the place of the worship of the Creator (Rom. 1:18–25; Acts 17:16–31). While religious symbolism and practices abound in the religious cultures of the world (Isa. 44:9–20; Acts 14:8–18), the signs and seals of the covenant of grace are those established by God.[16]

The *state* is clearly a legitimate institution in this world, but the state without God inevitably operates without his wisdom and is deprived of the true righteousness that alone can exalt a nation (Prov. 11:11; 14:34).[17] While the state can take several forms, such as monarchy, oligarchy, republic, and democracy to counter the opposing forces of tyranny and anarchy,[18] it ideally should have a covenantal or federal structure (2 Kings 11:4, 7) that protects the justice of all and preserves the rule of law.[19] Indeed, "By justice a king gives a country stability, but one who is greedy for bribes tears it down" (Prov. 29:4 NIV). Ideally, civil government should defend freedom of conscience and religious liberty. Such liberty marks biblical Christianity when its covenantal principles are applied to the public square.[20]

---

15. Gen. 2:18–25; Prov. 2:17; Hos. 2:18; Mal. 2:4–5; Matt. 19:3–9.

16. Gen. 17:7; Ex. 12:13; Matt. 28:19; 26:27–28; Rom. 4:11; 1 Cor. 11:25; Col. 2:8–15.

17. Gen. 1:28; 9:1–7; Matt. 22:21; Rom. 13:1–7; 1 Peter 2:13–17; 1 Cor. 2:6–14; Eph. 2:11–22.

18. Gen. 4:23–24; 1 Kings 12:1–15; 2 Kings 11:21–22; Judg. 2:21–25.

19. Ex. 22:21–22; Lev. 24:22; Deut. 8:10; Matt. 12:18; Luke 11:42; 18:8; 1 Tim. 1:8; Heb. 11:33; James 1:25; 2:8–10; 1 John 3:4; Rev. 19:11.

20. Lev. 25:10; Ps. 119:45; John 8:32, 36; Acts 5:29; Rom. 8:2; 1 Cor. 7:21;

It is evident from the global news that bribes and governmental corruption plague international business and national government practices, and world organizations such as the United Nations, UNESCO, and FIFA. Christian ethics, flowing from God's covenant law (Ex. 20), will help to end such practices.[21] It should be our prayer (Ezra 6:10; 1 Tim. 2:1–4) that the gospel of the covenant of grace will advance justice and mercy, so that they will make an impact on the governments of this world in the coming years.[22]

Signs of the Covenant

Believers in Christ are to be marked by God's signs of the covenant. Covenant theology asserts that God has always given covenant signs to his people to mark them as his own. There have been many divinely given signs in the history of the covenant, starting at creation and changing with the organic development of the covenant of grace through the history of redemption. These signs have varied with the progress of revelation:

- Adam before the fall—the Sabbath and the Tree of Life (covenant of works or the covenant of creation, Gen. 2:1–2, 8–9, 15–17; 3:22–24)
- Adam after the fall (the start of the covenant of grace)—animal sacrifice (Gen. 3:21) and the birth of sons (3:15–16; Isa. 9:6)
- Noah—the rainbow (Gen. 9:12–17)
- Patriarchs—circumcision (Gen. 17)
- Moses—Passover (Ex. 12) and the Sabbath (31:13)
- David—the Davidic dynasty, the throne of David (2 Sam. 7)
- Solomon—the temple (2 Chron. 7)
- Prophets—only the Ten Commandments were left in the ark of the covenant, pointing to the need for the new covenant, when the law would be written on the heart (2 Kings 8:9; Jer. 31:31–34).

---

2 Cor. 3:17; Gal. 5:1, 13; James 1:25; 2:12; 1 Peter 2:16.
   21. Ex. 23:8; Deut. 16:19; 27:25; Prov. 6:35; 19:28; Acts 20:35; Eph. 4:28.
   22. Jer. 29:4–7; Mic. 6:8; Isa. 29:18–21; 59:12–21; Rom. 13:1, 4; James 2:13.

- Christ—the Passover becomes the Lord's Supper (Matt. 26:26–30).
- Apostles—circumcision becomes Trinitarian baptism (Matt. 28:18–20; Col. 2:11–12); Christians take up their "cross" (Gal. 6:12–14).
- Apocalypse—the Tree of Life is restored (Rev. 22:1–5).

As the church is established around the world through mission activities, the biblical and especially the New Testament covenant signs are to replace of the signs of non-Christian faith. This means that as Christians become disciples and are trained in the Scriptures, they should set aside ancient folk religious symbols, or the religious objects of Buddhism and Hinduism, or the quasi-religion of Confucianism, as well as the religious practices of Islam. Such actions and elements are emblems that mark their past spiritual identity before knowing Christ.

Baptism is a major step for any new believer to take, but especially in a non-Christian culture, as this sign marks a new beginning of life in Christ's covenant of grace. Taking this step and sharing in the communion worship of the Eucharist indicate that the covenant community is being formed, even if it is costly to identify with it. Jesus taught that his followers would face persecution (Matt. 5:10–12; John 15:20).[23] The story of the early expansion of Christianity verifies this.[24] Nevertheless, the Christian is to be like an open book of Spirit-inspired Scripture in the new covenant ministry that flows from apostolic teaching due to the glorious and liberating ministry of the Holy Spirit (2 Cor. 3:1–18).

Cultural contexts engender disagreement over the propriety of worship practices and the covenant signs administered by the indigenous church. Mission leaders must prayerfully guide new believers, so that the application of God's covenant signs will issue in an authentic union and communion with Christ in the "new covenant in his blood."

---

23. See Barry Stricker and Nik Ripken, "Muslim Background Believers and Baptism in Cultures of Persecution and Violence," in *Missions in Contexts of Violence*, ed. Keith E. Eitel (Pasadena, CA: William Carey Library, 2008), 155–73.

24. Acts 9:1–2; 14:19–20; 16:16–24; 1 Cor. 4:12; 15:9; 2 Cor. 4:9; 1 Thess. 3:4; 2 Tim. 3:12; Heb. 11:37; Rev. 7:14.

The Scriptures as a Covenantal Book

The Scriptures are a covenantal book providing us with the message of justifying grace for sins and sanctifying wisdom for life. Covenant theology in this context means that we must not separate matters even if they are distinct. This touches a key principle of hermeneutics as well as a foundational truth of soteriology. So first, the Old and New Testaments are *inseparably* foundational for Christian faith and conduct, and second, the forgiveness of sins and the new life of the believer are *inseparable*.

The Old and New Testaments Are Inseparably Foundational for Christian Faith and Conduct

The issues raised by the relationship between missionary discipleship and covenantal hermeneutics are a vast field beyond the scope of this brief article. However, a few important observations are in order. First, the Great Commission is remarkably expansive in scope. Note each "all" in Jesus' mission mandate (Matt. 28:18–20):

> And Jesus came and said to them,
>   "*All authority* in heaven and on earth has been given to me.
> Go therefore and make disciples of
>   *all nations . . .*
> teaching them to observe
>   *all that I have commanded* you.
> And behold, I am with you
>   *always*, to the end of the age.

This authority inherent in the Christian missionary mandate extends to all nations for all times and is directly tied to the teaching of all that Christ commanded. This language argues for a mission pedagogy that is inclusive of the entire biblical revelation. This alone is compatible with the Gospels and Jesus' own use of the Scriptures, for he insisted that all the Scriptures point to him and his mission.[25]

---

25. Matt. 1:22; 22:41–46; John 1:45; 5:46; Luke 24:27, 44; Acts 13:27.

The continuity of the covenant in classic Reformed covenantal thought argues that the biblical covenants that comprise the covenant of grace are a unity that develop in a progressive, organic manner.[26] This means that they are the same in substance; that is, they always point to Christ (Gen. 22:7–14; John 1:29). The Scriptures, simply put, are Christ-centered.[27] Covenant theology emphasizes the unity of the Bible with its Christ-centered plan of salvation (2 Cor. 1:20; Rev. 22:13, 16).

Yet the unity of the covenant of grace does not discount the discontinuity in the development of the covenant of grace. The history of the covenant of grace shows that the epochs of the covenant of grace, while unified in Christ's saving work, are nevertheless distinct in administration.[28] A simple example is the ending of Old Testament sacrifices in the New Testament with the crucifixion and resurrection of Christ.[29] This means that the Scriptures as a whole are the inexhaustible repository of Christ-centered wisdom for our missions as we seek to impact the nations with our lives and ministries (Pss. 19; 119:130; 2 Tim. 3:16–17).

The Forgiveness of Sins and the New Life of the Believer Are Inseparable

The Old and New Testaments develop the covenant of grace with two primary benefits. Justification by faith alone is carefully harmonized with sanctification.[30] Thus, salvation is not only the forgiveness of sins, but also the renewal of the believer, transforming

---

26. Ex. 6:1–5; Ps. 105:8–11; Luke 1:67–75; 22:20.

27. See, for example, Peter A. Lillback, *The Binding of God: Calvin's Role in the Development of Covenant Theology* (Grand Rapids: Baker, 2001), 142ff.; Lillback, "Calvin's Interpretation of the History of Salvation: The Continuity and Discontinuity of the Covenant," in *A Theological Guide to Calvin's Institutes: Essays and Analysis*, ed. D. W. Hall and P. A. Lillback (Phillipsburg, NJ: P&R Publishing, 2008), 168ff. Korean translations of both volumes are available.

28. Gen. 17:1–14; Acts 15:19–30; Gal. 3:1–29; 5:2–6.

29. Ex. 12:1–11; 24:8; Lev. 17:11; John 1:29; 1 Cor. 5:6–8; Heb. 9:1–10:18.

30. Gen. 15:6; Matt. 7:21; 12:50; 25:31–46; John 3:16; 14:20–21; Acts 13:39; Rom. 2:23; 4:1–25; 10:9–13; Gal. 2:15–21; 5:6; Heb. 12:14; James 1:22; 2:14–26; 1 John 5:2–5; Rev. 22:14–15.

him into the likeness of Christ by the sanctifying work of the Holy Spirit.[31]

Justification and sanctification are different, to be sure, but they are inseparable and given simultaneously in salvation (Jer. 31:31–34).[32] The forgiveness of the sinner and the new nature of obedience in the new believer are the dual blessings of grace, acknowledging Christ as both Savior and Lord. Nevertheless, there is a foundational primacy to justification in Christ.[33] The good works of sanctification are always dependent upon justification for their value before God.[34] This is because even the best works of Christians, though empowered by the Holy Spirit, are yet imperfect and need to have their imperfections forgiven and purified by the justifying blood of the Lamb of God, who takes away the sin of the world.[35]

Thus, Reformed missions must apply covenant theology's understanding of the dual benefits of the covenant of grace in its discipleship and church building. This necessitates a firm grasp of the covenantal relationship between justification and sanctification. As the Westminster Confession of Faith declares, "Faith, thus receiving and resting on Christ and His righteousness, is the alone instrument of justification: yet is it not alone in the person justified, but is ever accompanied with all other saving graces, and is no dead faith, but worketh by love" (WCF, 11.2).

Calvin's articulation of the relationship between these two covenantal benefits is particularly helpful.[36] These benefits are:

- *Distinguishable*—justification is an accomplished act of the imputed righteousness of Christ, while sanctification is an ongoing process of renewal by the Holy Spirit that results in the believer's acts of righteousness.

31. Jer. 31:31–34; Rom. 8:26–32; 1 Cor. 3:9–17; 2 Thess. 2:13; Heb. 8:10–12; 1 Peter 1:2.
32. On this passage, cf. Robertson, *Christ of the Covenants*, 271–300.
33. Isa. 28:16; Matt. 21:42; Acts 4:11; 1 Cor. 3:11; Eph. 2:20; 1 Peter 2:7.
34. Eph. 1:6; 1 Peter 2:5; Heb. 6:10; 11:4; 13:20–21.
35. Job 9:20; Ps. 143:2; Matt. 25:21, 23; 1 Cor. 13:12; 1 John 1:7–10; 3:1–3.
36. See Lillback, *Binding of God*, 176–96.

- *Simultaneous*—justification and sanctification are both given to the new believer in the process of regeneration. The sinner is forgiven by faith, but that faith is imparted by the Holy Spirit's inner witness. The Spirit's work of renewal is ongoing to be sure, but it begins with justification.
- *Inseparable*—there can be no justification without sanctification, just as there can be no sanctification without justification. For them to be separated, we would have to tear the covenant of grace in pieces; we would have to tear Christ in pieces. Christ would then be either a prophet or a priest or a king, but not all three to the Christian. The Lord's Prayer would be torn apart, as we pray for both covenant benefits: "forgive us our debts" (justification) and "lead us not into temptation, but deliver us from evil" (sanctification).
- *Logically ordered*—with sanctification resting on justification. Justification is the foundation of the building of sanctification. Sanctification is the fruit that grows on the tree of justification. If we make sanctification primary, it would be like putting the foundation of a house on top of the roof.

As these two benefits of salvation emerge in the covenant of grace, they lead believers to the Scriptures, the inexhaustible repository of Christ-centered wisdom for life and ministry. Thus, God's gracious law is imparted in the covenant of grace by the Holy Spirit, who writes God's law upon the hearts of believers. This covenantal union of hermeneutics and soteriology has great implications for our global missionary efforts.

As "law in grace" is the Reformed paradigm of the covenant of grace, the missionary message preached worldwide will point to the Ten Commandments, the moral law of God. God's moral law either exposes human sin, and thus condemns, or is graciously written on the believer's heart by the Holy Spirit, who then begins a life of new obedience in the covenant of grace. Thus, both missionaries in China and Chinese disciples must remember that their new life in Christ is not defined by emulating either Western Christianity or Korean Christianity, but by loving God. Obedience to the law of God is summarized by our Lord as loving God with all our being and loving our neighbor as we love ourselves.[37] The first table of the Ten Commandments teaches us to love God. The second table instructs us to love our neighbor. The Westminster Confession of Faith describes believers' good works this way:

> Notwithstanding, the persons of believers being accepted through Christ, their good works also are accepted in Him; not as though they were in this life wholly unblameable and unreproveable in God's sight; but that He, looking upon them in His Son, is pleased to accept and reward that which is sincere, although accompanied with many weaknesses and imperfections. (WCF, 16.6)[38]

Here we have seen the covenantal principles of biblical law and good works taught from the whole Bible operating in union with the dual graces of justification and sanctification. As this model of missionary ministry is advanced, it will have a powerful, reforming influence on Chinese culture. This is timely, as Chinese Christians must confront the tensions created by the struggle between the arbitrary rule of power and the authentic rule of law under the Chinese Constitution.

The Promised Gift of the New Covenant of Grace

Global evangelization advances through the proclamation of the gospel by the powerful, regenerating witness of the Holy Spirit, the promised gift of the new covenant of grace. The new covenant in Christ and his giving of the Holy Spirit to the church have critical significance for missions.[39] The new covenant gift of the Holy Spirit is the *sine qua non* of global missions. All mission efforts must acknowledge the truth that the Holy Spirit is sovereign in his witness (John 3:3–15).

---

37. Matt. 22:34–40; Mark 12:28–31; Luke 10:25–28; John 13:34; 15:9–17; 1 John 2:7–11; 3:11.

38. Lillback, *Binding of God*, 194–97.

39. Acts 1:8; 2 Cor. 3:4–6; 7:16–18; Gal. 3:15; Eph. 2:12; Heb. 8:6–13; 10:16, 29; 12:24; 13:20.

For an unbeliever to believe, there must be more than teaching, apologetics, and ministries of love and compassion to overcome the lost soul's fatal incapacity. John Calvin, in his *Institutes of the Christian Religion*, affirms that "Scripture will ultimately suffice for a saving knowledge of God only when its certainty is founded upon the inward persuasion of the Holy Spirit."[40] But "the Spirit of truth" is one "whom the world cannot receive, because it neither sees him nor knows him" (John 14:17a). In contrast to the world, Jesus declares to his disciples that they "know him, for he dwells with you and will be in you" (John 14:17b). Jesus insisted that even his disciples were spiritually impotent without him, "for apart from me you can do nothing" (John 15:5). Covenantal missions proceeds, entirely dependent upon the work of God's sovereign Holy Spirit.[41]

Thus, the plan for the success of covenantal missions is timeless and without ethnic or national qualification. The new covenant vision for missions is to preach the gospel in the truth and power of the Holy Spirit.[42]

This aspect of the Spirit's ministry has been termed the internal witness of the Holy Spirit. James M. Boice writes,

> The idea of the witness of the Spirit in the Fourth Gospel has been central to that doctrine which reformed theologians have called the *internal* witness of the Holy Spirit (*testimonium Spiritus Sancti internum*). By this phrase is meant the supernatural and saving activity of the Holy Spirit on behalf of the one who hears the Gospel so that the reality of what is taught is conveyed to the mind, producing the conviction that this is truth and leading the soul to receive it to its consequent salvation.[43]

40. John Calvin, *Institutes of the Christian Religion*, ed. John T. McNeill, trans. Ford Lewis Battles (Philadelphia: Westminster, 1960), 1:92, 1.18.13.

41. John 20:22; Acts 1:8; 2:17; 4:3; 13:2; Rom. 8:9, 26; 1 Cor. 2:14; 2 Cor. 3:6; Gal. 5:25; Eph. 5:18; 1 John 3:24.

42. Joel 2:28–32; Acts 1:8; 2:1–4, 14–21.

43. James M. Boice, *Witness and Revelation in the Gospel of John* (Grand Rapids: Zondervan, 1970), 143.

For the truth of God to be received, the Holy Spirit is necessary, for he alone is the Spirit of truth (John 14:17; 16:13). The Spirit is the one who reveals God, since he is "sent by the Father" in Christ's "name." Thus, the sovereign Spirit is the church's, the evangelist's, and the missionary's "helper" (*paraklētos*, John 14:16, 26). And as such, he is the one who witnesses to Christ (John 15:26) and reminds the church of Christ's teaching, guiding the church into truth (John 16:13–14). The nations will be reached as the Spirit-inspired Word is taught with the convicting power of the Holy Spirit.[44]

To underscore the reality of the Spirit's inner witness, John 16:8–11 speaks of the *elenctic* work of the Holy Spirit in his mission to the world. "If the primary function of the Spirit to believers is that of teacher and interpreter, he is to the world an accuser."[45] This has significance for missiology. Bavinck declares:

> The Holy Spirit will convince the world of sin. The Holy Spirit is actually the only conceivable subject of this verb, for the conviction of sin exceeds all human ability. Only the Holy Spirit can do this, even though he can and will use us as instruments in his hand. Taken in this sense, elenctics is the science which is concerned with the conviction of sin. In a special sense then it is the science which unmasks to heathendom all false religions as sin against God, and it calls heathendom to a knowledge of the only true God.[46]

This Spirit is the heart of the new covenant promise taught by the Old Testament prophets. He blesses the church and gives power to missions. He is the dynamic of all the church's work. Saving faith is a miracle—the astonishing work of God's sovereign grace through his Holy Spirit. Such a spiritual revival began in Korea in 1907:

44. 1 Cor. 2:13; 2 Tim. 3:16; 2 Peter 1:19–21; John 16:7–8; 1 Thess. 1:5; Jude 15.

45. George E. Ladd, *A Theology of the New Testament*, rev. ed. (Grand Rapids: Eerdmans, 1993), 333.

46. Bavinck, *Missions*, 222.

On January 14, 1907, after a sermon on repentance, Graham Lee asked two or three people to lead in prayer. More than a dozen people started to pray. Lee said, "Then let's all pray together out loud." In his book, *The Korean Pentecost*, William Blair said, "The effect was indescribable—not of confusion, but a vast harmony of sound and spirit, a mingling together of souls moved by an irresistible impulse of prayer. The prayer sounded to me like the falling of many waters, an ocean of prayer beating against God's throne." The resulting revival spread to other parts of the country. . . . From that movement emerged the now mature mission outreach of the churches of South Korea, which report a total of over 16,000 cross-cultural Korean missionaries. (SIM website, 2007)

From this revival, kindled by the Holy Spirit's grace, Korea has witnessed the growth of more Presbyterians than any other country in the world, including the United States.

Conclusion

Our Lord Jesus, the very embodiment of the covenant as the God-man, will one day rule over all nations. He rules today in his own people by the Spirit of the new covenant. The Holy Spirit, the great blessing of Christ in the new covenant, is the power that builds the church. Our new covenant task in the global context is Spirit-filled preaching of the gospel worldwide.

The Reformed covenantal perspective has crucial implications for missions. Unlike a pietistic-individualistic approach, it forces us to view the mission of the church as broader than the salvation of individual souls. Indeed, the emphasis on the church underscores the need for church planting and the necessity for mission to include social, political, and cultural involvement. This involvement is informed by the continuity between creation and covenant alluded to in this chapter. But unlike liberal approaches, with their social concern and universalism, Reformed mission, informed by covenant theology, is centered on the preaching of the gospel of Christ.

We pursue our mission endeavors because God has declared in

his great formula of the covenant, "I will be your God, and you will be my people"! Our methods may vary, but the content of what we preach is ever the same. We preach in the power of the Spirit of the new covenant of grace, exalting Jesus Christ as King of kings and Lord of lords!

4

Mission and Gathering God's New Covenant People

Flip Buys

Abstract

This article describes the New Testament biblical-theological foundations of the new covenant and its implications for missions. Covenant theology has always been a vital aspect of Reformed theology, with its biblical basis. It provides a deep motivation for the church to be part of God's mission (*missio Dei*) and has concrete implications for the practice of global and local missions and for missional ecclesiology. The covenantal structure of the Great Commission is described, the implications of the forensic character of the new covenant for the proclamation of the gospel—including its promises, commands, and sanctions—are explained, and the collective and corporate character of the new covenant for family and household evangelism is presented. Finally, God's missional goal for the new covenant in ushering in the kingdom is emphasized.

The Importance of the Covenant in Reformed Tradition

The biblical teaching of the covenant has traditionally been seen as one of the pillars of Reformed theology. Geerhardus Vos wrote, "At present there is general agreement that the doctrine of the covenants is a peculiarly Reformed doctrine."[1] This view is echoed by many Reformed theologians.[2] According to John Hesselink, "Reformed theology is simply covenant theology."[3] Jacob Van der Schuit can even say that Reformed theology has always had the deepest conviction that true religion is expressed in the covenant relationship.[4] Covenant theology deals with the realization that God has revealed his truth, revealed himself, and revealed redemption through the covenant. It is the study of God's eternal, unchanging purpose to bring a people to himself in covenantal relationship.

Many people readily associate Reformed theology with the so-called five points of Calvinism, the famous TULIP acronym.[5] Michael Horton stresses that while some friends and critics of Reformed theology have reduced Calvinism to these five points—or further still to predestination—the confessions, catechisms, and standard doctrinal works of the Reformed tradition testify to a far richer, deeper, and all-embracing faith in the God of the covenant. Horton concludes: "Reformed theology is synonymous with covenant theology."[6]

In his assessment of Ursinus's development of the covenant of creation, Peter Lillback points out that the contraposition of covenantal thinking with predestination is a historical inaccuracy stemming from Heinrich Heppe's predilection for Melanchthon and German Reformed theology.[7] Although John Calvin's view of the covenant is

1. Geerhardus Vos, "The Doctrine of the Covenant in Reformed Theology," in *Redemptive History and Biblical Interpretation: The Shorter Writings of Geerhardus Vos*, ed. Richard B. Gaffin, Jr. (Phillipsburg, NJ: Presbyterian and Reformed, 1980), 236.

2. See Michael Horton, *Introducing Covenant Theology* (Grand Rapids: Baker, 2006), 11; Leon Morris, *The Apostolic Preaching of the Cross: A Study of the Significance of Some New Testament Terms* (London: Tyndale, 1972); Herman N. Ridderbos, *De Komst van het koninkrijk: Jezus' prediking volgens de synoptiese Evangeliën* (Kampen: Kok, 1972), 178; Jacob Jan Van der Schuit, *Het verbond der verlossing* (Kampen: Kok, 1982), 8.

3. I. John Hesselink, quoted in Horton, *Introducing Covenant Theology*, 11.

4. Van der Schuit, *Het verbond der verlossing*, 8.

5. TULIP: Total depravity, Unconditional election, Limited atonement, Irresistible grace, Perseverance of the saints.

6. Horton, *Introducing Covenant Theology*, 11.

7. Peter A. Lillback, "Ursinus' Development of the Covenant of Creation: A Debt to Melanchthon or Calvin?," *Westminster Theological Journal* 43.2 (Spring 1981):

less developed than the view of the post-Reformation theologians, there is a broad consensus that Calvin did express many concepts of the covenant idea.[8] M. Eugene Osterhaven explains: "Since Christ was the foundation of the covenant and both Testaments found their meaning in Him, that which was said by God to Israel was said to Calvin and us as well. The law was written for us, he is fond of saying in his explication of the Old Testament in commentaries and sermons."[9]

In the architecture of most buildings, the framework is largely hidden from view. The same is true in Reformed theology. The covenant is the framework, but it is far from being a central doctrine. Whenever Reformed theologians attempt to explore and explain the riches of Scripture, they often think covenantally about every topic they take up.[10] Christopher Wright presents an overarching view of the covenant in Old Testament theology as being "like a cable, with several closely intertwined wires, running along together at the core. . . . The covenant theme may be regarded as one of the core wires."[11]

In recent missiological literature, the covenantal basis for missions, according to the Old Testament, has been discussed thoroughly, and the church has been defined as *the covenant community of the King*.[12] Unfortunately the implications of the structure of the covenant and missions, as set forth in the New Testament, is an underdeveloped area in missiology. When David Bosch presents his definition of *missio*

246–88; Lillback, *The Binding of God: Calvin's Role in the Development of Covenant Theology* (Grand Rapids: Baker, 2001).

8. See Willem Balke, *Calvin and the Anabaptist Radicals* (Grand Rapids: Eerdmans, 1981), 310–11; J. Van der Vegt, *Het genadeverbond by Calvyn* (Kampen: Kok, n.d.), 30.

9. M. Eugene Osterhaven, "Calvin on the Covenant," in *Readings in Calvin's Theology*, ed. Donald K. McKim (Grand Rapids: Baker, 1984), 90–91, 103.

10. Horton, *Introducing Covenant Theology*, 15.

11. Christopher J. Wright, *The Mission of God: Unlocking the Bible's Grand Narrative* (Downers Grove, IL: InterVarsity Press), 325.

12. Charles E. Van Engen, *God's Missionary People: Rethinking the Purpose of the Local Church* (Grand Rapids: Baker, 1993), 101–8; Wright, *Mission of God*, 324–55; Walter Vogels, *God's Universal Covenant: A Biblical Study* (Ottawa: University of Ottawa Press, 1986), 67–68.

Dei, he mentions that its theological basis originated in the covenant theology of the post-Reformation era, but he fails to elaborate.[13] From this perspective, we will endeavor to apply core New Testament principles relating to the structure and character of the covenant and explore some practical implications for missions.

Old Testament Roots of the Structure and Character of the New Testament Covenant

Scripture, essentially a witness to Christ, coalesces around the revelation of Christ as the fulfillment of the Father's plan of redemption. We learn inductively that Christ stands at the center of the covenant, which is an architectonic structure, a matrix of beams and pillars, holding together the structure of biblical faith and practice. The concrete reality of God's covenantal dealings is laid bare, a context within which the unity of Scripture is recognized in remarkable variety. A broad consensus exists among Reformed biblical scholars that *diathēkē* in the New Testament cannot be understood apart from the structure of the covenant in the Old Testament.[14]

Herman Ridderbos makes this clear when he writes about the fulfillment in Christ of the promises of the new covenant in Jeremiah 31 and Ezekiel 11:19 and 36:27: "From the fulfillment in Christ all the designated privileges that Israel had as the people of God become part of the essence of the Christian church with new power and meaning."[15] The covenant structure in the New Testament is explained by that of the Old Testament. Reformed theology has been helped by the research of Meredith G. Kline in his groundbreaking work

13. David J. Bosch, *Transforming Missions: Paradigm Shifts in Theology of Mission* (Maryknoll, NY: Orbis Books, 1991), 8.

14. J. De Vuijst, *Oud en nieuw verbond in de brief aan de Hebreën* (Kampen: Kok, 1964), 72; Cornelis Van der Waal, *Het Nieuwe Testament, boek van het verbond* (Goes: Oosterbaan & Le Cointre, 1978), 102; Ridderbos, *De Komst van het koninkrijk,* 175; Leon Morris, *Apostolic Preaching of the Cross,* 97; O. Palmer Robertson, *The Christ of the Covenants* (Phillipsburg, NJ: Presbyterian and Reformed, 1980), 45; Wright, *Mission of God,* 354–56.

15. Ridderbos, *De Komst van het koninkrijk,* 375.

The Treaty of the Great King. He characterizes not only the content, but the very form, of Scripture in the light of the structure of the covenant. Building on George E. Mendenhall's *Law and Covenant in Israel and the Ancient Near East,* Kline points out that the covenants of the Old Testament can best be understood in the light of discoveries concerning ancient Near Eastern treaty diplomacy.[16] Of all the various forms of literature in the Bible, the treaty is the most basic. He emphasizes the parallels between ancient Hittite treaties and the covenantal structure of Old Testament thought and practice. These Old Testament historical records "are extensions of the treaty prologues . . . linked to both law and prophecy, and on both scores served as an instrument of covenant administration."[17] Covenant in Scripture often refers to the specific literary form common in the ancient Near East, of which extrabiblical examples from the Hittite culture are models. Covenants between Yahweh and Israel, says Kline, are analogous to Hittite suzerainty treaties of the second millennium B.C. between a great king and a lesser king. They had a fairly standard form, consisting of the following elements:

1. Name of the great king,
2. Historical prologue,

16. Meredith G. Kline, *The Treaty of the Great King* (Grand Rapids: Eerdmans, 1972). Mendenhall's research is presented in two articles: George E. Mendenhall, "Ancient Israel and Biblical Law," *Biblical Archaeologist* 17.a (1954): 26–46, and "Covenant Forms in Israelite Tradition," *Biblical Archaeologist* 17.b (1954): 50–76. Cf. Delbert R. Hillers, *Covenant: The History of a Biblical Idea* (Baltimore: John Hopkins University Press, 1969), 30. In the light of the research by Victor Korošec, *Hethitische Staatsverträge* (Leipzig: Weicher, 1931), Mendenhall compared the Sinai covenant with the structure of the vassal treaties of the Hittite kings, which stimulated renewed consideration of the structure of the covenant in the Old Testament, as pointed out by G. Van Rongen, *Zijn vast verbond* (Goes: Oosterbaan & Le Cointre, 1966), 9; Dennis J. McCarthy, "Covenant in the Old Testament: The Present State of Inquiry," *Catholic Biblical Quarterly* 27 (1956): 217–40; McCarthy, *Treaty and Covenant: A Study in Form in the Ancient Oriental Documents and in the Old Testament* (Rome: Pontifical Institute, 1963); and David M. Weinfeld, "Berit," in *Theologische Wörterbuch zum Alten Testament*, ed. G. J. Botterweck and H. Ringgren (Berlin: Kohlhamer, 1973).

17. Kline, *Treaty of the Great King*, 79.

3. Stipulations (laws): exclusive loyalty (love) and specific requirements,
4. Sanctions (blessings and curses), and
5. Administration.

Kline finds this literary form in the Decalogue (Ex. 20:1–17) and
identifies the book of Deuteronomy as a whole as a suzerainty treaty
between Yahweh and Israel. There is "an architectural aspect to the
Bible. . . . In this connection the imagery of God's 'house' comes to
the fore in the book of Exodus. That house is built by means of the
canonical Scripture which proceeds from the victorious Yahweh."[18]

The Structure of the Old Testament Covenant and the Hittite Suzerainty Treaties

In suzerain-vassal treaties, a great king (suzerain) would rescue a
vassal from impending doom and claim the right to annex the ben-
eficiaries of his kindness by covenant to his empire. The vassal king's
people would then be seen as the people of the great king, their suzerain. Their own king might continue to rule locally as a viceroy of the
emperor. The great king was the father adopting the captives he had
liberated from oppression. Consequently, he was not simply to be
obeyed externally, but loved, and not only feared, but revered—not
only as the legal lord of the realm, but as the rightful sovereign. Such
a treaty had distinguishing features, with several typical elements:

1. In the preamble, the name of the king was described ("thus
[saith] NN [name], the great king, king of the . . . land, son of
NN . . . the valiant"), identifying the one who made the treaty.
2. In the historical prologue, everything that followed was justified. It often referred to incidents where the suzerain had
rescued the smaller nation from an invading army, with the
implication that gratitude should follow. By telling the story

---

18. Meredith G. Kline, *The Structure of Biblical Authority*, 2nd ed. (Eugene, OR:
Wipf and Stock, 1997), 79.

of what happened, the suzerain showed that the lesser king was in no bargaining position. The lesser king and his people had been treated mercifully and had no claim upon the great king. The references to historical facts or incidences shaped the religious as well as the political life of the people. Similarly in God's covenant with his people, he claimed sovereignty over all of life and anchored this claim in historical facts, not in myth or general principles of truth and morality.

3. The third element of the Hittite treaties was stipulations. Based on the historical facts of his salvation, God commanded, "You shall have no other gods before me" (Ex. 20:2–3). Because certain things had happened, Israel was obligated to commit themselves wholeheartedly to him, implying a relationship of trust, love, and genuine faithfulness, not simply of external obligation and consent. Out of that flowed specific requirements: "Therefore, you shall not . . . You shall . . ." Those who kept the stipulations were covenant keepers, while those who violated them were covenant breakers. Far from being arbitrary dos and don'ts, the stipulations were a reasonable duty. They fit the character of the liberation experienced. Typically, they involved the following: no backroom alliances with other kings, no murmuring against the suzerain, and payment of an annual tribute. The vassal also had to pledge to raise a regiment to join the suzerain's army in any action taken against a fellow vassal under the suzerain's protection.

4. Consequently, the stipulations were followed by sanctions that spelled out what would happen should the vassal fail to uphold the treaty, including eviction and exile. The sanctions were then followed by a formula of blessings and curses. Although the suzerain was in no way obligated prior to the covenant, he pledged himself to guard his vassals. The political term for this was invocation. A vassal king in trouble could invoke the suzerain's pledge of rescue. Calling upon the name of the suzerain, he could be assured of his lord's swift protection.

5. A public ceremony sealed the treaty and put it into effect. Such ceremonies included an event in which the suzerain and the

vassal would pass between the halves of slaughtered animals, as if to testify, "May the same fate befall me should I fail to keep this covenant." In other rituals, the vassal king would walk behind the great king down an aisle as a sign of loyalty, service, and submission—hence the language of "walking after" God in the Scriptures. Celebratory meals at which the treaty was ratified were also held.

In the typical Hittite treaties, the covenant was regularly spoken of as that which the sovereign gave to his vassal as the sovereign's covenant—he was its author. The specific obligations imposed upon the vassal were called the "words" of the sovereign, for when the great king delivered his utterance, to speak was to command.

While the basic structure and elements of the covenant in the Old Testament texts bear close resemblances to Hittite treaties, what distinguishes Israel from other nations is that their God is the acting suzerain and not merely a witness to a human imposition of a relationship. It is this intimacy of the I-thou exchange between suzerain and vassal that is transposed into the form of the relationship between YHWH and Israel.

The Covenantal Basis of the *Missio Dei*

The Latin term *missio Dei* was coined already in the fourth century A.D. by Augustine to describe the sending acts within the Trinity, with God the Father sending Jesus Christ, the Son of God. From then on, *missio Dei* became a major term in Catholic and Orthodox dogmatics.[19] In 1952, the term was appropriated in the Protestant world at the Ecumenical World Missions Conference in Willingen to emphasize that world mission is rooted in the divine Trinity. It was popularized in Protestant missions theology by George Vicedom in his book *Missio Dei*, and by German Lutheran theologians and missiologists involved in ecumenical agencies, such as Karl Hartenstein and Walter Freytag. Vicedom wrote: "Missio Dei declares the sending

19. Karl Müller, *Missionstheologie* (Berlin: Reimer, 1985), 57–59.

to be God's own concern, which He began in His Son and which He continues through the Holy Spirit in His Church till the end of time."[20] The term is valid for Reformed and evangelical Christians also, because it belongs to the heart of Christianity, whether it is used for the fact that God came himself for the redemption of the world or for the fact that church mission is the outcome of God's mission.[21]

A Brief Description of the Covenant of Redemption

The older Reformed systematic theologies referred in Latin to the *pactum salutis* to designate the covenant of redemption. When we consider the *pactum salutis*, it becomes clear how the *missio Dei* is rooted in the intra-Trinitarian sending of God. It lies at the heart of the biblical plan of salvation shaping the earthly life of our Savior and continuing to shape his present heavenly life.

Definition

The covenant of redemption was contracted in eternity past between God the Father and God the Son when they covenanted together for the redemption of the human race. The Father appointing the Son to be the mediator—the second Adam—whose life would be given for the salvation of the world, and the Son accepted the commission, promising to do the work that the Father had given him and fulfill all righteousness by obeying the law of God.

Biblical-Theological Foundations of the Covenant of Redemption

In the New Testament, there is only one passage referring directly to the eternal nature of the plan of salvation as a covenant. In Luke 22:29, Jesus promises that he will make the disciples part of his kingdom in the same way as (*kathōs*) his Father has done for him. The verb used here, *diatithēmi*, can mean "to issue a decree" or "to make a covenant" (Acts 3:25; Heb. 8:10; 10:16).[22]

---

20. George F. Vicedom, *Missio Dei* (Munich: Chr. Kaiser, 1958), 352.
21. Thomas Schirrmacher, *World Mission: Heart of Christianity* (Hamburg: Reformatorischer Verlag Beese, 2008), 22.
22. Cf. Johannes P. Louw and Eugene A. Nida, *Greek-English Lexicon of the New*

Taking this meaning into consideration, Luke 22:29–30 may be paraphrased as follows: "As the Father has covenanted royal dominion [*basileia*] for me, so I covenant for you a share in my future reign as those who shall feast [*trapeza*] and rule [*thronos, kpivō*] with me." The verb *diatithēmi* here has the force of freely ordaining or authoritatively disposing—not of making a testamentary disposition, for the covenanting of Jesus corresponds to that of the Father, and the Father is certainly not making a will to be revealed after Christ's death.[23] Jesus makes it clear that the eschatological kingdom is ordained for him by the sovereign declaration of the will of his Father, and so it is covenanted by the sovereign resolve of Jesus that the disciples should reign with him.

This lays a New Testament exegetical foundation for the Reformed understanding of the covenant of redemption. In the eternal plan of God, it was decreed, or covenanted, that:

- The Father would plan the redemption through election and predestination.
- The Son would provide redemption through his atoning death.
- The Holy Spirit would effect the plan through regenerating and sealing believers (Eph. 1:3–14).

Numerous other Scripture passages emphasize the eternal nature of the plan of salvation.[24] Christ refers to his coming as a commissioning (John 5:30, 43; 6:38–40; 17:4–12). Christ is also regarded as the representative of the human race, the head of a covenant (Rom. 5:12–21; 1 Cor. 15:22).

The features of the covenant of redemption relate to the work assigned to the Son. To achieve the redemption of man, Christ had

---

Testament, 2nd ed. (New York: United Bible Societies, 1988, 1989), 1:452 (34.43); W. F. Arndt and F. W. Gingrich, *A Greek-English Lexicon of the New Testament and Other Early Christian Literature*, 4th ed. (Chicago: University of Chicago Press, 1974), 189; Robert E. Van Voorst, *Building Your New Testament Greek Vocabulary* (Grand Rapids: Eerdmans, 1990), 38.

23. Gerhard Kittel and Gerhard Friedrich, eds., *Theological Dictionary of the New Testament*, vol. 2 (Grand Rapids: Eerdmans, 1964), 105–6.

24. Eph. 3:11; 2 Thess. 2:13; 2 Tim. 1:9; James 2:5; 1 Peter 1:2.

to take on humanity in a genuine incarnation (Rom. 8:3). As man's representative, he became the guarantee of a better covenant—one that could genuinely effect salvation (Heb. 7:22). Christ subjected himself to the dictates of the law, perfectly fulfilling its requirements, so as to redeem humanity in bondage to the law (Gal. 4:4–5). Final release from enslavement to the law came through the atoning death of Christ (Gal. 3:13).

For the sake of missions, it is important to see the link between the covenant of redemption and the covenant of grace. The first provides the deepest foundation, because by it God effects the covenant of grace, providing a God-centered motivation and vision for world missions. Based on this understanding of *missio Dei* in the light of the *pactum salutis*, we can define missions as follows: Through Jesus Christ, and by the Holy Spirit, God, for his own glory, is uniting people from every tribe, nation, kingdom, and language to worship him forever in the new world.

The Covenantal Structure of the Great Commission

In the Old Testament, Israel, as God's covenant people, was a participant in YHWH's universal purpose for the whole world. To be the people of YHWH meant a commitment to be an instrument on behalf of all the nations within the scope of divine lordship over all the world. Daniel T. Niles sums up this universal relationship of God's Old Testament covenant people in four principles:[25]

- God's concern for the salvation of the nations underlies his call of Abraham.
- Israel is formed out of the nations, and so is not a nation like any other. Israel is a nation among and from the nations and turned toward them.
- The God who chose Israel out of the nations remains the God of the nations.

25. Daniel T. Niles, *Upon the Earth: The Mission of God and the Missionary Enterprise of the Churches* (New York: McGraw-Hill, 1962), 250.

- Consequently, Israel's life and mission affect not only its national history, but also the history of the world.

"Such a conception of Israel's life and mission," Niles says, "demanded on the one hand, that it guard its identity in the world, and on the other that it serve the world toward which its mission was set." The Old Testament background and the covenantal structure of the Great Commission in Matthew 28 reveal God's missional goal for his new covenant people.

Otto Michel demonstrates the parallels between the proclamation of Matthew 28:18–20 and the coronation hymns in other biblical passages, especially Daniel 7:13–14.[26] In the coronation ceremonies and comparative hymns, three elements can be recognized: elevation to royal or regal dignity, promulgation and proclamation of elevation to regal status, and coronation and transfer of authority to the new king. Richard De Ridder points out how these elements, which are inherent in Daniel 7:13–14, can also be seen in 1 Timothy 3:16, Philippians 2:9–11, Hebrews 1:5–14, and Matthew 28:18–20.[27] What makes the latter unique is that whereas the coronation is proclaimed in the other passages, Matthew 28 is the speech of the enthroned Lord.

When the covenantal structure of Genesis 12; 15–17; Exodus 20; and Deuteronomy 4:39; 31:8, 23 is compared with Matthew 28:18–10, 1 Timothy 3:16, Philippians 2:9, and Hebrews 1:5–14, it becomes clear that in the Great Commission Jesus is portrayed as the heavenly suzerain, the great king of the universe addressing his new covenantal vassal, and how thoroughly covenantal the form and content of Matthew's record is at this point.

Among the key elements of the Old Testament covenant form were:

- The preamble as the self-introduction of God as great king with all authority (often shortened simply to "I am YHWH"),

---

26. Otto Michel, "Der Abschluß des Matthäusevangeliums," *Evangelische Theologie* 10.1 (1950): 16–26.

27. Richard R. De Ridder, *The Dispersion of the People of God: The Covenant Basis of Matthew 28:18–20 against the Background of Jewish, Pre-Christian Proselyting and Diaspora, and the Apostleship of Jesus Christ* (Kampen: Kok, 1971), 170–75.

- The demands of the covenant relationship—the instructions given by the covenant Lord, and
- The covenant promises of blessing.

In light of the preamble in the covenantal structure of the Great Commission, it is clear that its theme is the sovereign Christ. What was affirmed of YHWH in the Old Testament is now claimed by Jesus, who identifies himself as the one who possesses all divine authority— he is the covenant Lord. Wright summarizes: "The Great Commission is nothing less than a universalized covenant proclamation. It could even be regarded as the promulgation of the new covenant of the risen Jesus, just as his words at the Last Supper were the institution of the new covenant in relation to his death."[28] Fritz Rienecker puts it like this: "This is the almighty word of the resurrected Lord."[29]

Put together in a table, this covenantal structure can be seen in several passages in figure 4.1. The same structure can be seen in other passages outlining the mission of the church in figure 4.2.

The covenantal command to make disciples is a sovereign command to proclaim him to all nations, an unqualified demand for universal recognition of his sovereignty. It is also a sure prophecy of the consummation of his sovereignty. When we acknowledge the covenantal structure of the Great Commission, mission is integral to normal covenantal obedience. One who responds to his personal call, "Follow me," will have to say to others: "Follow him with me." Mission is therefore an imperative, founded on the covenantal lordship of Christ our King. Its task is to produce self-replicating communities of covenantal obedience to Christ among the nations. Churches that are not involved in missions are covenant breakers. Missions is indeed the summons of the lordship of Christ.[30]

The command to make disciples by baptizing and teaching them to obey all things that Christ has taught his followers implies that new

28. Wright, *Mission of God*, 355.

29. Fritz Rienecker, *Das Evangelium des Matthäus* (Wuppertal: Brockhaus, 1975), 375 (my translation).

30. Johannes Blauw, *The Missionary Nature of the Church* (New York: McGraw-Hill, 1962), 84.

	Genesis 12	Genesis 15	Genesis 17	Exodus 20	Daniel 7	Matthew 28
Preamble	Now the LORD (YHWH) said to Abram,	"Fear not, Abram, I am your shield; . . ."	"I am God Almighty;	"I am the LORD your God	And to him was given dominion and glory and a kingdom,	"All authority in heaven and on earth has been given to me.
Covenantal demands	"Go from your country and your kindred and your father's house to the land that I will show you.	And he believed the LORD, and he counted it to him as righteousness.	walk before me, and be blameless.	You shall have no other gods before me. . . . You shall not . . ."	that all peoples, nations, and languages should serve him;	. . . make disciples of all nations, baptizing them in the name of the Father and of the Son and of the Holy Spirit, teaching them to observe all that I have commanded you.
Covenantal promises	And I will make of you a great nation, and I will bless you and make your name great, so that you will be a blessing. I will bless those who bless you, and him who dishonors you I will curse, and in you all the families of the earth shall be blessed."	"Look toward heaven, and number the stars, if you are able to number them." Then he said to him, "So shall your offspring be."	And I will establish my covenant . . . to be God to you and to your offspring after you."	Dt 29:13: ". . . that he may establish you today as his people, and that he may be your God, as he promised you, and as he swore to your fathers, to Abraham, to Isaac, and to Jacob."	his dominion is an everlasting dominion, which shall not pass away, and his kingdom one that shall not be destroyed.	And behold, I am with you always, to the end of the age."

Fig. 4.1. The Covenantal Structure of the Great Commission, Table 1

	Mark 16	**John 20**
Preamble	(The testimony of Jesus' resurrection in vv. 9–14)	"Peace be with you." . . . He showed them his hands and his side. . . . "Peace be with you.
Covenantal demands	"Go into all the world and proclaim the gospel to the whole creation.	As the Father has sent Me, even so I am sending you.
Covenantal promises	Whoever believes and is baptized will be saved, but whoever does not believe will be condemned. And these signs will accompany those who believe: in my name they will cast out demons; they will speak in new tongues; they will pick up serpents with their hands; and if they drink any deadly poison, it will not hurt them; they will lay their hands on the sick, and they will recover."	Receive the Holy Spirit."

Fig. 4.2. The Covenantal Structure of the Great Commission, Table 2

disciples become part of God's new covenant people. As in Genesis 17, it is part of the stipulations of the new covenant to receive the sign and seal of being part of God's new covenant people—but now through baptism. Baptism is the sign and seal of the promise of God's covenantal blessings, and it is received and internalized through comprehensive teaching. The recipient is thus brought under the promises and sanctions of the covenant through baptism and instruction. Baptism is the sign of consecration and discipleship in the new covenant. Its meaning is life, the new life, that has been made possible by participation in the death and resurrection of Christ.[31] Baptism *in the name* (*eis to onoma*) of the Father, the Son, and the Holy Spirit expresses proprietorship and conveys the meaning that new disciples enter into a forensic relationship with the triune God as their proprietor. In rabbinic literature, a slave has to be baptized when he

---

31. De Ridder, *Dispersion of the People of God*, 190.

becomes a part of a Jewish household and rebaptized in the name of freedom when released. In this way, baptism expresses the new covenant as a forensic relationship.[32]

Comparing the expression "in the name" in Matthew 28:19 with the way it is used in 18:20, it becomes clear that it signifies solidarity with Jesus and indicates a comprehensive commitment to him, what he has done, and what he stands for. Loyalty, belonging, submission, and intention to act on his behalf are involved.[33] In this way, the character of the new covenant corresponds to the character of the Old Testament covenant, where the total commitment of the covenant people to YHWH was required.

Considering the broader context in the Gospels, it becomes clear that Jesus' call to his disciples adopted the concept of YHWH's purpose with regard to Israel's special destiny and unique mission, which set her apart from all other races, cultures, families, and nations. He told them that they were in the world, but not of the world, because of their allegiance, values, goals, and hope. They were called out of the world and sent into the world as sheep among wolves, to be hated and persecuted as he had been, because they were uniquely separated from the world by God's call to discipleship (Matt. 10:16–25).

The same picture unfolds in the rest of the New Testament. Paul picked up this theme during his first missionary journey, when he preached his first sermon in Pisidian Antioch (Acts 13:16–41). He saw his mission as a mandate, derived from Jesus' messianic mission (Luke 4:17–27), now transferred to the disciples: to be "a light for the Gentiles" (Acts 13:47). Peter also reminded his readers that as a church they were "a chosen people, a royal priesthood, a holy nation, a people belonging to God, that you may declare the praises of him who called you out of darkness into his wonderful light." As a result, pagans will "see your good deeds and glorify God on the day he visits us" (1 Peter 2:9, 12 NIV). Light for the Gentiles, priests for the nations—this is

32. H. L. Strack and P. Billerbeck, *Das Evangelium nach Matthäus erläutert aus Talmud und Midrasch* (München: Beck, 1974), 1054.

33. John Nolland, *The Gospel of Matthew: A Commentary on the Greek Text* (Grand Rapids: Eerdmans, 2005), 1268–69.

the special calling and identity of missional congregations. They are the missionary people of God, whose uniqueness derives directly from God's instrumental purposes for them. They are his special people, who, because of God's call, emerge in human history as the covenant community of the King, a key part of the kingdom of God. Anyone who downplays the importance of the local congregation in relation to mission must carefully consider its unique identity and purpose in the world as a *covenant community of the King*.[34]

The term "disciple" also implies a supremely personal union where the Greek word *mathētēs* is used. There can be nothing in the life of the disciple that is separated from the Lord and his life. Disciples, with all they have and are, are drawn into personal fellowship with him.[35] According to Vos, participation in the covenant of grace refers to "a relationship between two parties with reciprocal conditions" (promises and warnings on God's side, faith and repentance on ours) and to the living fellowship between God and his people in the covenant of grace (participation in the covenant).[36] In other words, the covenant of grace involves first a formal, forensic relationship of mutual obligation, and when that relationship achieves its real purpose, it becomes a living fellowship between those bound by mutual obligation in the covenant. Vos's distinction does not posit two different covenants of grace, but rather a twofold sense of membership in the covenant of grace.

This distinction allows us to recognize as covenantally related to God as "his people" (Heb. 10:30) those who nevertheless do not enjoy a living fellowship with God in Christ and who do not enjoy the graces of justification, sanctification, and glorification—for example, Simon the Magician in Acts 8, the branches broken off in John 15, and the apostates of the Johannine community in 1 John 2:19. It allows us to take the warnings of the new covenant administration

---

34. Charles E. Van Engen, *God's Missionary People: Rethinking the Purpose of the Local Church* (Grand Rapids: Baker, 1993), 105.

35. De Ridder, *Dispersion of the People of God*, 186.

36. Scott Swain, "Geerhardus Vos on Membership in the Covenant of Grace," http://www.reformation21.org/blog/2015/06/geerhardus-vos-on-membership-i .php, accessed on June 8, 2015.

(Col. 1:21–23; Heb. 6:4–8; 10:26–39) with utter seriousness as God's righteous curse of the covenant on those who do not repent whole-heartedly, and without denying the perseverance of the saints. It also allows us to appreciate the organic connection between a formal cov-enant relationship with God (entered into by adult believers through baptism and confession, and by the children of believers on the basis of the covenant promise "to you and your offspring"—Gen. 17:7–8; Acts 2:39) and the living covenant fellowship that follows from it by God's grace, in the case of the elect. Baptism in the name of—

- The Father implies that the disciple has received the mark and seal that he/she has been placed under the regal rule and care of the Father.
- The Son implies that the disciple has received the mark and seal that he/she has become the possession of Jesus Christ. The disciple has been liberated from slavery to sin and death and has been placed under the rule of a new King, to live according to a new lifestyle.
- The Holy Spirit implies that the disciple has come under the authority, rule, and enabling power of the Holy Spirit. In the new covenant, Christ is not only our representative, who has fulfilled the commands of the covenant in our place; he also gives us the promise that he will enable us through his Spirit to obey the commands of the covenant. Humble obedience is thus sustained by the covenantal promise of the constant presence of Christ with his followers by the Holy Spirit.

Making disciples through teaching implies that dominion over the whole of creation must come to expression in a total dedication and submission to what Jesus commanded. De Ridder states:

> "All I have commanded you" includes not merely the thought of the content of the proclamation, but what is more central, it refers to the total scope of one's obedience and commitment to the Lord of the covenant. Nothing in all life's relationships lies outside the area of subjection to Him. It is as though Christ were saying

through the witnesses of all ages, "You have been made the object of salvation; prove now true that you know it to be true."[37]

Whereas a member of the covenant was circumcised in the Name of YHWH in the old covenant, the richer, more complete revelation of God in the new covenant makes it clear that covenant members are now baptized in the name of the triune God.

Covenant, Church, and Kingdom

Understanding the covenantal structure of the Great Commission and the missional goal of God's new covenant people makes it clear that there is no tension between the covenant and the kingdom in the New Testament. The kingdom of God should not be seen as identical with the church.[38] Charles Van Engen points out that Herman Ridderbos, George Eldon Ladd, Oscar Cullmann, John Bright, Jürgen Moltmann, and others have demonstrated that the kingdom, the rule of Jesus Christ, became a present, but not yet complete, reality through the coming, suffering, death, and resurrection of Christ: it has come, but it is also coming. So with the church.[39] Ridderbos puts it this way:

> *The basileia* [kingdom of God] *is the great divine work of salvation in its fulfillment and consummation in Christ; the ekklesia* [church] *is the people elected and called by God and sharing in the bliss of the basileia.* . . . The former, therefore, has a much more comprehensive content. It represents the all-embracing perspective, it denotes the consummation of all history, brings both grace and judgment, has cosmic dimensions, fills time and eternity. The *ekklesia* in all this is the people who in this great drama have been placed on the side of God in Christ by virtue of the divine election and covenant. . . . Insofar as the *basileia* is already a present reality, the *ekklesia* is also

37. De Ridder, *Dispersion of the People of God*, 194.
38. P. J. Buys, "Die verhouding tussen verbond en koninkryk bij Paulus—'n terreinverkenning," *In die Skriflig* 26.1 (1973): 7–20.
39. Van Engen, *God's Missionary People*, 107.

the place where the gifts and powers of the *basileia* are granted and received. It is, further, the gathering of those who, as the instruments of the *basileia*, are called upon to make profession of Jesus as the Christ, to obey his commandments, to perform the missionary task of the preaching of the gospel throughout the world. In every respect the church is surrounded and impelled by the revelation, the progress, the future of the kingdom of God without, however, itself being the *basileia*, and without ever being identified with it.[40]

The New Covenant Structure: Preaching, Challenge, and Comfort

Understanding the covenantal structure undergirding the gospel provides a biblical balance when proclaiming the promises of the gospel and confronting the audience with its claims—calling them to repentance and faith, and warning them of the judgment of God, should they not repent.

Many preachers seem to be out of balance when it comes to their sermons. Generally, when they go awry in this area, they do so by displaying one of the two following forms of imbalance. Some, in an effort to establish their authority in the pulpit, make the mistake of overloading their sermons with harsh application and threats. In fact, they browbeat their people week after week. On the other end of the spectrum are those who, out of a desire not to offend and be politically correct, eviscerate their sermons of all poignancy and obligation.[41] Both of these common errors are equally deadly in a congregation and on the mission field.

Preaching in an Established Church

An uncompassionate emphasis on the imperatives and the threats of God's imminent judgment in the new covenant, apart from the

40. Herman N. Ridderbos, *The Coming of the Kingdom* (Philadelphia: Presbyterian and Reformed, 1962), 354–56.

41. Anthony T. Selvaggio, "Preaching Advice from the 'Sermon' to the Hebrews," *Themelios* 32.2 (2006): 33–44.

promises of the gospel, leaves the congregation in despair. On the other hand, merely proclaiming the promises of the covenant and ignoring the imperatives to repent and the covenantal threats of God's righteous judgment, lulls the recipients into complacency and false assurance.

The preacher in the book of Hebrews displays a remarkable equilibrium and adeptly avoids these two common mistakes. He balances challenge and comfort in his sermon. Presenting the new covenant, the book of Hebrews contains some of the most fearful admonitions and challenges of the entire Bible. This preacher is not afraid to challenge people. For example, in Hebrews 3–4 he compares the congregation to the generation that died in the wilderness due to their unfaithfulness. He effectively places them in the shoes of that Old Testament generation and warns them that they are close to repeating the same deadly error: "Therefore, while the promise of entering his rest still stands, let us fear lest any of you should seem to have failed to reach it" (Heb. 4:1). However, after putting the fear of God in them for fourteen verses, and making them think they are on the verge of apostasy, he comforts them by reminding them: "For we do not have a high priest who is unable to sympathize with our weaknesses, but one who in every respect has been tempted as we are, yet without sin. Let us then with confidence draw near to the throne of grace, that we may receive mercy and find grace to help in time of need" (Heb. 4:15–16). He balances challenge with comfort.

Likewise, in Hebrews 6, the preacher warns once again of the threat of apostasy and goes so far as to say that it is impossible to recover from it (Heb. 6:6). However, after giving this stern warning, he balances the challenge with these comforting words: "Though we speak in this way, yet in your case, beloved, we feel sure of better things—things that belong to salvation" (Heb. 6:9). Anthony Selvaggio concludes:

> The preacher to the Hebrews is neither a blustering legalist nor a facile man-pleaser. Instead, the preacher powerfully drives home the full force of his warnings while never allowing his people to fall into despair. He calls them to persevere, but he always reminds

them that they can only do so by following Christ. He reminds them that God will never leave them nor forsake them (Heb. 13:5). Modern preachers should take a cue from the preacher to the Hebrews by adopting his pattern of balancing challenge with comfort in their sermons.[42]

This balance has been part and parcel of preaching in the Reformed tradition. Over against Roman Catholic misunderstanding, Reformed people have always believed that the church received the authority to minister the keys of the kingdom. In the original German translation of question 83 of the Heidelberg Catechism, we read: "Was ist der Ampt der Schlüssel?" In English, a good translation could be: "What is the task . . ." or "What do the keys of the kingdom of heaven do?" and not "What are the keys of the kingdom of heaven?" as many translations have it. If we understand the question in this way, the answer given makes more sense: "(Through) the preaching of the holy gospel . . . the kingdom of heaven is opened to believers, and shut against unbelievers."

When Jesus gave this authority to Peter in Matthew 16:18–19— and also to all who hold the same confession—to open and shut the kingdom, authority is not attached to specific persons; rather, their preaching of the gospel opens and shuts the entrance to God's kingdom. That is why the catechism states that the act of preaching does this. The emphasis is on the preaching and not on the preacher.

One of the words for preaching in the New Testament, *kēryssō*, was used for the proclamation of a king's messenger. When the king had a message for his people, the messenger went about the public places announcing the message of the king. This is what the church must do today. We should proclaim: "Thus says the King of the universe: All those who acknowledge their sins and believe in the complete forgiveness that Jesus Christ earned through his crucifixion and resurrection and accept him as their only Savior, Lord, and Master of their lives, will be part of the covenant community of the King, and receive eternal life. But all those who do not acknowledge their

---

42. Selvaggio, "Preaching Advice from the 'Sermon' to the Hebrews," 38; cf. 33–44.

sins and do not repent and humbly embrace Jesus as their Savior and Lord, will perish in everlasting punishment."

The goal of preaching is to make Jesus Christ present. Christ himself comes clothed in the gospel, and so the message is more than words—it is the power of God for salvation. This is not simply new religious doctrine to be affirmed and understood. It announces what God is doing through Jesus by the Spirit. The message itself is the power of God to transform lives (Rom. 1:16; 1 Cor. 1:18, 24; 2:4).[43] Where this everlasting gospel of salvation and judgment, of forgiveness and condemnation, is faithfully preached, Christ himself is at work, opening and closing the entrance to the kingdom of heaven.

Preaching is also a powerful means by which God's people are nurtured and empowered for their missional calling. Faithful biblical preaching will be missional. The various books of the Bible were written to form a missional people. To overlook this original intention of Scripture is to miss the aim of the text. Scripture is first of all not about delivering salvific benefits to individuals, important though this be, but is rather concerned with forming a people that embodies the good news of the kingdom for the sake of the world. Thus, preaching should always orient us outward. Faithful preaching moves from Christ to mission because "there is no participation in Christ without participation in his mission."[44]

Preaching on the Mission Field

It is not only the preaching in the church building that shuts or opens the kingdom, but everywhere the gospel is preached faithfully. Preaching to pagans who have never heard of Christ should also proclaim the promises of the gospel and then summon hearers to repent and believe. One of the best examples of contextualization with the aim to connect with and confront pagans is Paul's preaching on the Areopagus in Athens (Acts 17:22–34). His sermon builds up to the

43. Michael W. Goheen, *A Light to the Nations: The Missional Church and the Biblical Story* (Grand Rapids: Baker, 2011), 212.

44. Norman Goodall, ed., *Missions under the Cross* (London: Edinburgh House Press, 1953).

climax of verses 30–31: "The times of ignorance God overlooked, but now he commands all people everywhere to repent, because he has fixed a day on which he will judge the world in righteousness by a man whom he has appointed; and of this he has given assurance to all by raising him from the dead."

The Heidelberg Catechism (answer 84) says that the gospel is declared and publicly testified to every believer or unbeliever. In other words, Christ opens or shuts his kingdom on the mission field and in personal evangelistic discussion. This also has an awesome implication: where unbelievers come under our preaching, if they do not hear in it the gospel and come to repentance and faith through the warning of the judgment of God (John 3:36), an opportunity to open the doors of heaven for them has been missed, and their blood is on the hands of the preacher (Ezek. 33:7–9; Acts 20:26–27).

The teaching of the proclamation of the gospel as an act of ministering the keys of heaven also implies that preaching should not only be an opening up of heaven, but also a closing. Faithful proclamation of the gospel must proclaim judgment as well as grace. We must also shut the gates of heaven by explaining the awful judgment of God and the eternal damnation of unrepentant sinners and unbelievers. It is comforting to preach God's tremendous forgiveness, but true preaching should also announce his awful curses on those who reject the gospel. The gospel is not merely a sentimental story to soothe people's consciences, while never telling them of the awesome holiness and justice of God. Real compassion and genuine love constrain us to warn people about the judgment of God. Too many evangelistic programs and popular preachers handle the keys of heaven in an unfaithful way by not proclaiming the threats of the new covenant and God's eternal judgment on those who do not believe and repent.

The Heidelberg Catechism (84) also states that God judges in this life, as well as in the life to come, through the preaching of the gospel. God is already drawing the boundary lines of eternal judgment in this life. According to 2 Corinthians 2:16, the gospel is a fragrance of life, as well as a smell of death. When people reject the gospel of God's wonderful forgiveness in Christ and do not repent and believe, they are already condemned. That is why we read in Hebrews 2:3, "How shall we escape if we neglect such a great salvation?" Preaching that fails to invite God's people to embody a different story of the world than the one offered by the dominant culture will leave them vulnerable to the idolatrous stories of the culture.

Missional Implications of the Corporate Character of the New Covenant

Continuity as well as newness must be recognized in the relationship between the new covenant and the old. In terms of the collective or corporate character of the covenant, there is no discontinuity between the two: corporateness is an essential reality and part of the new covenant community, and it functions as complementary to individuality, as they are not mutually exclusive principles. Problems arise in the covenant community when either is excluded from an understanding of the covenant relationship. Presumption occurs when corporateness is recognized apart from individuality, and isolation occurs when individuality is recognized apart from corporateness.[45]

Unless both principles are understood aright, a true appreciation of the promise of the new covenant cannot be comprehended. Jeremiah, in his prophecy about the remnant, states both principles and their roles in the new covenant community. Although it is better and richer than the old covenant, the new nowhere indicates a covenant excluding little children. After the exile, God wanted a people, and to a thousand generations, which is quite different from a collection of reborn individuals pulled out of their family ties. The genealogical principle, as a gracious promise, is an integral aspect of biblical understanding of the covenant corporateness.

In the book of Acts, the realization of the promises of the new covenant through faith and repentance is described. The Holy Spirit, as the great gift of the covenant (Ezek. 36:26ff.; Jer. 31:32; Joel 2:28–32), was poured out on the church, as the new covenant community, to reside in the hearts of believers. In his sermon in Acts 2, Peter points out that, in accordance with Joel 2, the Holy Spirit is poured out on

45. Robertson, *Christ of the Covenants*, 290.

all people, including sons and daughters, young men, old men, and even on servants, both men and women. Lambertus Floor points out with reference to Joel 2:16—now fulfilled with the outpouring of the Holy Spirit—that even nursing infants were included in the promises to God's people of the outpouring of the Holy Spirit.[46] Acts 2:38–39 should be interpreted in this context as teaching that the promise is for believers, for their children in the generations to come, and also for the Gentiles who will become believers. Peter concludes his appeal in verse 21 with the promise of Joel 2:32: "Everyone who calls upon the name of the Lord shall be saved." The universal scope of the promise is emphasized. Salvation is not only for the group of Jews present at Pentecost, but for future generations, "your children" as well. It is not only for Jews, but for Gentiles, for those "who are far off."[47]

The collective character of the new covenant is affirmed in the way whole households of new disciples were included in receiving baptism as the sign and seal of becoming part of the people of God (Acts 10:44–48; 16:15; 16:33; 18:8; 1 Cor. 1:16). In his study of the household in the New Testament, Jean-Jacques von Allmen concludes:

> In accordance with the custom of the time, which the New Testament nowhere disputes, the family (also called by the beautiful name *house*) comprises parents, children and also servants, often designated in Greek by terms which show they belong to the particular "house" (Matt. 10:25, 36; 24:45; Luke 16:13; Acts 10:7; Rom. 14:4; Phil. 4:22; 1 Peter 2:18). When the father is alive, or when he is a Christian, the house takes his name, and this social unity is so closely bound up with him that he is also able to make decisions on behalf of the whole household which have eternal effects. This is seen for example in the narratives of conversion or of baptism (Acts 10:2; 11:14; 16:31; 18:18; 1 Cor. 1:16, cf. again Acts 16:15; John 4:53; and Matt. 18:25).[48]

46. Lambertus Floor, *Die heilige doop in die Nieuwe Testament* (Potchefstroom: Potchefstroomse Teologiese Publikasies, 1983), 34.

47. John B. Polhill, *Acts* (Nashville: Broadman & Holman, 1992), 117.

48. Jean-Jacques von Allmen, "Family," in J.-J. von Allmen and H. H. Rowley, eds., *Vocabulary of the Bible* (London: Lutterworth, 1958).

The forensic position of children within the covenant becomes a relationship of intimate fellowship when a child—through the work of the Holy Spirit—comes to the point of personally embracing Jesus as Lord and King. In this way, the forensic relationship is deepened to become a relationship of mutual, loving fellowship, without wiping out the forensic stipulations of the covenant.

Household Evangelism

The emphasis in the new covenant on the importance of households coming to faith in missions and evangelism is of great importance. Conversion is not merely an individual issue, but interwoven with the corporate character of the covenant in which household and family are important aspects. The family did not just happen; it is ordained and instituted by God. The household is a fundamental biblical concept; God willed the family and the home. It is the original divinely instituted, natural, social, and specific unit, essential to the well-being of the human race. In this regard, Timothy Monsma rightly states that God saves his people, not individualistically, but organically and covenantally, parents together with their children.[49] Along the same lines, he adds:

> Stress family work. The same organic covenant works through the family channel. We seek individuals, yes, but we hasten to add "and thy house." This is biblical. This is distinctively our reformed contribution in evangelism and mission work. We are more committed to neighborhood evangelism—bringing the gospel to the family. We should be especially strong in that.[50]

In his research on evangelism in the early church, Michael Green discovered that Christian missionaries made a deliberate point of gaining whatever households they could as lighthouses from which

---

49. Timothy M. Monsma, *Household Evangelism* (Grand Rapids: Board of Evangelism of the Christian Reformed Churches, 1948), 38.

50. Monsma, *Household Evangelism*, 79.

the gospel could illuminate the surrounding darkness. Although he is of the opinion that Ethelbert Stauffer may have gone too far when he claimed that there is an almost ritual *oikos*-formula in the New Testament, he agrees with him in stressing the centrality of the household to advance the cause of Christ.[51] Green also gives examples, from the second century, of how slaves became Christians and even established house churches. According to him, this gives concrete attestation to the process of the gradual infiltration of the middle and upper classes of Roman society by Christianity through the lives and words of slaves and freed men in their employment. This is how the Christian home as a unique institution began to make an impression on surrounding paganism.[52]

In his book *A Light to the Nations*, Michael Goheen stresses the vital importance of a church with parents trained to take up the task of nurturing children in the faith. He makes it clear that if families are not taught to make radical, costly, and time-consuming commitments to nurturing their children, the future of the church as a missional community in the West will be bleak. He then gives a moving testimony about family devotions in a healthy missional church:

> I remember trembling at the baptism of my oldest two children as I felt the enormous weight of my responsibility to enable them to know the promises, the commands, and the warnings of the covenant. At that time my wife and I committed to taking whatever radical steps were needed to be faithful in this calling. I want to briefly note some of those measures that eventually materialized.
>
> The first is *family worship*. We started this early, and none of our children can remember a time when we didn't have family worship as central to our evenings. We set aside an hour to an hour and a half for family worship five nights a week (Monday through Thursday and Saturday). It was important to set a time and remain unswerving in a commitment to guard it at all costs against other

51. Michael Green, *Evangelism in the Early Church* (London: Hodder and Stoughton, 1970), 209, 260.

52. Green, *Evangelism in the Early Church*, 209, 260.

intrusions. It meant starting other meetings later and not planning other evening events. During this time we taught our children the true story of the world in Scripture, using books and methods appropriate to their ages. We spent significant time in singing and praying together. We memorized and discussed sections of *Our World Belongs to God: A Contemporary Testimony*. Using *Operation World* we talked about and prayed for the world church. I would regularly take each of my children on my knee and pray for her or him. All of this made family worship one of our favorite times of the day.[53]

Group Conversions and People Movements

Donald McGavran and other leaders in the Church Growth Movement argue fervently for group conversions of tribes and homogeneous people groups: "The people movement is the God-given way by which social resistance to the gospel can be surmounted."[54] Elsewhere he states: "What is called for today, then, is to break the chains of Western individualism so that the ingathering that runs through caste, becomes the normally expected outcome of evangelism. The goal then is that each of the three thousand and more ethnic units should find flowing within it a strong movement becoming disciples of the Lord Jesus, and to feed on his revealed Word in the Bible."[55]

Some Reformed missiologists also consider that such a practice is an acknowledgment of the collective character of the covenant. In this regard, Roger Greenway agrees with Harry R. Boer, who has stated: "The great merit of McGavran in emphasizing the place of the *oikos* in missionary strategy can hardly be overestimated."[56] However, others

53. Goheen, *A Light to the Nations*, 250.

54. Donald A. McGavran, *Understanding Church Growth* (Grand Rapids: Eerdmans, 1980), 336.

55. Donald A. McGavran, *Ethnic Realities and the Church: Lessons from India* (Pasadena, CA: Carey, 1979), 247.

56. Roger S. Greenway, "Winnable People," in *Theological Perspectives on Church Growth*, ed. Harvey M. Conn (Nutley, NJ: Presbyterian and Reformed, 1976), 46, quoting Harry R. Boer.

have warned that group conversions do not take into consideration that the covenant does not only have a corporate character, but is also a personal relationship between the disciple and the living Christ. If the aspect of personal commitment to, and intimate fellowship with, Christ is ignored, the result is often the rise of a nominal, syncretistic Christianity, where the claims of the gospel are clouded by traditional tribal worldviews and culture. In this regard, John Young asks about people who have become Christians through group conversion strategies: "Have they been brought by a strategy or by the convicting power of the Holy Spirit? Have they substituted new rites for old with their faith still in externals and their sense of security still basically in their tribal identity?"[57]

It is therefore important to take both the corporate approach and the appeal to personal fellowship with Christ into consideration in mission work.

Conclusion

The following characteristics of the covenant in the New Testament impact the understanding of the practical aspects of global missions:

1. The covenant is a forensic relationship between God and his new covenant people, and therefore has promises, commands, and sanctions.
2. The covenant has a collective or corporate character, so that the relationship between God and the individual includes families and households and the church as God's larger family.
3. The forensic and collective character of the new covenant reaches its peak when individuals enter into a personal relationship of loving commitment and fellowship with the triune God.
4. God's goal with the covenant is missional, so that his covenant people will be his witnesses to the ends of the earth and participate in the final coming of his kingdom.

57. John M. L. Young, "The Place and Importance of Numerical Church Growth," in *Theological Perspectives on Church Growth*, ed. Conn, 72.

5

Mission in the Light of Covenantal Eschatology

Paul Wells

Abstract

Jesus Christ, as mediator between God and man, fulfills the covenant promises and heralds the arrival of the eschatological period that will be concluded by his return in glory. Mission in the interim is therefore *missio Christi* in the power of the Spirit and in the hope of the new creation. The triune God sends the Son, who in turn sends ambassadors to all nations, proclaiming the love of God and the good news of salvation to lost humanity. New communities of faith are united to and in Christ by the Spirit and by the apostolic truth, announcing the coming of God's kingdom, to the glory of God.

Introduction

Eschatology is often taken to be the knowledge of the last things (*ta eschata*) associated with end-time events and the *telos* of history. This approach has served to accentuate the impersonal aspect of eschatology related to chronologics, time lines, signs of the end, and suchlike. However, another approach exists, which considers eschatology as an aspect of biblical theology and therefore of the history of redemption and the covenant. It focuses on the mediator, Jesus Christ, who is the *eschatos*, the last one in person, whose presence, as the second Adam, marks the climax of the historical purposes of God and his dealings with humanity.[1] In this respect, it can be defined as the orientation and the objective of God's covenant faithfulness to the created order and human beings, in order to bring renewal and salvation in Christ.[2]

In recent years, the mission of God model (*missio Dei*) has been prominent in missiological debate and policy. David Bosch indicates that in this model the church has to be committed to

> service to the *missio Dei*, representing God in and over against the world, pointing to God, holding up the God-child before the eyes of the world. . . . In its mission, the church witnesses to the fullness of the promise of God's reign and participates in the ongoing struggle between that reign and the power of darkness and evil.[3]

While there are definitely positives to be found in this approach, problems arise mainly due to the pluralistic and relativistic presuppositions of some of those using it.[4] For instance, critical analysis and evaluation need to be made of the idea that mission is an attribute of God himself, or that the mission of a mutable God moves in step with the historical process, or that the acts of God are more missional than simple word evangelism, or even that the hidden Christ of non-Christian religions is an expression of God's global mission.[5] Furthermore, it is also remarkable that the proclamation of God's

---

1. Paul Wells, "Eschatologie," in *Dictionnaire de théologie biblique* (Cléon d'Andran: Excelsis, 2013), 561–71, translated as "Eschatology," *Reformed Theological Journal* 24.1 (2008): 59–75.

2. Kent E. Brower and Mark Elliott, eds., *The Reader Must Understand: Eschatology in the Bible and Theology* (Leicester, Downers Grove, IL: InterVarsity Press, 1998), 119.

3. David J. Bosch, *Transforming Mission: Paradigm Shifts in Theology of Mission* (Maryknoll, NY: Orbis, 1998), 391.

4. Christopher J. H. Wright, *The Mission of God: Unlocking the Bible's Grand Narrative* (Downers Grove, IL: IVP Academic, 2006), 45–47, 61–68.

5. Tormod Engelsviken, "*Missio Dei*: The Understanding and Misunderstanding of a Theological Concept in European Churches and Missiology," *International Review of Mission* 92 (2003): 481–97.

judgment through Christ is ignored by many publications about the mission of God.[6] A covenantal approach, integrating biblical law, provides a viable way to proclaim the reality of eschatological judgment and how it is related to response to the gospel message.[7]

A covenantal model of mission and eschatology can provide a viable corrective to these pitfalls. The covenant provides the context for both the words and the acts of God. In contrast to the *missio Dei* model, it encourages a full recognition of the diversity of Trinitarian action. God's saving acts have a beginning and an end, and run on historical trajectories. Their content is salvation, with Christ as the central actor, the Alpha and Omega, the incarnate servant, and the risen Lord and King of the new creation.[8] Centered on the person of Christ, eschatology is the direction and purpose of God's faithfulness through his covenant promises. From Adam to Abraham to Moses to Christ, the covenant has a Christ-oriented centripetal direction; from Christ forward, it is a centrifugal force of mission to the nations, to the end of the world.[9]

From this perspective, eschatology is not limited to the presentation of the last things of systematic theology; it seeks to show how, in Christ, the ultimate reality of God's plan guides human history through the covenant promise and how at each stage the will of God—Father, Son, and Holy Spirit—intervenes. The mission of Christ and of his witnesses is vital in the implementation of God's purposes.

Presuppositions of Covenantal Eschatology

Three biblical assumptions guide covenantal eschatology: the *goodness* of God in salvation, the divine *wisdom* of God's promises, and the *power* of God to achieve his purposes, which seem impossible

---

6. Acts 17:31; Heb. 10:26–30; 2 Peter 3:11–13; Rev. 20:11–15.

7. Joseph Boot, *The Mission of God: A Manifesto of Hope* (St. Catherines, ON: Freedom Press, 2014), 14–17.

8. Adrio König, *The Eclipse of Christ in Eschatology: Toward a Christ-Centered Approach* (Grand Rapids: Eerdmans, 1989).

9. Johannes Blauw, *The Missionary Nature of the Church* (London: Lutterworth, 1963).

to human immanentism. The acts of God in salvation history are contrary to worldly versions of the good life, to the wisdom of Athens, and to the evanescent powers of this age. The history of the covenant presents God doing the impossible to achieve his promise. Mission in this context is undertaking daring acts against totalitarian worldly logic, because what is impossible for men is possible for God. Think of Paul's witness to his missional apostolate in 2 Corinthians 11:16–33, which even includes escapes in laundry baskets!

God's people confess that mission is carried out in all periods of the history of salvation, which centers on the incarnation, the cross, and the resurrection, giving focus to God's life-giving goodness and forecasting a new creation of peace, life, and justice in communion with God.[10]

Covenantal eschatology saps the premises of both determinism and indeterminism, the twin enemies of the divine promise. Determinism undermines dynamic narrative and the historical contingency which is the context of the victory of the Lamb.[11] For determinism, the temporal process is less meaningful than the forces governing it. Narrative loses its features of novelty, the unexpected, freedom, and tragedy. Covenantal prophecy, by way of contrast, has all these features; it announces future events, but their performance always surpasses expectations. It is contrary to the Stoic notion of the eternal return (i.e., that the universe goes through an eternally repeating life cycle). Indeterminacy, on the other hand, moves the outcome of the historical process into the realm of mystery and the unknown, as nothing can be stated with certainty concerning the future. Pure chance eliminates the possibility of a future whose outcome is foreseen as the finality of present events. In other words, there is no plan of God and nothing to expect. The radical contingency of the narrative makes it like a puzzle made up of undecipherable fortuities.

10. See the illustration of the basic covenantal-eschatological structure of the work of Christ and mission in the appendix at the end of this article. See also Paul Wells, "La chaîne d'or de l'eschatologie biblique," *Revue réformée* 54.4 (2003): 25–42.

11. Paul Wells, "Story, Eschatology and the Agnus Victor," in *Strangers and Pilgrims on the Earth: Essays in Honour of Abraham van de Beek*, ed. E. Van der Borght and P. van Geest (Leiden: Brill, 2012), 343–56.

In contrast to these views and their correlates—pure rationalism or irrationalism—Christian eschatology, with a covenantal structure, espouses both divine sovereignty and human freedom, recognizing the complementarity of the divine and the human factors in historical narrative. God accomplishes his plan in a way that respects the conditions of "two-factor theology." The counsel of God concerning "all things" that come to pass (Eph. 1:11) is behind developments in space-time history. The complementarity of divine initiative and human response, with man's answer to the divine call, makes the covenant a launching pad for mission in the extension of Christ's kingdom.

Covenantal Eschatology as the Structure of Mission

From a theological point of view, taking Christ as the center of God's purposes has two perspectives. In the vertical sense of John Calvin's *Institutes* (2.6.1), Christ occupies geographically the unbridgeable space between God and man, as the one mediator (1 Tim. 2:5).[12] In the horizontal diachronic sense, the fulfillment of the covenant promise in Christ opens a perspective going back to Adam as the end of a period of expectation. However, covenant fulfillment also opens a new horizon to the future, because of the new creation present in the resurrection and the empty tomb. The fullness of time leads to the new creation in Christ. As Oliver O'Donovan states,

> The triumph of the Son of man prepares the way for the future triumph of his "brethren," mankind as a whole. But this eschatological triumph of mankind is not an innovative order that has nothing to do with the primal ordering of man as creature to his Creator. It fulfils and vindicates the primal order in a way that was always implied, but which could not be realized in the fallen state of man and the universe.[13]

12. Pierre Gisel, *Le Christ de Calvin* (Paris: Desclée, 1990), 29–37.

13. Oliver O'Donovan, *Resurrection and Moral Order: An Outline for an Evangelical Ethics* (Grand Rapids: Eerdmans, 1986), 66. Cf. Colin Gunton, *Christ and Creation* (Carlisle: Paternoster, 1992), 93–98; William J. Dumbrell, *Covenant and Creation* (Carlisle: Paternoster, 2013), 46–47.

The centrality of the resurrection in the biblical story of salvation, Christ as firstfruits, prepares for the final revelation.[14] And this is implemented through the mission of those whom Christ sends, the apostles and their successors, who preach the gospel of Christ. The mandate for the mission of the church is not in the attributes of God and the fact that God himself is considered a missional God. The focus is more precisely in redemptive history—in salvation accomplished in the fulfillment of the covenant by the one who was sent. The mission of the church is a christological covenantal activity with eschatological salvation as its goal. We need go no further to found this mission than the use of *apostellō* in the gospel of John, linked with the promise of the Holy Spirit, for instance in the Johannine Pentecost (John 20:21): "As the Father has sent me (*apestalken me*), even so I am sending you (*pempō hymas*)."

In what follows, we will consider the covenant fulfillment as the content, the message, the perspective, and the hope of missional activity, all of which have an eschatological focus in the already–not yet pattern of salvation in Christ.

Covenantal Fulfillment as the Content of Mission

Since the beginning of Christian tradition, Jesus has been presented as *ho eschatos, the last*. The person of Jesus *himself* is the goal toward which all creation and the covenant progress to find fulfillment in him (Col. 1:15–20). The incarnation causes the end of history to enter time, for in Jesus the divine plan of salvation and judgment is present and already played out at Calvary and the garden tomb. As Jesus is the climax of the covenant, he himself is the content of mission in four respects.

First, *Jesus Christ is the* telos *in person, for he accomplishes God's eschatological plan historically*. In the New Testament, there exists a juxtaposition between the last days and the last day, for example in Matthew 24. The first expression concerns the present period,

---

14. Richard B. Gaffin, Jr., *The Centrality of the Resurrection: A Study in Paul's Soteriology* (Grand Rapids: Baker Book House, 1978), 33–41.

while the second never refers to present time, but to the future day of judgment. According to Hebrews 1:2, God has spoken "in these last days" (*ep' eschatou tōn hēmerōn toutōn*) by his Son. Hebrews 9:26 equally indicates that the incarnation of Christ is the watershed of history: "He has appeared once for all at the end of the ages (*epi synteleia tōn aiōnōn*) to put away sin." Immanuel, by his appearance, marks the arrival of the eschatological day and inaugurates a different time, that of the end. In 1 Peter 1:20, we read that he was "foreknown before the foundation of the world but was made manifest in the last times (*ep' eschatou tōn chronōn*) for the sake of you"—a striking contrast between the beginning and the end of time. The link between the two is established by the presence of Christ. In other words, in the person of Jesus, and because of his coming, the end of time is transparent.

Second, *the ministry of Jesus marks the beginning of the end.* In him, God's year of grace is announced and begun (Luke 4:18–21). Captives are liberated as Satan is bound, dethroned, and falls from heaven, since the kingdom has come (Luke 11:20; Matt. 12:28). Jesus' power over demons is a reorganization of cosmic forces. The kingdom of God is redemptive and dynamically active in establishing his kingship over men. The kingdom, which will appear as God's apocalyptic act at the end of the age, has already come in human history in the person and the mission of Jesus, who conquers evil, delivers men from its power, and grants access to the covenant blessing. The kingdom unites two great moments: its accomplishment in history and its consummation at the end.

Furthermore, *the crucifixion of Jesus is an eschatological event of covenant fulfillment.* The evangelists record the eschatological discourse of Jesus before his passion, and subsequently the crucifixion. The loss of the love of many, injustice, and the supernatural phenomena of the Old Testament day of the Lord are present at the moment of Christ's death. *Tetelestai* in John 19:30 can be translated either by "it is finished" or "it is accomplished," indicating that the end has begun at Calvary. The crucifixion is the judgment of the world (John 12:31). "The cross . . . cut through the bond which for a definite period of time had tied [Christ] to the kosmos; it threw Him out from the world, and He departed from it to enter another world, which was his real home. . . . It made Him not so much a 'new creature,' as the veritable beginner of a 'new creation.'"[15] The *eschaton* already happened in Christ and reveals the secret of a new world. This means that mission in the name of Jesus is new-creation activity.

Finally, *Jesus inaugurates the eschatological judgment of the covenant.* Since he is, in his incarnate life, the truth of God made manifest in human history, the judgment of the last day already takes place in people's response to him.[16] In John's presentation, while Jesus condemns no one, his message of salvation is a witness against those who reject him and is their judge (John 3:17–21; 12:46–48). Between the incarnation and the return of Jesus in glory, God's policy does not change; it provides the content of the missional message of the church. The blessing and curse to be revealed at the last judgment are already present in reaction to the good news. The life-and-death principles of the end are proleptically present in Christ and in the gospel message. "The astonishing coincidence of God's utter condemnation of sinners and his radical grace for sinners occurs definitively in the cross and will recur at the last judgment. The last judgment will implement what has been decided once and for all at the cross."[17] The content of mission is already definitively mapped out; the wheat will be separated from the chaff.

This highlights that Jesus, in his incarnation, is the culmination of the covenantal *magnalia Dei.* All that is going to happen at the end has *already* happened in him and continues to be the determinative factor in the relationship between God and human beings. Every person covenantally united to Christ, the Head, through the proclamation of salvation in him, is united, in principle, to the end, and lives in the light of the kingdom to come.

---

15. Geerhardus Vos, *The Pauline Eschatology* (Grand Rapids: Eerdmans, 1961), 48–49.

16. Richard Bauckham and Trevor Hart, *Hope against Hope: Christian Eschatology in Contemporary Context* (London: Darton, Longman and Todd, 1999), 141.

17. Bauckham and Hart, *Hope against Hope*, 143–44.

Covenant Salvation as Missional Gospel

The incarnation is without precedent. As William Manson states,

> When we turn to the New Testament, we pass from the climate of prediction to that of fulfillment. The things which God had foreshowed by the lips of His holy prophets He has now, in part at least, brought to accomplishment. The *Eschaton*, described from afar . . . , has in Jesus registered its advent. . . . The supreme sign of the *Eschaton* is the Resurrection of Jesus and the descent of the Holy Spirit on the Church. The Resurrection of Jesus is not simply a sign which God has granted in favour of His Son, but is the inauguration, the entrance into history, of *the times of the End*.[18]

Each stage of the ministry of Jesus—incarnation, crucifixion, resurrection, ascension, the sending of the Spirit, his glorious parousia—is characterized by his active presence. Together they form an eschatological triptych in which each panel, past, present and future, is a part of the one vast picture. In him the covenant achieves its personal goal.[19]

The incarnation modifies the structure of eschatological expectation. Old Testament hope embraced a simple movement from this age to the age to come at the end of time, an expectation illustrated by the disciples' question in Matthew 24:3. This two-step eschatology gives way to a more complex structure. The future has already entered history and is present in the appearance of the Messiah. Between the present and the future, the messianic epoch is inserted with its own missional character. As Oscar Cullmann states, "The new element in the New Testament is not eschatology, but what I call the tension between the decisive 'already fulfilled' and the 'not

---

18. William Manson, "Eschatology in the New Testament," in *Eschatology: Four Papers Read to the Society for the Study of Theology*, ed. T. F. Torrance and J. K. S. Reid, Scottish Journal of Theology Occasional Papers, 2 (Edinburgh: Oliver and Boyd, 1953), 6, quoted by Anthony A. Hoekema, *The Bible and the Future* (Grand Rapids: Eerdmans, 1979), 14.

19. König, *The Eclipse*, 64–68. Cf. the appendix to this article.

yet completed', between present and future."[20] Cullmann speaks of a new division of time: "The proclamation of that event on the cross, together with the resurrection which followed, was the already concluded decisive battle."[21]

The interim period, the time between the resurrection and the future parousia, has four innovative aspects that define the mission of the church and the good news of salvation. The gospel proclaims the present reality of salvation, with healing reconciliation, victory over death, and entry into the age of the Spirit. Together they constitute the *raison d'être* of mission.

The presence of salvation: The cross calls for its consequence in resurrection, the justification and sanctification of Jesus. The order is not one of temporal succession, but a manifestation of the inherent logic of the redemption accomplished. Because of the perfect obedience of Jesus, salvation is according to the covenant's principle of justice; the resurrection *must* follow the cross as the seal of divine approval.

The New Testament weaves a complex web in which past, present, and future are interdependent in the perspective of the covenant of grace. The author of the Epistle to the Hebrews uses the words *hapax* and *ephapax*[22] to show that the once-for-all work of Christ brings about the eschatological situation in which he now intercedes and procures salvation for his people though his heavenly ministry. The past, present, and future are conditioned by one another. The saving witness of mission is that "God's victory in the future is based on a victory already achieved in history. It proclaims not merely hope, but a hope based on events in history and its own experience."[23]

Reconciliation: The wall of hostility between God and man and between men is broken down by the mission of Christ (Col. 1:20; Eph. 2:15–16). It is not a question of two enemies making peace, because God was never man's enemy. The covenant between God and man is an agreement involving two parties, and only one of them has broken it.

20. Oscar Cullmann, *Salvation in History* (London: SCM, 1967), 172.

21. Oscar Cullmann, *Christ and Time* (London: SCM, 1962), 84.

22. Heb. 7:27; 9:11–12, 26–28; 10:10; 12:26–27; Rom. 6:10; 1 Peter 3:18.

23. George E. Ladd, *The Presence of the Future* (Grand Rapids: Eerdmans, 1966), 337.

The message of the gospel is that our enmity toward God is dealt with. God reconciles the world to himself in Christ (2 Cor. 5:19). If man has broken the covenant and brought about his own disaster, the breach is abolished by the obedience of Christ in our place, destroying hostility at the cross by his death, while men were still his enemies (Rom. 5:10).

Reconciliation through the cross of Christ has a cosmic dimension. It is global, as the sacrifice of Christ, as an act, has no limits, and the world is reconciled with God already by the work of Christ. This calls for the spread of the gospel to every creature and salvation by faith to those who believe (John 12:32, 36).

If reconciliation has a universal aspect—for the good pleasure and the mercy of God are vouched for by the cross toward the entire creation—it becomes a reality when the sinner is reconciled to God by trust in Christ. God's disposition toward his creation becomes a reality in the act of faith, which brings the believer into the kingdom of the Son and into a new relationship of peace, according to the conditions of the covenant of grace. Reconciliation is not a change in God, who remains constant in his disposition toward justice and sin. Man is the one who changes when he is reconciled by a new covenant relationship with God in Christ. The enmity abolished by Christ's act of reconciliation calls for conversion to the new state by repentance and faith.

Victory over death is already accomplished by the resurrection: Christ is the conqueror of death and, as such, delivers believers from its inevitability and its power (Rom. 6:9–10). He destroyed the power of death in newness of life as the resurrected one, bringing immortality to light (2 Tim. 1:10). Death can now be conjugated in the past tense: death died in the death of Christ. Believers now experience the victory of the kingdom because nothing can separate them from the love of God in Christ (Rom. 8:39). For the suffering Christians of Revelation 1:17–18, Christ is not only the first and the last (*ho prōtos kui ho eschatos*), but also the living one (*ho zōn*): "I died, and behold I am alive forevermore, and I have the keys of Death and Hades." He is their master because he defeated them both.

The age of the Spirit: The eschatological Spirit, promised to bless the messianic work (Isa. 61:1–2; 42:1), the Spirit of final communion between God and his people (John 17:24–26), was received by Jesus and poured out on his apostles on the day of Pentecost. On the wings of the Spirit, the gospel flies to the ends of the earth. Hence, their mission is under Christ's authority (Acts 2:16–17; Matt. 28:16–20). Christ's witnesses already possess the future blessings, if not in their fullness, because the Spirit is a seal and guarantee (2 Cor. 1:22; 5:5; Eph. 1:14). Living forever (John 14:16) with the people of God, the Spirit of adoption helps them to recognize the Father (Gal. 4:4–6; Rom. 8:14–16) and to receive the title of sonship. They are born from on high and receive the seal of the Spirit (Eph. 1:13; 4:30), who transforms them into the image of Christ (2 Cor. 4:6; 5:17; Eph. 4:4; Col. 3:10). The new people of God is formed by the Spirit as a holy nation to proclaim the excellences of salvation among the Gentiles (1 Peter 1:15; 2:9). While waiting for the resurrection of the body (1 Cor. 15:55), this is faithful witness even in the midst of hatred and tribulation, following in the footsteps of the master (John 15:18–25; 16:33).

From the new covenant perspective, eschatological time begins with the coming of Christ and his becoming the risen Lord of the Spirit. The present is therefore situated in the last times, with the constant activity of the Spirit in the gospel mission to the ends of the earth and to the end of the age.

Covenantal *Telos* as Missional Perspective

The stage is set for the eschatological future of creation by the fact that the covenant between God, creation, and man will arrive at its terminus in the parousia of Christ. At that time, as a renewed reality, the new creation in Christ will blossom out into eternity.

The covenant waits to be sealed in perfect, eternal, and permanent communion between God and his creatures. Communion with God throughout the history of salvation, even under the new covenant with the effusion of the Spirit, is always only a foretaste of eternal glory. The promise repeated throughout covenant history, "I will be their God, and they will be my people," will see its final realization (Rev. 21:3; Lev. 26:12, etc.).

When God makes "all things new" (Rev. 21:5), he will be the "all in all" of the new creation.[24] If the old creation alludes to this perfection, the new world reaches the fullness of joy, life, knowledge, holiness, and justice in the New Jerusalem. Zion is the dwelling place of God; all that falls short of perfection has no place there (Ps. 24; Rev. 21:27).

Jesus Christ, "the founder and perfecter of our faith" (Heb. 12:2), is the craftsman and the substance of the consummation. In John's Revelation, his visiting card, in the first person singular, is: I am *the Alpha and the Omega*.[25] This title indicates his sovereignty over all history (Rev. 1:8, 11; 21:6; 22:13), but it also points to the summit and the beginning of a new and final economy of the created order. Under the lordship of Christ, redemption encompasses the created order in its final revival, a covenant of fulfillment. Already in the Old Testament, the future accomplishment sends us back to the beginning:

> "I am he; I am the first,
>   and I am the last. . . .
> "From the beginning I have not spoken in secret,
>   from the time it came to be I have been there."
> And now the Lord God has sent me, and his Spirit. (Isa. 48:12,
>   16; cf. 3, 7)

God is the one who declares "the end from the beginning and from ancient times things not yet done" (Isa. 46:10; cf. Prov. 8:22). The Amen, the faithful and true witness, the author (*archē*) of the creation of God, he who is preeminent (Col. 1:18), will reign over the renewed universe.

As the mediator of salvation, Christ remains eternally the mediator of the communion between God and his people in the new creation.[26] The kingdom of God will be characterized by life, knowledge,

---

24. Rom. 11:38; 1 Cor. 8:6; 15:28; Rev. 21:6.

25. Meredith G. Kline, *Kingdom Prologue: Genesis Foundations for a Covenantal Worldview* (Overland Park, KS: Two Age Press, 2000), 23–41.

26. John Calvin, *Commentary on the Epistles of Paul the Apostle to the Corinthians*, trans. John Pringle, Calvin's Commentaries (repr., Grand Rapids: Baker Book

and justice; the ontological, epistemological, and ethical attributes of God will shine forth in the eternal jubilee. Thus the covenant between God and man, which will be realized at the end in the New Jerusalem, is nothing other than the conclusion of the covenant of life presented in Eden. Between the two paradises, man's life with "the knowledge of good and evil" is tragic, but Christ, who is wisdom and life, links the two ends of the spectrum. It is possible, as Meredith Kline suggests, to think that creation is a *primal parousia* of God: "The Glory-Spirit was present at the beginning of creation as a sign of the *telos* of creation, as the Alpha-archetype of the Omega-Sabbath that was the goal of creation history."[27]

The *telos* is God's kingdom of life, which, like all divine creation, depends on his ontological presence and eternity. Heaven is a supernatural world that comprises the renewed totality of visible and invisible created reality. In Hebrews, it is a sanctuary where the high priest dwells in the spiritual tabernacle (Heb. 8:1–2). It is also the place where the martyrs, having achieved perfection, are alive and wait for the end (Rev. 20:1, 4), and where Christ dwells to prepare for his own (John 14:1–2). The new creation follows the old. Second Peter 3:10, 12 and Revelation 20:11 announce the dissolution of the elements, which will happen at the moment of the new creation.[28] Present reality will be dissolved at the moment of the second coming of Christ and be transformed, by the Spirit, into another renewed reality. This

House, 1979), 2:33 (comm. on 1 Cor. 15:28). Calvin seems to think that mediation will cease at the consummation and that there will be direct enjoyment of the vision of God when Christ will "yield to the Father his name and crown of glory, and whatever he has received from the Father" (*Institutes of the Christian Religion*, ed. John T. McNeill, trans. Ford Lewis Battles [Philadelphia: Westminster, 1960], 1:485, 2.14.3). Cf. Paul Wells, "Calvin and Union with Christ," in *Calvin: Theologian and Reformer*, ed. Joel R. Beeke and Gary Williams (Grand Rapids: Reformation Heritage Books, 2010), 71.

27. Meredith G. Kline, *Images of the Spirit* (Grand Rapids: Baker Book House, 1980), 20.

28. Klaas Schilder, *Heaven* (Grand Rapids: Eerdmans, 1950), 41ff., says that the new creation comes out of the old in a certain continuity, but there is also a jolt, a *diastasis*, as the old violently disappears and the new comes forth. Cf. Herman Bavinck, *Reformed Dogmatics* (Grand Rapids: Baker Academic, 2003–8), 4:716–20.

metamorphosis is neither natural nor the result of evolution, but the cataclysmic work of the Spirit. It calls for a certain violence: the death of the old, the disappearance of present reality, and the general resurrection. Paul, in 1 Corinthians 15, presents Jesus' resurrection as that of a glorified body; it is the firstfruits that precede the resurrection of all in Christ. Heaven is therefore the final place where Jesus is now, the *Omega* in person, and in bodily form. The renewal of heaven and earth has already taken place in Jesus, who has new physical form as a prototype and pioneer of the new life, the fulfillment of the covenant.

Thus begins the story of the new creation, where "his servants will worship him. They will see his face" (Rev. 22:3–4). In God's presence, the cultural mandate entrusted to Adam will be realized eternally, in justice and holiness, by the people of the last Adam.

Missional Hope and Cultural Mandate

Critical exegesis links salvation history, at the very most, to the Abrahamic covenant and hesitates to see eschatology in creation, doubtless because it finds no formal covenant there.[29] Nevertheless, within the scope of canonical interpretation, the role of the first Adam in relation to the second Adam indicates the incomplete, eschatological situation of the first creation.

In the new creation, the imperishable takes the place of the perishable, because of the incorruptible nature of Christ's resurrection body (1 Cor. 15:50). The regularity of the weekly structure will be replaced by an eternal Sabbath in Christ (Heb. 4). The possibility of disobeying, doing evil, and destroying life, will disappear in the holy Zion (Isa. 2:2; 11:9). Present marriage and procreation will be abrogated (Matt. 22:30). Adam is found at the beginning of history, the natural preceding the spiritual. The state of creation displays the glory of the Creator, but does not compare with the glory of the New Jerusalem.

The fact that Christ is the last Adam (1 Cor. 15:45) indicates that there were many "Adams" before the true Son of the covenant

---

29. Cf., for example, James Barr, *The Garden of Eden and the Hope of Immortality* (Minneapolis: Fortress, 1992).

appeared—Noah, Abraham, Moses, Elijah, David—who all failed in the mission to lead the people of God into the promised rest.[30] The heavenly theocracy will establish the last Adam, the victor over Satan, as prophet, priest, and king of his people, who will join him in the holy calling of beautifying the glory of God. Fulfillment in Christ does not exclude the cultural mandate, but renews it in the heavenly context during the eternal Sabbath, when service of the Lord will be unsullied by sin and fear of death.

In this respect, the missional mandate of the church, which is of primary importance in Christian witness, does not exclude the cultural mandate, but encompasses it, as the gospel renews fallen culture in the hope of the coming kingdom. The future encourages us to lead a life of hope and obedience now, in the present. That implies a way of being in the world: "Do not love the world or the things in the world. If anyone loves the world, the love of the Father is not in him. . . . The world is *passing away* . . . but whoever does the will of God abides *forever*" (1 John 2:15–17). As Herman Bavinck comments, "The contrast in 1 John 2:17 teaches us that the first statement does not imply a destruction of the substance of the world, but a vanishing of the world in its present sin-damaged form."[31] Doing the will of God in creational activities is not against the gospel mandate, but something durable that proclaims that God's rule is eternal, and that life is worship. *Soli Deo gloria.*

Conclusion

Sometimes it is asked whether the "Go" of Matthew 28:18–20 is a command or a participle of attendant circumstance.[32] No doubt there is a contrast between the Great Commission and the sending of Matthew 10:5, where Jesus instructs his disciples not to go to the Gentiles, but to the lost sheep of the house of Israel. After the

---

30. Rowland S. Ward, *God and Adam: Reformed Theology and the Creation Covenant* (Wantirna, Aus.: New Melbourne Press, 2003), 17–48.
31. Bavinck, *Reformed Dogmatics*, 4:717.
32. Wright, *Mission of God*, 34–35.

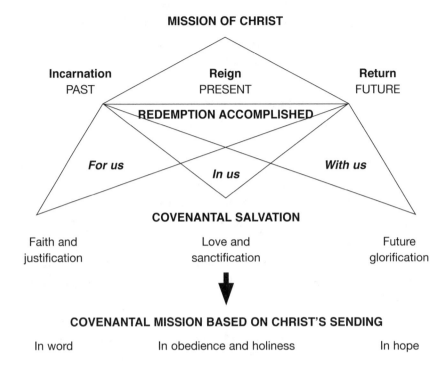

Fig. 5.1. The Mission of Christ as the Foundation of Covenantal Eschatology

resurrection, universality replaces particularity. Jesus sends out messengers in a new mission to the nations to disciple them, with the authority ("therefore") given him in heaven and on earth. His words authorize the mission of God's people; true witnesses do discipling, and a true church is one that goes out with the intent of extending Christ's kingdom. The disciples are sent to the nations in fulfillment of the covenant promises concerning the messianic kingdom. Thus, mission is covenantal activity based on Christ's fulfillment of the divine promise, and on the gift of his Spirit. Just as Christ was sent into the world, so those who are his, united to him under his headship, are sent out as he was, and their witness is part of his Spirit-anointed mission.

Because Christ has fulfilled the messianic hope of salvation and the dwelling place of God among his people, those united to him by faith partake of his eschatological mission to the nations, as the prophecy of Ezekiel 37:26–28 predicts:

I will make a covenant of peace with them; it will be an everlasting covenant. I will establish them and increase their numbers, and I will put my sanctuary among them forever. My dwelling place will be with them. I will be their God, and they will be my people. Then the nations will know that I the LORD make Israel holy, when my sanctuary is among them forever. (NIV)

Mission is therefore *missio Christi*, in fulfillment of the covenant. The triune God sends the Son, who in turn sends ambassadors to all nations, proclaiming the gospel of salvation to a lost humanity. New communities of faith are united to and in Christ by the apostolic truth, announcing the coming of God's kingdom, to the glory of God. Mission and evangelism are inherent in the covenant of grace as Christ's witnesses universally proclaim the day of salvation and do so until this age ends.[33]

33. Rienke B. Kuiper, *God-Centered Evangelism: A Presentation of the Scriptural Theology of Evangelism* (Grand Rapids: Baker Book House. 1961), 46.

PART 2

COVENANT THEOLOGY AND
THE MISSION-MINDED CHURCH

6

Missions in the Fear of God

Flip Buys

Abstract

There has been new interest in missional spirituality since David Bosch published *Spirituality of the Road* in 1979. The spirituality of missionaries, the staff of mission organizations, and churches that want to be part of the *missio Dei* has a vital impact on their zeal, motivation, perseverance, and methods for missions practice. This article considers the biblical concept of *the fear of God* as a vital but often missing aspect of covenantal missional spirituality. This concept is explained and then applied to attitudes, approaches, and methods of mission in the practice of mission work.[1]

Introduction

There is a growing interest among missiologists in the relation-ship between spirituality and missions at both the popular and the academic levels.[2] In his book *A Spirituality of the Road*, David Bosch

---

1. This is an edited version of a presentation given at the International Missions Conference of The Gospel Coalition in Orlando, Florida, April 2013.

2. David J. Bosch, *A Spirituality of the Road* (Eugene, OR: Wipf & Stock, 2001); Charles Fensham, "A Missional Spirituality: Understanding God's Call," http://presbyterianrecord.ca/2011/12/01/a-missional-spirituality, accessed on October 13, 2014; Leonard Hjalmarson and Roger Helland, *Missional Spirituality: Embodying*

criticizes the notion that spirituality is analogous to withdrawal. The idea is sometimes expressed that devotional practices are like fuel that burns up as we go about our work; prayer fills you up, and missions work drains you out. Bosch pleads for a more cyclical understanding of spirituality, where engagement with the world deepens experience of God and engagement with God deepens compassion for the world. Several authors on missional spirituality emphasize that spirituality struggles to integrate emotional and spiritual aspects with real life on the mission field. Barry Fischer states that spirituality is like a reservoir from which a person or a community can draw to motivate action, keep on track, bolster commitment, and avoid discouragement when times get rough: "To speak of spirituality is not to speak about a part of life but rather about the whole of one's life."[3]

Spirituality or Godliness

The term *spirituality* indicates the quest for a full and authentic religious life, involving the bringing together of the ideas distinctive to it and the experience of living on the basis of it and within its scope.[4] This article uses the comprehensive biblical term *godliness* to indicate reverent awareness of God's sovereignty over every aspect of life and the attendant determination to honor him in all of one's conduct. *Godliness* and *holiness* denote one reality, and the terms are joined in 1 Timothy 2:2 and 2 Peter 3:11. In the last two decades, several publications have outlined the specific characteristics of Reformed spirituality, but little exists on Reformed spirituality and missions.[5]

God's Love from the Inside Out (Downers Grove, IL: IVP, 2011); J. A. Ricci, "What Is Missional Spirituality?," http://missional.ca/2012/09/what-is-missional-spirituality, accessed on February 6, 2014; Darren Cronshaw, "Re-envisioning Theological Education and Missional Spirituality," *Journal of Adult Theological Education* 9.1 (2012): 9–27.

3. Barry Fischer, "Towards a Precious Blood Spirituality of Mission," http://www.mission-preciousblood.org/docs/index.php?option=com_docman&task=cat_view&gid=21&Itemid=5, accessed on February 6, 2014.

4. Alister E. McGrath, *Christian Spirituality: An Introduction* (Oxford: Blackwell, 1999), 25.

5. Howard L. Rice, *Reformed Spirituality: An Introduction for Believers* (Louisville, KY: John Knox, 1991); W. Van't Spijker et al., *Spiritualiteit* (Kampen: Goudriaan de

A Transformed Heart

All mission work flows from a transformed heart. A growing irritation with shallow techniques and a hunger for a deeper missional spirituality have recently led Len Hjalmarson and Roger Helland to publish a guide to a spirituality that is deep and yet practical, mystical (in the best sense of the word) and yet missional.[6] Their goal is to lead the reader into the depth of a spiritual life that does not escape from the world, but rather engages and subverts it, with a life rooted in the Trinitarian life of God.

Effective evangelism, holistic missions, and faithful perseverance in spite of intense opposition, suffering, and even persecution go hand in hand with the continued practice of biblically based godliness and spiritual growth. The book of Acts describes the remarkable growth of the church under the guidance and power of the Holy Spirit, and it is clear that growth was not simply quantitative, but also qualitative.[7] There was not just an increase in numbers and in geographical outreach, but a radical transformation of the personal lives of the individuals in developing Christian communities throughout the Roman Empire. Wherever the gospel was preached, there was an increase in living that was driven by heartfelt godliness.

This article will consider the biblical concept of the fear of God as a central aspect of genuine Christian godliness, providing a deep inner motivation and drive for missions, and its influence on missional methodology.

Groot, 1993); James I. Packer, *A Quest for Godliness: The Puritan Vision of the Christian Life* (Wheaton, IL: Crossway Books, 1994); Francis A. Schaeffer, *The Complete Works of Francis A. Schaeffer: A Christian Worldview*, vol. 1 (Westchester: Crossway Books, 1982); John Copper, "A Reformed Perspective on Spirituality: All of Life Is the Lord's," http://www.ccel.org/node/13458, accessed on June 19, 2015; Natalie Brand, *Complementarian Spirituality: Reformed Women and Union with Christ* (Eugene, OR: Wipf & Stock, 2013); T. Schwanda, "Amazing Grace, A Paradigm for Piety," http://reformedspiritualitynetwork.org/Amazing%20Grace%2C%20A%20Paradigm%20for%20Piety, accessed on June 19, 2015; Paul Wells, "Union with Christ and Sanctification," in *In Christ Alone: Perspectives on Union with Christ*, ed. Stephen Clark and Matthew Evans (Fearn, UK: Christian Focus, 2016), 175–234.

6. Hjalmarson and Helland, *Missional Spirituality*.

7. Allison A. Trites, "Church Growth in the Book of Acts," *Bibliotheca Sacra* 145 (1988): 162–73.

Missions, Evangelism, and the Overflow of Godliness

After many years of studying evangelism in the early church and comparing it with later stages of church history, Michael Green came to the conclusion that the essence of evangelism may be summarized by one word: *overflow*.[8] It gives the right nuance for someone who is so full of joy, reverence, worship, and admiration for Jesus Christ as a mighty Savior, and so concerned about the glory of a majestic God, that evangelism flows from their life. Michael Horton uses "intoxicating grace" as a better term for "irresistible grace" to indicate how the Spirit, through the word of the gospel, overwhelms us with his love and grace, liberating us to freely embrace what we had previously freely rejected.[9] When Paul writes in 2 Corinthians 5:14 about his motivation for seeking to persuade men, he states that Christ's love *compels* him (cf. Acts 18:5). The verb *synechō*, used here, has the connotation of someone's attention being occupied intensely, or being *absorbed*, so that evangelism then becomes a natural thing.[10]

The words *overflow* and *being compelled* have qualities that are lacking in many evangelistic approaches: *spontaneity* as well as *reverence and awe*. Incidentally, "overflow" is a good paraphrase for the Greek words *parrēsia* ("confidence") and *plērophoria* ("full assurance") in Hebrews 10:19, 22. These terms are used a good deal in the New Testament to describe the liberated confidence of a Christian. Paul, for example, reminds the Thessalonians that "our gospel came to you not only in word, but also in power and in the Holy Spirit and with full conviction"—that is, with much *confident overflow* (*plērophoria*, 1 Thess. 1:5). *Parrēsia* and *plērophoria* flow out of the new covenant, which declares that Christ, its mediator and initiator, has entered into heaven itself to appear in the presence of God on

---

8. Michael Green, *Evangelism through the Local Church: A Comprehensive Guide to All Aspects of Evangelism* (Nashville: Nelson, 1992), 8.

9. Michael Horton, *Putting Amazing Back into Grace: Embracing the Heart of the Gospel* (Grand Rapids: Baker Books, 2011), 127.

10. W. Arndt, F. W. Danker, and W. Bauer, *A Greek-English Lexicon of the New Testament and Other Early Christian Literature* (Chicago: University of Chicago Press, 2000), 971.

our behalf.[11] It is also important to note that the confidence and full assurance of access to God through Christ do not exclude the warning of a fearful expectation of judgment for those who break the new covenant.

This note is enhanced in Hebrews 12:22–24, where God's new covenant people are warned that they have come "to Mount Zion and to the city of the living God, . . . to the assembly of the firstborn who are enrolled in heaven, and to God, the judge of all, and to the spirits of the righteous made perfect, and to Jesus, the mediator of a new covenant, and to the sprinkled blood that speaks a better word than the blood of Abel." That should motivate them to be grateful in receiving a kingdom that cannot be shaken, so that they may offer acceptable worship to God with reverence.[12] Boldness and assurance, as well as reverence and awe, describe the godliness of a member in the new covenant.

In this respect, Francis Schaeffer warned against irrational, emotional Christianity in which evangelical Christians slip into a dichotomy, separating an encounter with Jesus from the content of Scripture. That produces a kind of spirituality in which "it is now Jesus-like to sleep with a girl or a man, if she or he needs you. As long as you are trying to be human—at the cost, be it noted, of breaking the very morality that Jesus taught."[13]

A biblical fear of God provides a correlate to biblical godliness that has an impact on the whole life of an individual and determines the motivation, as well as the methodology, in our approach to missions.

Genuine Godliness Expressed in the Fear of God

The overflow and constraint of God's love needed for missions is a mixture of love and reverence, of abundant joy and deep respect, which the Bible calls *the fear of God*—and which produces genuine

11. Cf. "therefore" (*oun*), linking Hebrews 10:1–18 and 10:19–39.

12. Arndt, Danker, and Bauer, *Greek-English Lexicon*, 218: *deos* indicates an emotion of profound respect and reverence.

13. Schaeffer, *Complete Works*, 1:259–60.

godliness. The Greek words for godliness (*eusebeia*; *theosebeia* from *theos*, "God," and *sebomai*, "to worship") have this nuance of fear or reverence. In Timothy and Titus, godliness is connected with the fact that Paul always has in view the impression that the walk of Christians makes on non-Christians.[14] We read in Acts 9:31 of the churches that grew by walking in the fear of the Lord and in the comfort of the Holy Spirit.

For many current-day Christians, though, one of the most perplexing commands in the New Testament is found in 1 Peter 2:17: "Fear God!" They feel uncomfortable with such an exhortation. Now that through Christ we call God "Father," is there any room left for fearing him? Are we not meant to love God, not to fear him? And doesn't perfect love drive out fear (1 John 4:18)?

In the Bible, however, the primary meaning of the fear of God is veneration and honor, reverence and awe. As John Murray wrote, "The fear of God is the soul of godliness."[15] It is the attitude that elicits from our hearts adoration and love, reverence and honor, focusing with awe, not primarily on the wrath of God, but on the majesty, holiness, amazing love, forgiveness, and transcendent glory of God. This concept is often given as a key to a holistic godly life, and is clearly not an option:

1. The fear of the Lord is the beginning of wisdom (Prov. 9:10).
2. Live in the fear of the Lord always (Prov. 23:17).
3. Fear him who is able to destroy both soul and body in hell (Matt. 10:28).
4. In all things obey, fearing the Lord (Col. 3:22).
5. Since you call on a Father who judges each man's work impartially, live your lives as strangers in reverent fear (1 Peter 1:17).

God's wish for his covenant people is that they should fear him. He says to Moses, "Oh, that their hearts would be inclined to fear

---

14. See 1 Tim. 3:7; 6:1; Titus 2:5, 8, 10; see also *anenklētos* in 1 Tim. 3:10. Titus 1:6–7 points in the same direction.
15. John Murray, *Principles of Conduct* (Grand Rapids: Eerdmans, 1957), 229.

me and keep all my commands always, so that it might go well with them and their children forever!" (Deut. 5:29 NIV).

The deepest wish of any true child of God is to obtain an existential knowledge of this fear of God. Therefore, it is part of David's desire for the experience of godliness in Psalm 86:11, "Teach me your way, O LORD, and I will walk in your truth; give me an undivided heart, that I may fear your name." Jesus also carried out his ministry in the fear of God (Isa. 11:2–3; Heb. 5:7).

The Meaning of the Fear of God

It is not always easy to describe the exact meaning of the Hebrew word *yir'at*, usually translated as "fear." It is sometimes translated "reverence," "service," or "terror."[16] In various genres of the Old Testament, the expression has different shades of meaning.[17] In several contexts, the verb not only describes a sense of awe toward God, but also is used for faith in God demonstrated through obedience.[18]

Genuine fear of God almost defies definition, because it is really a synonym for the heartfelt worship of God for who he is and what he has done. Thus, the biblical concept of fear embraces a much wider dimension than the common English word, which denotes some sort of dread or terror. While this meaning forms an essential part of the scriptural picture, it is by no means the primary significance, especially when the fear of God, an awe-inspiring reverence, is referred to.

It is true that the Bible uses the expression "fear of God" in different ways. We are told, "It is a fearful [terrible] thing to fall into the hands of the living God" (Heb. 10:31). Jesus taught that we should fear God, who has power to punish sin and consign men to utter

16. R. Laird Harris, ed., *Theological Wordbook of the Old Testament* (Chicago: Moody Press, 1980), 1:399.

17. Richard Schultz, "Integrating Old Testament Theology and Exegesis: Literary, Thematic, and Canonical Issues," in *The New International Dictionary of Old Testament Theology and Exegesis*, ed. Willem A. VanGemeren (Carlisle: Paternoster, 1996), 1:192.

18. Daniel I. Block, "Grace of Torah: The Mosaic Prescription for Life (Deut. 4:1–8; 6:20–25)," *Bibliotheca Sacra* 162 (2005): 15.

destruction (Luke 12:4–5). Sometimes this does mean "terror" or even "horror" of God. The first occurrence of such fear may be found in Genesis 3, where Adam and Eve recoil from the presence of the holy God, whose commandment they have blatantly spurned. Their fear is entirely reasonable, for they were warned that disobedience would incur a grave judgment. Fear in this sense is quite naturally the logical consequence of sin (Gen. 3:10; 4:13–14; Prov. 28:1). Anxious fear seizes the wicked (Job 15:24), surprises the hypocrite (Isa. 33:14), and consumes evildoers (Ps. 73:19); their faithless lives are characterized by fear (Rev. 21:8). Some people have such fear for God, but at the same time, deep in their hearts, they also carry animosity toward him, just as a slave would toward a cruel master. He serves the master, but only out of fear of punishment.

True fear of God is a *childlike fear*. The Puritan Wilhelmus à Brakel speaks of a *filial fear* that children have for their parents: "They cannot bear to hear someone speak a dishonoring word about their parents; it grieves them at their heart and they will defend them with all their might."[19] Proper fear of God is a combination of holy respect and glowing love. It is at the same time, writes Sinclair Ferguson, "(1) a consciousness of being in the presence of True Greatness and Majesty; (2) a thrilling sense of privilege; (3) an overflow of respect and admiration; and perhaps supremely, (4) a sense that His opinion about my life is the only thing that really matters."[20]

To someone who fears God, fatherly approval means everything, and to lose it is the greatest of all griefs. To fear God is to have a heart that is sensitive to both his awesome deity and his graciousness. It means to simultaneously experience great awe and deep joy, understanding who God really is and what he has done for us.

To think that love for God and fear of him are incompatible is to fail to see the richness of his character and to ignore the way in which knowing him in all of his attributes, and responding appropriately

19. Wilhelmus à Brakel, *The Christian's Reasonable Service* (Morgan, PA: Soli Deo Gloria Publications, 1993), 2:430–31.
20. Sinclair Ferguson, "The Fear of the Lord: Seeing God as He Is," *Discipleship Journal* 9 (July-August, 1989): 41.

to him, stretches our emotional capacities to their limit. Scripture portrays the fear of the Lord and the love of the Lord as emotions that go together. Frederick W. Faber saw this clearly when he wrote:

> They love Thee little, if at all,
> Who do not fear Thee much:
> If love is Thine attraction, Lord,
> Fear is Thy very touch.[21]

In the Dutch and Afrikaans Reformed traditions, the fear of God is a concept expressed in many psalms and hymns. We see this same combination of *fear* and *love* in the Afrikaans psalms of Totius of the Reformed Churches in South Africa, for example Psalm 119:44 and 60:

As ek dink aan U gestrengheid,	(When I think of your strictness,
dan meng liefde en vrees deureen.	then love and fear blend in me.)
Tot U loop ek, op U hoop ek,	(To you I walk, on you I hope,
op U wette gee ek ag;	to your laws I give attention;
en ek hou wat U getuig het	and I keep what you have testified
vol van liefde en stil ontsag.	full of love and silent awe.)

The fear of God is an emotion of awe and respect for the magnitude of God. It provides a deep inner peace and calm and lets one cry out in amazement, "O Lord, our Lord, how majestic is your name in all the earth! You have set your glory above the heavens" (Ps. 8:1).

Such awareness not only leads to true wisdom (Ps. 111:10; Job 28:28), but also provides direction for the child of God throughout life. When God works in you, both to will and to work for his good pleasure, you work out your own salvation with fear and trembling (Phil. 2:12). This kind of spiritual experience drives a person to kneel before God in amazement and adoration, with deep gratitude for his

---

21. Quoted by Ferguson, "The Fear of the Lord," 41.

indescribable mercy. It causes one to cry out in amazement: "How great is the love the Father has lavished on us, that we should be called children of God!" (1 John 3:1 NIV).

In the light of the understanding of the biblical meaning of the fear of God in traditional Reformed circles, it is appropriate that the new Statement of Faith of World Reformed Fellowship expresses true Christian spirituality in terms of the fear of God: Christian spirituality is a lifelong process of deep reverence and love for God, which translates into a right relationship with fellow human beings.[22]

The fear of God is therefore awe, admiration, wonder, and love, experienced simultaneously in the presence of his glorious majesty. Unless there is personal awareness of the awesome and majestic sovereignty of God, it is impossible to have a meaningful faith in one's heart (Pss. 5:7; 89:7). An experience of this childlike fear influences every aspect of a person's life, including the approach to missions.

What, then, is the impact of this spirituality on our lives and specifically on our zeal for, and methods in, missions?

The Effects of the Fear of God in the Christian Life

The true fear of God is holistic, influencing all of life. The most obvious impact is that it produces holiness, in which spirit we work out our salvation (Phil. 2:12) and purify ourselves as we grow in holiness (2 Cor. 7:1). A valid comprehension of the fear of God will not only cause us to worship God aright, but will also regulate our conduct. As John Murray says, "What or whom we worship determines our behaviour." Albert N. Martin adds that the essential ingredients of the fear of God are correct concepts of God's character, a pervasive sense of God's presence, and a constant awareness of our obligation to God.[23] The Bible abounds in illustrations of the sanctified lifestyle that the fear of God produces.

---

22. World Reformed Fellowship, "Statement of Faith," http://wrfnet.org/about /statement-of-faith#life, accessed on April 9, 2016.

23. Jerry Bridges, "What Is Godliness?," quoting Murray and paraphrasing Martin, https://bible.org/article/what-godliness.

Motivation for Christian Morality

To truly revere the Lord entails avoiding sin, as clearly expressed in Exodus 20:20 NIV: "God has come to test you, so that the fear of God will be with you to keep you from sinning." Therefore the fear of God is a motivation for genuine Christian morality. If we have some insight into God's infinite holiness and his hatred of sin, coupled with a sense of God's presence in all of our actions and thoughts, then a fear of God will influence and regulate all our conduct. An example is seen in the history of Joseph, when the wife of Potiphar tried to seduce him. She blatantly invited him to have sexual intercourse with her, but he resisted. What was the secret of his moral power? The answer shows clearly in his words: "How then could I do such a wicked thing and sin against God?" (Gen. 39:9 NIV). His fear of God kept him from sinning.

James Draper points out that the calamity of educational systems that no longer include the fear of God is reflected in violent crimes, mounting divorce rates, teenage pregnancies, abortions, illegal drug use, high illiteracy rates, and the AIDS epidemic.[24] These plagues, on the increase since 1960, witness to the disaster that ensues when God and the fear of his name are rejected in society.

Childlike Fear of God Produces Integrity

Nehemiah was a model of integrity. The governors of his time ruled through bribery and corruption. Nehemiah 5:15 says that the preceding governors placed a heavy burden on the people. Their assistants also lorded it over the people. But out of the fear of God, he did not act like that. If we remain aware that we live *coram Deo*, in the presence of God, a new honesty will mark our speech and make us stand out in the world.

Childlike Fear of God Promotes Obedience

Godly fear is characterized by total allegiance to the one true God. The fear of God should provide a motivation for, and result in,

---

24. James T. Draper, "The Ground of All Truth: Deuteronomy 6:4–9," *Faith and Missions* 15.2 (1998): 53.

obedience to him. If we truly revere God, we will obey him, since every act of disobedience is an affront to his dignity and majesty. Noah is portrayed as such an example in Hebrews 11:7. When he received the command to build an ark, he obeyed, and despite scorn built the ark on dry ground. Noah "in reverent fear" built an ark to save his family.

An Antidote for the Fear of Others

A holy fear is a source of joy (Ps. 2:11) and a fountain of life (Prov. 14:27). Therefore, it produces boldness and bravery. In times of persecution, the fear of God will dominate the fear of man, and cause God's children to speak out, although fear of man bids them be silent (Acts 4:18–21). Many Christians are afraid to show that they are followers of Christ. Here is the answer to our lack of courage in witness. In the context of his exhortation in Matthew 10:28, Jesus says: "But whoever denies me before men, I also will deny before my Father who is in heaven" (Matt. 10:33). The great reformers in history all acted with undaunted bravery. For example, friend and foe alike said of John Knox that he feared no man because he feared God.

The Fear of God and Missions

Those who fear the Lord and who have been gripped in awe by his majestic, transforming grace will want to deploy their energies and gifts to bring others to trust such a gracious Savior. This happened in the early church; it was strengthened and encouraged by the Holy Spirit, and it grew in numbers, living in the fear of the Lord (Acts 9:31). The early Christian fellowship, marked in this way, did not diminish in size, but was joined by others! The fear of God makes us part of the *missio Dei*, empowered by the Holy Spirit.

The Missional Impact of Corporate Worship in the Fear of God

The quest for transcendence is a challenge to the quality of the church's public worship. John Stott asks about it:

> Does it offer what people are craving—the element of mystery, the
> "sense of the numinous," in biblical language "the fear of God," in

modern language "transcendence"? My answer to my own question is "Not often." The church is not always conspicuous for the profound reality of its worship. . . . We seem to have little sense of the greatness and the glory of almighty God. We do not bow down before him in awe and wonder. Our tendency is to be cocky, flippant and proud. We take little trouble to prepare our worship services. Sometimes they are slovenly, mechanical, perfunctory and dull. At other times they are frivolous to the point of irreverence. No wonder those seeking Reality often pass us by![25]

Sometimes worship services are slovenly, mechanical, perfunctory, and dull; at other times, they are frivolous to the point of irreverence. No wonder those seeking the reality of God's presence often pass us by!

The New Testament makes it clear that true fear of God among his worshipping people has a missional impact on unbelievers. In 1 Corinthians 14:24–25, Paul says that there should be such a consciousness of God's presence when Christians worship that unbelievers will be so touched that they will fall down on their knees and declare that God is really present.

The call to be missional churches means listening to the biblical criticism of religion. No book is more scathing of empty religion than the Bible. The prophets of the Old Testament were outspoken in their denunciation of the formalism and hypocrisy of Israelite worship. Jesus applied their critique to the Pharisees of his day: "These people honor me with their lips, but their hearts are far from me" (Matt. 15:8 NIV). This indictment of religion by the prophets and by Jesus is uncomfortably applicable to many churches today. Too much worship is ritual without reality, form without power, or fun without the fear of God, ultimately religion without God.

For a church to be an instrument in the *missio Dei*, worship that is intense, earnest, authentic, God-centered, hope-giving, and life-changing is of the essence. It is the goal and fuel of world mission:

25. John Stott, *The Contemporary Christian* (Downers Grove, IL: InterVarsity Press, 1992), 227–28.

the goal is gladness in the glory of God, the fuel is joy in our majestic God. If in worship we are not real, deep, and fervent with reverence and awe, how can we say to the nations, "Be glad in God"?[26] That is why we read in Acts 19:17 that the name of the Lord was greatly honored after a solemn fear descended on a city.

The Fear of God, a Vision, and Zeal for Mission

Paul explains what made him such a zealous missionary: "Since, then, we know what it is to fear the Lord, we try to persuade men" (2 Cor. 5:11 NIV). Involvement in mission was not a special hobby for Paul, as some view it today, but part and parcel of his life, as natural as breathing, an outflow of his fear of the Lord. The connection between the fear of God and zeal for missions is a key concept in the Reformed tradition; it is well formulated in the Totius version of Psalm 22:8 of the Reformed Churches in South Africa:

> Laat wie God vrees, uit altyd wyer kringe sy lof vertel.
> (Let those who fear God proclaim his glory in always wider
>   circles.)

The Fear of God, Boldness, and Gentleness in Witness

The Bible combines the apologetic task to testify to hope in Christ with filial fear of God as a precondition for spiritual lives characterized by boldness and gentleness: "In your hearts set apart Christ as Lord. Always be prepared to give an answer to everyone who asks you to give the reason for the hope that you have. But do this with gentleness and respect" (1 Peter 3:15 NIV).[27] Witnessing can suffer from one of these two problems: people are either too timid to speak boldly about their own hope of salvation in Christ, or they are full of pride and lack the fear of God, and so they witness more about themselves than about the Lord.

---

26. John Piper, *Let the Nations Be Glad! The Supremacy of God in Missions* (Grand Rapids: Baker Books, 1993), 20.

27. It is noteworthy to see that the original Greek reads *meta praytēros kai phobou*, which the ESV and the NIV translate "with gentleness and respect."

Proclaiming God's Judgment

Those working in the fear of God are not afraid to preach the certain coming judgment of God as part of their missional message. Jesus sent out the seventy on their first missions assignment and said to them:

> When you enter a town and are not welcomed, go into its streets and say, "Even the dust of your town that sticks to our feet we wipe off against you. Yet be sure of this: The kingdom of God is near." I tell you, it will be more bearable on that day for Sodom than for that town. (Luke 10:10–11 NIV)

Paul preached the gospel on the Areopagus and concluded his message:

> In the past God overlooked such ignorance, but now he commands all people everywhere to repent. For he has set a day when he will judge the world with justice by the man he has appointed. He has given proof of this to all men by raising him from the dead. (Acts 17:30–31 NIV)

God-Centered Work

When churches and mission workers are involved in missions without true fear of God, their approach tends to become man-centered. They gather numbers as fast as they can and plant as many churches as possible, without making sure that those who follow have truly committed to Christ as their only hope. This may flatter their ego or even impress the mission board.

Spiros Zodhiates describes the Greek term *theosebeia* (genitive, *theosebeias*) as God-fearing, reverence toward God, godliness, devotion in action.[28] It is not just warm emotion from singing some grand hymn or from modern-day worship, but love, fear, and desire for God. From this Godward attitude grows the fruit of godliness in character and behavior.

Sometimes mission workers worry about losing their reputation in the eyes of their senders more than they fear God. To prove that their

---

28. Spiros Zodhiates, *The Complete Word Study Dictionary: New Testament* (Chattanooga, TN: AMG Publishers, 2000), 55.

work is worthwhile, they are quick to accept people as full members of a church, without having clear evidence of genuine repentance and faith. Without realizing it, they exhibit their converts as trophies to their supporters. They may publish sentimental articles in mission magazines with photos of their successes. When local people read such reports, they may smile or even be disgusted by the false impression given.

Missions without the Fear of God Produces Syncretism

When mission work lacks the fear of God and new converts do not learn to live in reverence and awe, new Christians sometimes accept teachings while retaining old pagan legacies, resulting in syncretism.[29] This is a real problem in Africa, with large congregations of baptized pagans. Many churches are weak because they are packed with unfaithful Christians who walk with one leg in paganism, continuing to venerate ancestral spirits and consult traditional healers (*isangomas* and *inyangas*) who rely on witchcraft.

It is also becoming clear that the most important problem in effective intervention in the HIV/AIDS pandemic, namely stigmatization, is to a large extent caused by the witchcraft legacies of traditional African religion.[30] Some missionaries have a greater fear of losing numbers than they have a genuine fear of God, and they concoct a "contextualised theology of missions" that allows for the accommodation of paganism in the Christian church.[31]

No Self-Supporting Churches without the Fear of God

Many churches in Africa with fairly large congregations were established over fifty years ago, but they are still unable to support their own pastor. There are even churches which, after several decades

29. David J. Hesselgrave, *Planting Churches Cross-Culturally: A Guide for Home and Foreign Missions* (Grand Rapids: Baker Book House, 1980), 246–47.

30. P. J. Buys, "Shame, Guilt and HIV/AIDS in Rural Communities," *Praktiese Teologie in Suid-Afrika / Practical Theology in South Africa* 23.3 (2008): 35.

31. S. T. Kgatla, "The Perspectives of 'Undersiders' and 'Topsiders' on African Religions," *Missionalia* 25 (1997): 634–46. For a summary of valid views on contextualization, see Harvey M. Conn, "Contextual Theologies: The Problem of Agendas," *Westminster Theological Journal* 50.1 (Spring 1990): 52–66.

of existence, are in such deep bondage to a culture of dependency, that they still appeal to mission boards overseas for new pastors when a serving missionary retires from the work. The painful reality is that often they do not really want a missionary, but they want the money that flows as a by-product. In some cases, the sponsoring organizations go through a financial crisis and are forced to cut funds. Consequently, pastors who are not supported by their churches have to take secular employment. Abandoned churches and scattered congregations are the result. It is difficult to escape the conclusion that there was something fundamentally wrong from the outset. Surely God does not wish the church anywhere to be so dependent upon foreign sponsoring that when help is withdrawn, the young church becomes moribund.[32]

In the New Testament, we see the reverse pattern: young churches financially supporting older churches. Paul was almost embarrassed by the willingness of the church in Macedonia to make financial sacrifices to help the poor in the mother church in Jerusalem:

> I testify that they gave as much as they were able, and even *beyond their ability*. Entirely on their own, they urgently pleaded with us for the privilege of sharing in this service to the saints. And they did not do as we expected, but they *gave themselves first to the Lord* and then to us in keeping with God's will. (2 Cor. 8:3–5)

They first gave themselves to the Lord! That is where many missionaries, evangelists, and church workers initially err. Because they do not walk in the fear of the Lord, they do not lead people to *first give themselves to the Lord*. Instead, they allow new "converts" to become members without real evidence of having started to walk in the fear of God. Those who are not led to a filial fear of God will not be willing to sacrifice in order to seek first the kingdom of God. David Hesselgrave therefore strongly accents the need for genuine conversion in church planting.[33]

---

32. Roland Allen, *Missionary Methods: St. Paul's or Ours?* (London: World Dominion Press, 1956), 5–30, gives many biblical arguments that demonstrate this.
33. David J. Hesselgrave, *Planting Churches Cross-Culturally*, 231–68.

Missions Not Christ-Centered Enough

When a missionary does not really do his work in the fear of God, converts are trained to depend on him, rather than becoming responsible to Christ. Sometimes missionaries may be overprotective of new converts, at other times they may unconsciously desire to build their own kingdoms and have people look to them as indispensable, or they may even lack faith in the Holy Spirit to do his work in causing new converts to mature.

A "pearl of great price" in building the church on the mission field is a sense of responsibility on the part of new converts, because through it the church will prosper.[34] Without it—although a thousand other reinforcements are tried—it will surrender in the end to the spirit of the world. Only God can produce this sense of responsibility in the hearts and minds of members of an infant church, but the attitude of a missionary will either open doors for indigenous people to become responsible or hinder them from being children of God walking in the fear of God and in the comfort of the Holy Spirit (Acts 9:31).

The Origin of Man-Centered Missions

Why is it that the fear of God is not at the heart of true Christian living, even in the hearts of mission workers? The answer lies in people's ideas about, and their concepts of, God. We have made God small and man great in missions. During the last two centuries, the Western world has been intoxicated with the notion that man is the measure of all things, and the god believed in is a pagan god, made in man's image, to suit his taste. No wonder the sense of awe has gone from our spirits.

Martin Luther once put his finger on the issue when he told the great humanist scholar Erasmus, "Your God is too manlike." Only when we share Luther's other great cry, "Let God be God," is God feared, because only when he is seen as the Glorious One, are hearts hushed in reverence before him. If we do not fear God today, it is not

34. Melvin L. Hodges, *The Indigenous Church: A Complete Handbook on How to Grow Young Churches* (Springfield, MI: Gospel Publishing House, 1976), 17.

because we have been set free from "Old Testament religion," as we sometimes mistakenly assume, but because we do not really know him as God. For to know him as God is to fear him—to be "stunned," as A. W. Tozer put it—by the *splendor of his presence.*[35]

Achieving a Filial Fear of God

There is an infinite gap in worth and dignity between God the Creator and man the creature, even though man was created in the image of God. The fear of God is a heartfelt recognition of this. After God revealed something of his preeminent majesty to Job and asked, "Do you have an arm like God's, and can your voice thunder like his?" (Job 40:9 NIV), Job replied: "I know that you can do all things; no plan of yours can be thwarted. . . . My ears had heard of you but now my eyes have seen you. Therefore I despise myself and repent in dust and ashes" (Job 42:2, 5– 6 NIV).

A realization of our insignificance before God Almighty brings us to our knees in awe and true fear. Thereafter, Job could pray for his friends. But this realization alone is not in itself enough for true fear of God to emerge in our lives. The realization of God's amazing mercy for a lost sinner is capital for growth in a filial fear of God. Psalm 130:4 puts it like this: "But with you there is forgiveness, that you may be feared." The Totius version of Psalm 130:2 formulates it:

Maar nee, daar is vergewing	(There is forgiveness with you
altyd by U gewees;	always
daarom word U met bewing	so that with trembling
reg kinderlik gevrees.	we have a childlike fear of you.)

Understanding God's mercy and loving-kindness evokes true fear of God in our hearts. The realization that the great and almighty God, who should condemn us because of sin, has forgiven us, sent his Son

35. As quoted by Ferguson, "The Fear of the Lord," 42.

to save us, adopted us, and made us heirs, brings a true filial fear of God. As John Newton wrote in his hymn "Amazing Grace," "'Twas grace that taught my heart to fear." We mistake Newton's meaning if we understand that grace removes the fear of the Lord. Rather, it is fears that grace removes by teaching us the fear of the Lord, brought about by a realization of God's loving-kindness!

The Holy Spirit works true fear of God in our hearts through the gospel proclaimed. Where Jesus Christ is preached faithfully, God brings people to look into his heart: a heart filled with such love for a lost, condemned world that he sent his only Son, whom he dearly loved, to rescue sinners and have fellowship with them, drawing them into fellowship with him in true fear.

It is of the utmost importance for mission workers and churches that aspire to be missional as part of God's mission, to learn to walk in the fear of God and the comfort of the Holy Spirit.

7

Christ's Dominion over Creation and Spiritual Warfare in Mission

Henk Stoker

Abstract

Is it necessary for Christians in covenant with God to engage in spiritual warfare while Christ is reigning over the whole of creation? Certain evangelical churches have adopted the idea that an essential part of apologetics and mission work is to use spiritual warfare to break through the power of demons over certain areas. This view implies a breaking away from traditional Christianity with regard to the relationship between human sin and salvation. Individual sins are not seen as the main factor in the alienation between God and man, but rather territorial sins. According to this understanding of salvation, the "conversion" of territories precedes individual conversions. Although advocates of this idea rely on texts of Scripture, the conclusions are hermeneutically untenable. Furthermore, the numerous claims of success are not supported by research. Biblically speaking, the belief that territories must *first* be claimed for God *before* the gospel can bring salvation to individuals undermines the saving power of the gospel (Rom. 1:16), Christ's omnipotence and dominion over creation, and the Great Commission itself (Matt. 28:18–20).

Apologetics and Spiritual Warfare

Christians experience different situations where the truth of the gospel is directly or indirectly under attack. Opposition may even be disguised as a request for information or care for you and what you believe—as seen in Genesis 3:1–5. To say what God really said is important for demolishing these arguments and opinions—and that is doing Christian apologetics.[1]

From the beginning to the end of the Bible, we read of spiritual opposition to God and his people. "Every New Testament writer draws our attention to the spiritual conflict that rages about us. In these profiles, God pastorally alerts us and equips us to engage the spiritual enemy."[2] The apostle Paul is not afraid to use the analogy of warfare in his letters, as in 2 Corinthians 10 and Ephesians 6. This is understandable because "an attack on the Christian faith is a declaration of war . . . against the truth of Christianity, and thus against the One who is the truth (John 14:6)."[3]

When God's Word calls Christians to do apologetics and to go into spiritual battle to save people from lies, false doctrine, sinful lives, false worldviews, or lives without God, it uses strong military language (2 Cor. 10:3–5). Yet the same passage emphasizes that this warfare must be conducted "full of grace and truth" while defending and making a way for the gospel into the individual heart, opened up by the Holy Spirit.

Spiritual Warfare and the Sovereignty of God in Salvation

Spiritual warfare is part of following Christ, the only one who saved and can save the inhabitants of this world (John 3:16). Since

---

1. K. Scott Oliphint, *Covenantal Apologetics: Principles and Practice in Defense of Our Faith* (Wheaton, IL: Crossway, 2013), 29, describes Christian apologetics as "the application of biblical truth to unbelievers."

2. Stanley Gale, *What Is Spiritual Warfare?* (Phillipsburg, NJ: P&R Publishing, 2008), 10.

3. K. Scott Oliphint, *The Battle Belongs to the Lord* (Phillipsburg, NJ: P&R

the time of the Reformation, spiritual warfare has focused on the responsibility of those who stand in a covenant[4] with God,[5] to bring the gospel of salvation through grace and faith in Christ to the world, while resisting the influence of the devil, the world, and the selfish self.

However, in the twentieth century a new view on spiritual warfare grew in influence. It focuses on

> an offensive attack against evil spirits who wage war in a cosmic battle. This new theology of spiritual warfare has been widespread both in its acceptance and in its scope. Its acceptance is manifested by the fact that Pentecostalism has quickly spread across the global South, especially in Traditional Africa Religion where evil spirits are thought to be involved in everyday life. . . . Many evangelicals who sense that Christians have downplayed the unseen reality of demons and spirits have also been drawn to this approach of spiritual warfare. . . . In this new perspective, the battle territory shifted away from the individual mind and heart to focusing on the unseen world of demons and evil spirits. The method likewise shifted from confronting people about their moral evil and the truth of God's Word to the need of binding evil spirits by command of Spirit-filled believers. This new approach to spiritual warfare also brings a new vocabulary to the table. Bound up with the

---

Publishing, 2003), 86.

4. Mark Karlberg: "Covenant theology sprang up naturally as the most consistent expression of Calvinism, in which the idea of the self-sufficient, ontological Trinity is the final reference point in all predication. It is this idea that lies at the center of covenant theology. The three persons of the Trinity have exhaustively personal relationship with one another. And the idea of exhaustive personal relationship is the idea of the covenant" (*Covenant Theology in Reformed Perspective* [Eugene OR: Wipf & Stock, 2004]), 105). Karlberg quotes Van Til's article on covenant theology in *Twentieth Century Encyclopedia of Religious Knowledge* (Grand Rapids: Baker Book House, 1955).

5. God created all men in his image and brought them into a covenant relationship with him. The harmony in this relationship changed to rebellion against God when the first humans sinned, but the relationship still continues. Scott Oliphint sees it as a crucial part of apologetics to defend the faith against covenant breakers who deny their relationship with God and thus do not fulfill their part of the covenant (*Covenantal Apologetics*, 42).

idea of binding spirits are concepts like identificational repentance, territorial spirits, and strategic level spiritual warfare (SLSW)."[6]

This view of spiritual warfare by proponents of the so-called "third wave of the Holy Spirit" forces Christian theologians, especially those in the field of mission, to answer the following question: Does the Lord want his church and his people to shift their missional apologetics away from a focus on the heart of the individual, to this new way of conducting warfare against territorial spirits to liberate certain areas from demonic influences, in order for a city or country to prosper and its people to have the possibility to start listening to the gospel? Defending the third-wave view in the book *Understanding Spiritual Warfare: Four Views*, Peter Wagner and Rebecca Greenwood see the task of "responsible spiritual mapping" to "unveil sins of a people, city, nation, or government that have been perpetrated in the past, often generations ago."[7] As an example, they claim that if spirits behind broken treaties are combatted, "a new measure of freedom, breakthrough and transformation" can be the result.

For those who are conscious of the fundamental tenets of the Reformation and the Reformed faith, it should be clear from the outset that any doctrine challenging the sovereignty of God in salvation is to be rejected. Nevertheless, as the true (invisible) church of Christ transcends denominational boundaries in the communion of the saints with the triune God, we should stand in the gap for brothers and sisters as in the time of the Reformation and preach that faith in the redemptive work of Christ is sufficient for every believer (1 Cor. 15:1–5).

Therefore, the main goal of the following presentation is to present Reformed perspectives on a specific view of spiritual warfare that has permeated many churches. It is assumed that this view may seriously harm individuals, in the sense that their ultimate trust is

6. Peter Aiken, "Should Reformed Believers Engage in Spiritual Warfare?," *Puritan Reformed Journal* 7.1 (2015): 245–55.

7. Peter Wagner and Rebecca Greenwood, "The Strategic-Level Deliverance Model," in *Understanding Spiritual Warfare: Four Views*, ed. J. K. Beilby and R. E. Eddy (Grand Rapids: Baker Academic, 2012), 187.

directed away from the gospel and the peaceful state of mind that is granted to man through his reconciliation with God in Christ and through the Holy Spirit (Rom. 5:1–5).

The Bible and Territorial Spirits

The passage in the Bible that is commonly cited as the main evidence in support of the concept of "territorial demons" is Daniel 10:13–21, where the angel says that he should first fight against the "prince of Persia" and then the "prince of Greece." In his explanation of this passage, George Otis states that the prince of Persia is "an evil spiritual being ruling over an area with explicitly described boundaries."[8] From that, Timothy Warner assumes that because there is a prince of Persia, there should also be "princes" of other geographical areas.[9]

Chuck Lowe rightly points out that the passage does not speak about forces ruling in specific geographical areas, within fixed limits.[10] It is a description of two world powers that ruled over several countries, first the one and then the other. At the time of Daniel, the Persian Empire ruled over a large part of the known world. Thereafter, the Greek empire ruled over an even larger area (which included Persia). The "areas" of the "princes" thus grew and shrunk. They were not fixed geographical units.

The view that demons would respectively be in charge of the Persian and Greek empires also creates problems.[11] Lowe points out that this would mean that the war that threatened to be fought between the two world powers was also a struggle between two demons about the size of their dominion and who would be in control. One could ask whether the "prince of Greece" obtained power over the "prince

8. George Otis, "An Overview of Spiritual Mapping," in *Engaging the Enemy: How to Fight and Defeat Territorial Spirits*, ed. Peter Wagner (Ventura, CA: Regal, 1993), 35.

9. Timothy M. Warner, "Power Encounter with the Demonic," in *Evangelism on the Cutting Edge*, ed. Robert Coleman (Old Tappan, NJ: Fleming Revell, 1986), 98.

10. Chuck Lowe, *Territorial Spirits and World Evangelisation?* (Kent: OMF International, 1998), 34.

11. Peter Wagner, *Warfare Prayer: How to Seek God's Power and Protection in the Battle to Build His Kingdom* (Ventura, CA: Regal, 1992), 66.

of Persia" by the reign of the Greeks over Persia. These ideas sound a lot like the pagan idea in biblical times that each nation had its own god or gods and that the power of the gods was measured by how the different nations performed in wars.

The "prince of Persia" was replaced by the "prince of Greece." It was by no means an improvement for the people of the Lord. Not many were misled by the Persian ways of thought, but millions were led astray by the Greek philosophies. Even if there was a main demon who reigned over Persia and whom Daniel wanted to bind with a war prayer (as the exponents of the new spiritual warfare argue), it would not have benefitted the gospel in any way when a stronger demon (that of the Greeks) filled the gap left by the weaker demon (that of the Persians). However, in the extended portion of the book of Daniel, which describes Daniel's experiences, we do not read that he tried to subdue or bind the "prince of Persia" in any way.[12]

Although exponents of the new idea appeal to various Scriptures, it soon becomes clear that the Scriptures do not say that God wants believers to be involved in such a spiritual struggle in this way. The advocates of the new movement try to compensate for the lack of real biblical proof by highlighting empirical data which, according to them, shows the immense success achieved by this new spiritual warfare.[13] It is therefore good to have a clearer look at this so-called success.

Demons and Territories

These days many pastoral and especially evangelistic programs of Christian churches focus on determining which demon reigns over what area. It is believed that this knowledge can help to limit the demons' powers, so that the gospel can take its course and people's crises can be solved. But this directs people's trust away from Christ and the gospel and emphasizes the need for a supplement to it.

An advocate of this idea, Bennie Mostert, wrote that research must be done before one can meaningfully pray for a city.[14] This research

---

12. Bill Randles, *Making War in the Heavenlies: A Different Look at Spiritual Warfare* (Pietermaritzburg: Plumbline Publishing, 1998), 26.

13. Lowe, *Territorial Spirits and World Evangelisation?*, 27.

14. Bennie Mostert, *Verander jou wêreld deur gebed* (Ferndale, South Africa:

is needed because "there are territorial spirits that live and work in certain geographical areas. . . . Those demons and their strongholds (as well as whatever gave them the right to raise up those strongholds) must be identified in order to pray for the demolition of these strongholds." Mostert then gives practical tips for research on these spirits, their operations and strongholds.

Under the heading "Recent examples of spiritual warfare," Mostert speaks about different countries of which he has heard, where churches grew dramatically after the power of evil forces was broken.[15] One example he refers to is the town of Arroyo Seco in Argentina, which a group of pastors supposedly discovered was the "seat of Satan in that region."[16] A few of them agreed to place the whole area under spiritual authority, and some of them went to Arroyo Seco. They stood in the street opposite the headquarters of the followers of Mr. Meregildo (a magician) and served an eviction order on the forces of evil. An unconfirmed report shows that today all the villages have a church or Christian witness. It is clear that no evidence could be provided for the claims. This hearsay evidence is accepted and even published, because it fits the ideas promoted.

Hendrik Venter claims that an awareness of the involvement of certain demons in specific geographical areas, organizations, workplaces, schools, churches, and the like is necessary to create an atmosphere where people can repent and where public sins can be effectively put to a stop.[17] His views imply that whether other people repent is in human hands, as it depends on whether territorial spirits are handled correctly. A consequence of this view, however, is that Paul, who preached the gospel wherever he went and at all times, should have attempted to find out what territorial spirits were active and bind them, so as to create the necessary atmosphere for conversion.

Otis and Wagner teach that territorial demons can be restricted

---

Kratos Uitgewers, 1995), 143–46.

15. Bennie Mostert, *Geestelike oorlogvoering* (Vereeniging, South Africa: Christelike Uitgewersmaatskappy, 2004), 88–93.

16. Mostert, *Geestelike oorlogvoering*, 91.

17. Hendrik Venter, *Strategiese gebed: Hoe om te bid vir jou gesin, werk, skool, kerk, ens* (Vereeniging, South Africa: Hendrik Venter, 1999), 8.

to a valley, a mountain, a river, some rocks, or specific trees.[18] This description makes one think of the old European pagan notion that there are devils in rivers and forests of which one should be aware. According to Wagner, the power of territorial spirits is tremendously strong in specific areas, but at the same time limited to that area to such an extent that it could not even cross a man-made border.[19] He describes a few examples where people just crossed a land border or even a nature reserve boundary and were free of the terrible hold that the demon of that region had over them. People who could not receive the gospel literally crossed a street to another part of town where it was possible for them to convert outside the influence of the territorial spirit.

If it were true that territorial demons can prevent the conversion of humans in a certain area, the conversion of the inhabitants of Nineveh in the time of Jonah would be incomprehensible. Of all pagan cities, Nineveh was so bad that God wanted to destroy it. Yet God used Jonah to bring the entire wicked city to repentance. Jonah was a reluctant preacher who wanted the city to be destroyed unconverted. His first step was certainly not to bind the city's territorial spirits to enable the people to come to repentance. In fact, he was angry about the conversion that occurred (Jonah 4). It is not man and his prayers, or his bondage to demons, which gives others the opportunity to come to repentance. It is almighty God who makes people, wherever they live or work, change radically when they hear the gospel.

Territorial Spirits, Spiritual Mapping, and Sin

According to Mostert, spiritual mapping is an attempt to describe the spiritual powers behind what is visible: "Spiritual mapping gives us an image or spiritual picture of how the situation in the spiritual realm above a city or geographical area looks."[20] To achieve this,

---

18. Otis, "An Overview of Spiritual Mapping," in *Engaging the Enemy*, ed. Wagner, 35; Wagner, *Warfare Prayer*, 77–79.

19. Peter Wagner, *Wrestling with Dark Angels* (Eastbourne, UK: Monarch, 1990), 92.

20. Mostert, *Verander jou wêreld deur gebed*, 226.

prayer expeditions are sent to a particular city or town. It is believed that when people move through an area praying, territorial spirits and other evil forces working in the area are revealed to the prayer travelers. In addition, they pray for revelation from God and his plan for what should be done in the area.[21]

As a part of spiritual mapping, research is done on the normal and religious history of the place, so the names of the spirits ruling over the area can be discovered. As an example, Randles quotes Dick Bernal, who claimed that the Holy Spirit gave him the title of the prevailing power over his area, namely "Self."[22] Frank Hammond also claims that one must determine which demon rules over your area.[23] He says that in a vision God revealed to him that the main demon in his area was an octopus-like creature called "Jealousy." He then tells how the demon of jealousy caused other church leaders in the region to have negative feelings toward him. His task in spiritual warfare was to wrestle against these powers by loudly emphasizing that he had authority over the demonic forces. From this description, it would seem rather (in this terminology) that Hammond does indeed have a problem with "Self," because he sees himself as the one to save the spiritual leaders who disagree with him from "Jealousy."

According to Wagner and Greenwood, a primitive hit-and-miss approach to spiritual warfare must be abandoned.[24] Likewise, Venter warns that spiritual mapping should only be done by specialists.[25] He stresses that research on the area is very important. First, an area that forms a unity geographically, historically, spiritually, and culturally is targeted. By researching these different aspects, prayer warriors can find out which demons they will be facing. For example, in a village that grew following the discovery of gold, one can be sure that the demons of materialism, alcohol abuse, promiscuity, and violence will have obtained the right to operate in the area.

---

21. Wagner and Greenwood, *Understanding Spiritual Warfare*, 193–97.

22. Randles, *Making War*, 13.

23. Frank Hammond and Ida Hammond, *Pigs in the Parlor: A Practical Guide to Deliverance* (Kirkwood, South Africa: Impact Books, 1973), 17–18.

24. Wagner and Greenwood, *Understanding Spiritual Warfare*, 182.

25. Venter, *Strategiese gebed*, 35.

These considerations are based on the false idea that people and their actions give demons the right to rule over certain areas. On the contrary, the Bible teaches that the earth in its fullness belongs to the Lord, and that Christ is "far above all rule and authority and power and dominion" (Eph. 1:21).

Wiaan van Schalkwyk is head of the interdenominational "Spiritual Mapping Task Team" in Kempton Park, South Africa. According to him, the aim of spiritual mapping is to find out what spiritual powers are responsible for the unique character of a city. This demands research of historical events and curses relating to the city. He asks people to come forward with facts about it. This research is necessary to drive out the evil spirits that have the city in their grip by war prayers, and to enable the Holy Spirit to do his revival work: "Spiritual mapping allows for informed intercession. It exposes the reasons, roots or origins of prevailing conditions, which hinder the working of God's Spirit. . . . The spiritual forces behind this must be identified . . . must be exorcised. Only if this has been done will a city be spiritually prepared for a Holy Spirit driven revival."[26]

The whole idea of spiritual mapping turns the redemptive work of God upside down. God the Holy Spirit is made dependent on the research and prayers of vain people who have to drive out the evil spirits. Nothing like this is found anywhere in the New Testament when the gospel is preached from city to city and region to region. Revival comes when the Spirit works in people's hearts and when they break with what is wrong in their lives, under his guidance. Johan Malan rightly points out that by this new view of spiritual warfare, the emphasis in the Bible on the sinfulness of man is moved to the pagan concept of sinful areas.[27]

The "research" done to determine the demon in charge of a specific area is based on the idea that certain sins and human failures are actually demons. Lists and lists of names of demons are given for

26. Wiaan van Schalkwyk, "Spiritual Mapping of Kempbisa," in *Kempbisa News*, July 2001, 6.

27. Johan Malan, "'n Valse herlewing brei ook na Suid-Afrika uit," in *Evangelies-Gereformeerde Kerkblad*, May-June 2001, 8.

things that the Bible describes as sins or faults of people. Hammond, for example, distinguishes fifty-three such "common demon group-ings," each with subdivisions.[28] The first of these demon groupings is bitterness. Under this heading, he classifies demons of resentment, hatred, unforgivingness, violence, temper, anger, revenge, and mur-der. In this way, a few hundred demons are distinguished. Thus, the responsibility for what a person has done is taken from him and placed on demons as perpetrators to be cast out, instead of the person confessing guilt before God.

Because of the belief in territorial spirits holding people in bond-age in a certain territory, it is important in third-wave thinking to find out what corporate sins give these spirits the right to operate there, and then to focus prayers on these things.[29] Advocates of the new kind of spiritual warfare see Daniel 10 as important proof that believers must fight demons through war prayers. Wagner, for exam-ple, says this passage "shows us clearly that the only weapon Daniel had to combat these rulers of darkness was warfare prayer."[30] The passage however, does not say that. Although Daniel is talking to an angel of God, he does not ask the angel about the names of the demons that threaten. Neither does he use names in his prayers. If the references to the demonic forces as "prince of Persia" or "prince of Greece" were really important, Daniel would have used them in his prayers. It is clear that not even Daniel 10 advocates war prayers against territorial spirits.

Bill Randles asks what difference the identification of the power of spirits over a specific area really makes.[31] He says that the time and effort of so-called spiritual warfare against the spirits of greed in New York, power in Washington, pornography in Los Angeles, etc., which were pinpointed by Wagner, had no impact. He writes that one of the pastors who attended a conference in Alabama excitedly told them

28. Hammond, *Pigs in the Parlor*, 113–15.
29. Michael Pocock, Gailyn van Rheenen, and Douglas McConell, *The Changing Face of World Missions: Engaging Contemporary Issues and Trends* (Grand Rapids: Baker Academic, 2005), 187.
30. Wagner, *Warfare Prayer*, 66.
31. Randles, *Making War*, 56.

that the impact of spiritual warfare in a city already became visible during the conference, because a small piece of the giant statue of Volcano (the Greek god of fire) broke off. Randles asks if anything really changed in the city. There is no evidence of it. He also mentions another advocate of the new kind of warfare, who told him that during a meeting in Washington it was determined that "deception" was the demon controlling the city.[32] They attacked "deception" with war prayers. The success of the prayers was apparently clear the next day, when a newspaper had the headline: "Deception exposed in the city government." He rightly asks whether there was less "deception" in Washington two or three years later.

The devil's strategy is to take our focus away from the real spiritual battle going on. The kingdom of God is not about statues that crumble, newspaper headlines, or similar signs. It is about sinful hearts that crumble in repentance and grateful praise to God for his grace.

Mostert also believes that it is important to specifically determine the evil spirits working in an area. He says "when we know the name of the evil spirit, he is kind of caught out and then it is easier for us to resist him and bind him in the name of the Lord and then we also know how to plan a counter-strategy."[33] However, these claims are directly in contrast to what we read in the Bible about how the gospel spreads to pagan areas. Paul, the apostle to the Gentiles, did not undertake spiritual warfare against Hermes in Athens, Zeus in Corinth, or Romulus in Rome. No statues cracked and broke while he was walking among the idols and altars in Athens. When it was necessary to drive out the spirit by which a woman predicted the future (Acts 16), Paul did not use the opportunity to break the demonic bondage holding the people of Philippi, in order to make it possible for them to receive salvation. The opposite happened. The residents got angry, they beat Paul and Silas terribly, and cast them into the maximum security section of the prison. We do not read that while in prison they bound the strong man of the city. No, they prayed and sang to God. It is God who, by his almighty decision, shook the

32. Randles, *Making War*, 59.
33. Mostert, *Geestelike oorlogvoering*, 67.

earth to give them the opportunity to preach the great consequences of the gospel.

With the Heidelberg Catechism (Lord's Day 52), Reformed theology confesses that through the redemptive work of Christ and the sanctification of the Holy Spirit, believers can overcome their three deadly enemies that work together: the devil (and his demons), the deceitful world, and their own sinful nature. The responsibility to do what God calls us to do stays with man, even if the devil comes to us in a deceitful way, as happened in the garden of Eden. Human beings remain responsible for their deeds as image of God.

The new-wave thinking concerning territorial spirits and their power over areas takes the focus away from the victory of Christ, who has all power in heaven and on earth (Matt. 28:18) and makes prayer a weapon in human hands. It is foolish to change the trust and certainty of our covenantal relationship with God to a type of prayer that uses God and his name to manipulate spirits. Prayer that is an expression of the covenantal relationship of believers with their heavenly Father—"prayer, as submission to and communicating with God"—should not be "redefined as a spiritual power-tool," which "virtually reduces God to an impersonal source of power that can be manipulated at will, as long as we use the right techniques."[34] Those who believe in the Lord Jesus share in his victory (Col. 2:15; Matt. 12:29). Therefore, the devil has no legal authority over Christians. The devil is not afraid of believers who walk around with eviction commands. He is not even afraid of praying believers. He is in fear and awe of almighty God, the One to whom believers pray, their heavenly Father to whom they belong and with whom they are in a covenant relationship.

Covenantal Spiritual Warfare

In Acts 17, God teaches us what real spiritual warfare is among the strongholds of idolatry, heresy, and pagan lifestyle. After only three weeks in Thessalonica, the persecution of believers escalated so much that Paul and Silas had to flee the city by night. We do not

---

34. Aiken, *Should Reformed Believers Engage in Spiritual Warfare?*, 252.

read that Paul bound the demons (e.g., of envy, v. 5) there. He used Scripture to argue with the people and pointed out that Jesus is the Christ (Acts 17:2–3). A large number came to faith in those difficult circumstances on the basis of the gospel and not by releasing the area from its bondage to demons (Acts 17:4; 1 Thess. 1:9–10). The congregation that developed also became powerful in the preaching of the gospel (1 Thess. 1:6–8). The people in Berea were more receptive to the gospel (Acts 17:10–15). It was not due to human prayer teams that first determined where the demons' headquarters were and then prayed until God had an opening to convert people in the city. It was the Lord who gave the people of Berea the desire to examine the Scriptures on the basis of Paul's preaching.

If there was one place where Paul should have bound idolatry and the demons behind it as well as false philosophical wisdom and the demons behind that, according to the new idea of spiritual warfare, it would have been Athens. As we read in Acts 17:16–34, even in this capital of pagan idolatry (v. 16) and Greek philosophy (v. 18), Paul still fought the spiritual battle by simply preaching and appealing to the people to repent of their wrong ways (v. 30). This occurred while Paul was indignant about all the idols in the city (v. 16). Paul gave his sermon and the call to repentance at the Areopagus (v. 19), at the foot of the Parthenon, the gigantic temple of the Greek gods. He did not bind the gods or demons behind it, and in his preaching he even quoted from the pagan doctrine of the time, to convince the Athenians that the sculptures they prayed to were human creations and their ideas were human imaginings (vv. 27–29).

Reacting to the views of Wagner and Greenwood on spiritual warfare, David Powlison emphasizes that "spiritual mapping has no biblical precedent or warrant."[35] It didn't even take place when Paul went into one of the "strongholds" in his time of Greek idolatry. When you read Paul's speech on the Areopagus in Acts 17, it is clear that Paul knew a lot about the thoughts and spiritual background of the people of Athens. He knew what to say to confront their belief

---

35. David Powlison, "Response to C. Peter Wagner and Rebecca Greenwood," in *Understanding Spiritual Warfare*, ed. Beilby and Eddy, 205–6.

and worldview. He proclaimed Jesus Christ as the only Savior of the world, in the midst of heathen practices.

Paul does recognize that demons are behind the idolatry of the Gentiles (1 Cor. 10:18–22). This is understandable because idolatry is essentially rebellion against God. The honor due to God is given to vain idols and illusions. For this reason, Paul says we should have nothing to do with idolatry.

When it is clear that demonic forces stand in the way of the gospel, we can ask the Lord to take them away, and in exceptional circumstances the demon could even be addressed in the name of the Lord (Acts 16:18). In the 1990s, two Reformed church members who were on an outreach in Malawi experienced such exceptional circumstances. They were preaching the gospel to a group of children when the children suddenly stood up in a trance and started to walk toward them swaying (as mentioned by an author at that time). After the evil spirit was commanded to stop it in the name of the Lord, the children came out of the trance, sat down again, and continued to listen to the gospel. Even in this direct confrontation, the focus remained on the gospel, which is about the only One through whom redemption can take place.

An Animistic Worldview and the Tearing Down of Strongholds

A huge problem with third-wave thinking is that it diminishes human responsibility and takes us back into animism. Powlison puts it as follows:

> We learn (and need to know) that the animistic, occultic, super-stitious view of demonic agencies is false. Animism exaggerates the personhood and autonomy of the forces of darkness. It locates the human drama within a haunted universe. It diminishes the significance of personal and sociocultural evils. One of the consistent purposes of the Old Testament is to demythologize the superstitious worldview.[36]

36. David Powlison, "The Classic Model," in *Understanding Spiritual Warfare*, ed. Beilby and Eddy, 91.

Lowe describes the twentieth century's shift in worldview to focus on spirits as a reaction to the mechanistic worldview of modern times.[37] Spiritual warfare through combatting territorial spirits "is an embodiment of post-modernity's spiritistic worldview." It is true that demons are behind idolatry (1 Cor. 10:19–20), but to ascribe everything that happens to their doing is not the biblical view of reality.

Based on 2 Corinthians 4:3–4 and 10:3–5, Randles shows that true spiritual warfare is about confronting false life and thought and about bringing the glorious gospel of Jesus Christ to people, while praying that God will change their hearts.[38] He says it is less threatening to tear down strongholds in cities through so-called war prayers than to confront people with the gospel to overthrow the strongholds of their false belief systems.

When referring to the tearing down of strongholds in 2 Corinthians 10, Paul uses a term already used in Proverbs 21:22: "A wise man scales the city of the mighty and brings down the stronghold in which they trust." Spiritual warfare is conducted through applying wisdom to pull down the fortresses falsely erected in someone's mind. Part of bringing the good news of the gospel is to tear down those things that hinder people from putting their trust in God, to live trustingly in covenant with him. Part of our responsibility, in covenant with God, is to demolish false views and arguments, and by so doing to "defend and commend the gospel."[39]

When Paul wrote about what had to be destroyed in spiritual warfare, he called it "arguments and every lofty opinion raised against the knowledge of God" (2 Cor. 10:4–5). "Destroy" is a very strong word that shows the seriousness of this apologetic fight. Arguments raised against the knowledge of God can be destructive to all who believe them. This provides an opportunity to answer false opinions, and, by so doing, to bring others to consider scriptural truths. This must be done, not by one or two people, but by all believers.

Aiken emphasizes the need for spiritual warfare when he describes

---

37. Lowe, *Territorial Spirits and World Evangelisation?*, 151.
38. Randles, *Making War*, 22–23.
39. Oliphint, *The Battle*, 83.

it as necessary for both believers' spiritual health and their maturity.[40] In the Bible, God teaches Christians about the attacks of Satan in order to prepare them for assaults, to let them grow in truth and in relationship with him, and to react faithfully to what they and others experience.

Active Spiritual Warfare

Ed Gross states that, based on Ephesians 6:16 and 1 Peter 5:8–9, the fact that believers hold on to the promises of God in his Word neutralizes the devil's onslaught on them.[41] The certainty believers have on the basis of God's promises to them as his children gives them great peace and security, but should not make them passive. The task of believers is to be on their guard and vigorously fight what is wrong and do what is right, with the certainty of salvation. This must result in them radically breaking with what is wrong, as well as fulfilling the task to which God calls every believer.

Gross also points out that the Bible is clear, not only that the devil and his demonic forces exist, but also that these forces, together with the world and our own sinful nature, continually engage in attacks on every believer.[42] They are embroiled in a struggle (Eph. 6:12–13). Although this is a spiritual battle, it is not a supernatural battle. Therefore, according to Ephesians 6:14–18, the armor needed to remain standing in this struggle is nothing supernatural, but rather a life based on truth, righteousness, gospel-preaching, faith, salvation, Scripture, and prayer. To counteract and resist the devil, you cannot rely on human power or pagan ideas; rather, victory comes through the truth of God's Word (Jer. 23:28–29; Eph. 6:17; Heb. 4:12).

This missional calling of the church is key to the Reformed understanding of faith. To follow Christ is to be a part of an active spiritual war. Instead of promoting a vision of spiritual warfare where believers fight "spiritually" in a "supernatural dimension," the

---

40. Aiken, *Should Reformed Believers Engage in Spiritual Warfare?*, 248.

41. Ed Gross, *Miracles, Demons, and Spiritual Warfare* (Grand Rapids: Baker Book House, 1990), 114–15.

42. Gross, *Miracles, Demons, and Spiritual Warfare*, 112–14.

Reformed faith proclaims that the spiritual war is to be fought spiritually within the confines of God's world and his creation order. Powlison emphasizes that when Paul describes the "complete weaponry" of the Christian soldier in Ephesians 6, it is based on spiritually being in Christ and that "we are to image the Lord God in person." The belt of truth refers to Isaiah 11, where the coming Messiah is described by truth and faithfulness, coming to destroy lies and to bring justice and mercy in God's created order for human existence. And Jesus told Pilate that he was born into this world to testify for the truth (John 18:37).

According to Powlison, other parts of the weaponry described in Ephesians 6, such as righteousness and salvation, are also based on Isaiah.[43] In Isaiah 59:1–21, we find the description of the Lord who will come armed to make right what is wrong, and through his words and Spirit wrench people out of darkness, sin, and condemnation. In the same way, the shoes used to take the gospel of peace refer to Isaiah 52, where the feet of the Lord bring good news, peace, happiness, and salvation—which shall be seen by the ends of the earth. All this is fulfilled in Jesus Christ and can be lived out and proclaimed by those who are in him.

While the shield of faith is used in Ephesians 6 in a defensive role against evil flaming arrows, the defense of the shield is needed in order to fight offensively. In Psalm 18, the Messiah is described as going out shielded and strengthened to wage war. David also calls the Lord our shield in this psalm. Against ideas of this "faith-movement," it is important to understand that we should not put our faith in faith to protect us in spiritual warfare. We have to put our faith in our Lord and Savior to protect us while fighting the good fight.

Scott Oliphint emphasizes that apologetics includes a mindset that knows that nothing is more true or special "than the truth of Scripture in all its richness and fullness."[44] With the truth of Scripture, Jesus reacts to Satan in the wilderness. With the truth of Scripture as the sword of the Spirit in human hands (Eph. 6:17), the

43. Powlison, "Classic Model," 94.
44. Oliphint, *The Battle*, 85.

Holy Spirit is changing millions of people's lives, until the end of times and the end of the world.

The covenant with God includes "me and my house" (Josh 24:15). In Deuteronomy 6:4, God teaches us to use every opportunity to teach his Word, especially to young ones who are part of our house, part of God's covenant. That will prepare them to understand and live as new creations, and, by so doing, make an impact for the kingdom of God. The covenant with God includes everything I possess, because we are what we are and we have what we have through God's grace and according to his purpose.

The Christian Victory

The Bible teaches believers not to try to resist or be victorious by themselves, but to live and work on the basis of the victory already achieved in and through our Lord Jesus Christ. This becomes apparent through the following two passages, among others:

- Ephesians 1:21–23: Christ is "far above all rule and authority and power and dominion, and above every name that is named, not only in this age but also in the one to come. And [God] put all things under his feet and gave him as head over all things to the church, which is his body, the fullness of him who fills all in all."
- Romans 8:37–39: "In all these things we are more than conquerors through him who loved us. For I am sure that neither death nor life, nor angels nor rulers, nor things present nor things to come, nor powers, nor height nor depth, nor anything else in all creation, will be able to separate us from the love of God in Christ Jesus our Lord."

All areas belong to the Lord. People trying to claim territorial areas for God are acting contrary to Christ's Great Commission in Matthew 28, which states that he has all power in heaven and on earth (v. 18). Based on his omnipotence, he instructs believers to go out and preach the gospel. It is not man who, by binding the power of the devil or territorial spirits, sets God in a position to bring people to repentance.

It is God who, on the basis of his omnipotence, sends out believers to gather in those whom he has called to himself.

Toward a Reformed Covenantal Response

Territorial spiritual warfare is not biblical. Scripture is clear with regard to Christ's dominion over the whole of creation, his triumph over demonic powers through his redemptive work (Col. 2:15), the believer's deliverance from the power of darkness (1:13), and the inability of every alien power to separate the elect from the love of God in Christ (Rom. 8:37–39). Also, conversion comes solely from the preaching of the gospel (Rom. 1:16; Acts 17:4; 1 Thess. 1:6–8). Thus, the Bible is clear in presenting the centrality of the redemptive work of Christ (1 Cor. 15:1–5) and the absolute sovereignty of the triune God in salvation.

In spite of the given scriptural evidence and arguments, and the books and articles written in recent years, many churches worldwide still embrace this wrong understanding of spiritual warfare. We should stand in the gap for those who are deceived and preach the liberating truth of the gospel to those who want to follow Christ in his mission.

We should not assume that everyone with an unbiblical understanding of spiritual warfare is an unbeliever, for knowledge of God is essentially different from having a sound theology; to know God and Christ *is* eternal life (John 17:3). Sound theology, as the suffix suggests, is the fruit of theoretical-scientific activity and shouldn't be confused with the knowledge of God in Jesus Christ, for the latter *is* eternal life and is primarily based on a personal relationship, not man's rationality. Good theology on the other hand, is essentially based on a deepened experience of faith and a personal relationship with God. In other words, when it comes to the relationship between faith and theology, life and faith precede structure and theology as "organized" faith. Now if sound theology isn't to be equated with knowledge of God, what does this mean for the current approach of territorial spiritual warfare? And how can Reformed believers help others who are oppressed by harmful and unbiblical beliefs in a biblical and constructive way?

The answer is manifold. Drawing on fundamental tenets of the Reformed worldview, some basic distinctions can be pointed out, in the hope that they may shed some light on central issues at stake. A covenantal Reformed perspective, which is rooted in the Reformational (specific, transcendental) understanding of the created order and correlated to the Reformed (ultimate, transcendent) covenantal understanding of God's relationship to man and to the cosmos, can be sketched briefly.

According to the Reformed covenantal (transcendent) perspective, creation and its constitution are ultimately dependent upon the triune God, including human beings and human consciousness. Based on this presupposition, Cornelius Van Til stresses that Christian apologists must speak to men so as to "make men self-consciously either covenant keepers or covenant breakers."[45]

On the other hand, this Trinitarian and covenantal understanding of God's relationship to man and creation in an ultimate sense has inspired Reformed thinkers to develop a radically Reformed philosophy, which has become generally known as Reformational philosophy. Most prominent in this philosophy is its nonreductive ontology, which can basically be seen as an all-encompassing covenantal and transcendental approach to the radical diversity and coherence of created reality.[46] In his attempt to reconcile Van Til's Reformed apologetics and Reformational philosophy, my grandfather, Hendrik G. Stoker, demonstrated how the former's emphasis on ultimate (transcendent) meaning moments are to be seen as correlative to specific (transcendental) meaning moments.[47] The latter involves a theory of

45. Cornelius Van Til, *Christian Apologetics* (Nutley, NJ: Presbyterian and Reformed, 1976), 62.

46. Oliphint says that "covenantal apologetics is transcendental," for it "asks questions about the basic foundations of an unbelieving position" (*Covenantal Apologetics*, 46).

47. For further exploration of the relation between Stoker, Dooyeweerd, and Van Til on Reformed apologetics, see G. Braun, "A Trinitarian Modal-Spherical Method of Apologetics: An Attempt to Combine the Vantilian Method of Apologetics with Reformational Philosophy" (MA thesis, North-West University, 2013), www.allofliferedeemed.co.uk/braun.htm. See also Hendrik Stoker, "Reconnoitering the Theory of Knowledge of Prof. Dr. Cornelius Van Til," in *Jerusalem and Athens:*

reality (ontology) that accounts for the different facets of human existence from a nonreductive perspective.[48]

Considering the difficulty of persuading people who believe in territorial spiritual warfare on theoretical and theological grounds, due to their dualistic "supernatural" treatment of the subject, their unwillingness to follow Scripture exclusively as the rule of faith (*regula fidei*), and their depreciation of any interpretation that doesn't rely on supernatural experiences of spiritual warfare, how can the Reformed covenantal perspective come into play?

According to the Reformed covenantal perspective, I'd like to suggest that a radically Reformed and Reformational approach is to stress the pre-theoretical and personal nature of knowledge of God and Christ (John 17:3).[49] This pre-theoretical starting point can be easily translated into a narrative discourse, which emphasizes man's personal reconciliation with God in Jesus Christ, through the Holy Spirit and the integral effect of it.[50] Thus, by unpacking personal stories and giving testimonies of faith, the Reformed believer and situational apologist can preach an integral gospel and demonstrate how the whole of Christian life is spiritual warfare, not in a "supernatural"

Critical Discussions on the Theology and Apologetics of Cornelius Van Til, ed. E. R. Geehan (Nutley, NJ: Presbyterian and Reformed, 1971), 48.

48. Although this transcendental view won't be expanded upon, it is implied in upcoming distinctions between the theoretical and pre-theoretical "biblical view concerning the correlation and mutual irreducibility of law and subject" (Herman Dooyeweerd, "Cornelius Van Til and the Transcendental Critique of Theoretical Thought," in *Jerusalem and Athens*, ed. Geehan, 79. See also Hendrik Stoker, *Philosophy of the Creation Idea* (unpub. translation of Hendrik Stoker, *Oorsprong en Rigting*, vol. 2, sect. 6 [Cape Town: Tafelberg, 1970], 31, 35, 38).

49. Stoker and Vollenhoven usually spoke of the pre-theoretical in the sense of prescientific. See Stoker, *Philosophy of the Creation Idea*, 7, 12, 15, 18. Thereby they convey a similar meaning as Dooyeweerd when he speaks of naive experience. For instance, Dooyeweerd explains how, prior to abstract thinking, human beings experience reality as a whole, i.e., aspects of reality then seen in irreducible coherence. And it is in this pre-theoretical coherence that man experiences God's revelation and stands in a covenantal relationship with him (*In the Twilight of Western Thought* [Grand Rapids: Paidea Press, 1960], 32).

50. For instance, Herman Ridderbos's redemptive-historical method is closely related to this approach.

and dualistic sense, but because Christians are now rooted in Christ (Rom. 5) as new creatures (2 Cor. 5:17). They are called by God to participate in his Great Commission, to proclaim Christ's triumph over demonic powers through his redemptive work, and to display the hope of the glory to come (Col. 1:27).

The covenantal perspective is an all-encompassing and personal one, reaffirming the sovereignty of the triune God in his works of creation, redemption, and transformation. On a personal level, this covenantal view reminds Reformed Christians that they must humble themselves before God and present their lives as a testimony to the saving power of the gospel (Rom. 1:16), so that when engaging others on issues such as spiritual warfare, the glory of Christ's gospel may shine through the darkness and fully restore people's lives in their relationship with God, with creation, and with each other.

Conclusion

With what attitude must Christians go into apologetics, into a battle for the truth, and at the same time for the hearts of people? When Paul's focus turns to apologetics in 2 Corinthians 10, he emphasizes in the first verse that we must work with "the meekness and gentleness of Christ." It is important to see that "meekness" and "gentleness" are defined as the same meekness and gentleness that we find in Christ. We are not just nice guys trying to convince others. We are people who are part of a covenant with God, following and imitating our leader, our Lord Jesus Christ, who came to bring salvation to those in bondage.

When the idea of the authority that Christians have in Christ becomes too prominent, the truth they articulate can be harsh, and the emphasis swings from defending the truth in Christ to defending the truth in myself, a task that needs me and my wit to do the fighting and win the contest. Although it is very difficult to attain the proper balance between authority and gentleness in apologetic conversations, it can be done in Christ. He is the one who is "full of grace and truth." Through our handling of apologetic warfare, we must do as our leader did, working visibly in grace and truth (John 1:17). This does not mean avoiding confrontations. It is a war about saving lives. We must not give the wrong impression that Christ, our Savior, is not interested in converting people, and that he doesn't mind sin, as long as people love or respect each other.

Paul uses strong words in 2 Corinthians 10:3–5, words that speak of both defensive and offensive warfare. The passage begins with the defensive and offensive task to demolish arguments. An important part of the defense against those who are hostile to the Christian faith is to prevent them from advancing. To stop them from "advancing . . . is a significant and crucial part of apologetics. . . . But we must also be offensive. We must take up our weapons and march against the enemy. . . . The offensive team is determined to advance."[51]

To always be prepared to give an answer (1 Peter 3:15) in accordance with the Word of God, Christians must read and rethink the content of the Word in such a way that the covenantal knowledge of God and what he gave us is truthfully burned into our hearts and minds. Then those who stand in covenant with God will be fully equipped for every good work (2 Tim. 3:17) through his Word and Spirit, ready to proclaim the gospel in different situations in a world that belongs to God.

---

51. Oliphint, *The Battle*, 78.

8

Missional Preaching
and the Covenant

Robert Norris

Abstract

The term *missional* is derived from a series of ecumenical dialogues confronting the increased secularization of society. While it underlines the urgency of the evangelistic task, the term is used broadly to justify many pragmatic techniques for church growth. The Reformed understanding of covenant provides a biblical justification for preaching as a God-appointed means of communicating the gospel. It also provides an understanding of the content of preaching and a critique of pragmatism. The theology of the covenant provides a sense of definition and direction to the God-given task of proclaiming his gospel. Covenantal missional preaching demands a preacher, is Trinitarian and Christocentric, proclaims a clear gospel, emphasizes corporate sanctification in the context of corporate worship, is concerned with both the proclamation of spiritual truths and authenticity of life, confronts the church and the world, and stimulates evangelism.

Introduction

Scripture attests the covenantal way in which God reveals himself in relationship with his people. The idea of a covenant developed in history before it was formally revealed as the primary means of unfolding the revelation of redemption. Covenants had been made among men long before God established his covenants with Noah and Abraham, as is clear from the language used to describe marriage. This prepared people to understand the significance of a covenant in a sinful world and helped them understand the divine revelation that presented man's relation to God as a covenant relation. The significance of this is displayed in the biblical record of the covenants established with Noah, Abraham, Moses, and David.

Peter Craigie has established that in ancient Near Eastern practice, when a covenant was made between a suzerain and a vassal, it was expected and demanded that the terms of the covenant be announced and repeated regularly. This has been demonstrated by Meredith G. Kline.[1] Indeed, it was the duty of the vassal to rehearse the terms of the covenant, so that it would be remembered. For this reason, "solemn assemblies" were called. Hughes Old has argued further that "we have in the covenant theology of the Pentateuch the rationale for the reading and preaching of the Scripture and worship—namely that it is demanded by a covenantal understanding of our relationship to God and each other."[2] For this reason, the nature of the covenant is announced in worship and becomes the central motif of proclamation as it reflects the way in which God has chosen to address himself to his people.[3]

The Reformed tradition stands alone in having a consistent understanding of the use of covenant in its preaching and its interface with the church's calling. Craig Van Gelder has argued that evangelicalism has adopted a "cross-centered gospel message that focuses on an individual's personal relationship to God," which leads, he believes, to a diminished and ineffective ecclesiology and often makes the church

1. Peter Craigie, *The Book of Deuteronomy*, NICOT (Grand Rapids: Eerdmans, 1967); Meredith G. Kline, *Kingdom Prologue: Genesis Foundations for a Covenant Worldview* (Overland Park, KS: Two Age Press, 2000), 1–7, 15.

2. Hughes Oliphant Old, *The Reading and Preaching of the Scriptures*, vol. 1 (Grand Rapids: Eerdmans, 1998), 29.

3. This is clearly affirmed in the second article of our "Missions Declaration," where it is stated, "Mission has its origin in God's eternal being and plan."

just one option among others for Christians. At the same time, theologically liberal approaches to covenantal thinking have reduced salvation to the social gospel and economic liberation by seeking to harmonize covenant with creation, giving rise to a human and social understanding of redemption.[4]

Defining *Missional* in a Reformed Context

Martin Kähler's dictum that "mission is the mother of all theology" may also be applied to the church's proclamation. True preaching has always been seen in the light of the mission of the church to proclaim the gospel.[5] The term *missional* has of late been adopted as the watchword for thinking about the task of the church, although the word is relatively new. Darrell Guder has argued in his book *The Missional Church* that the idea had its origin in the ecumenical dialogues of the 1950s.[6] Under the influence of Karl Barth, the concept of the *missio Dei* developed. Mission is not one function of the church, nor is the church the outcome of mission; rather, the emphasis is placed on the mission of the triune God in the world. Mission is then to be understood in relation to all three persons of the Godhead—Father, Son, and Holy Spirit. The basic premise of the missional church is that "missions" is not just one of the departments or programs of the church, but rather that it constitutes the very nature and essence of the church.

Theologically, this means that the church itself is a sign that the kingdom of God has begun on earth, and is a foretaste of the consummated reign to come. The implication for the self-understanding of the church is that the church exists, not to draw people to it and so perpetuate its own institutional life, but to announce the kingdom of God among men and women. It also suggests that the gospel is not to be understood merely as the news of what God has done in Christ to

4. Craig Van Gelder, "The Covenant's Missiological Character," *Calvin Theological Journal* 29 (1994): 190–92.

5. David J. Bosch, *Transforming Mission: Paradigm Shifts in Theology of Mission* (Maryknoll, NY: Orbis Books, 1991).

6. Darrell L. Guder, ed., *The Missional Church* (Grand Rapids: Eerdmans, 1998).

pardon sinners; rather, salvation and conversion are to be construed in a broader way to include justice, peace, healing, and liberation.

This has given rise to various understandings of what it means practically to be "missional." Some use the word to describe "Seeker Sensitive Church"; others use it to describe the Church Growth Movement and the world of mission.[7] Yet others use the term to call for evangelicals to live more authentically.[8] Some use it simply to describe techniques for adding to the church by a variety of approaches that will reach those outside the church. It is a term that has been used to justify any number of outreach practices that are based on management techniques or human activity.

In view of the confusion resulting from the various uses of this broad term, the Reformed understanding, drawn from the core concept of covenant, becomes ever more imperative as it shapes the discussion of what being "Reformed and Missional" means, and how that is reflected in the task of proclamation. Sometimes it has been suggested that "Reformed" focuses on the inward life of the church and "Missional" on the outward task or vision of the church. This is to misunderstand the nature of the Reformed faith, which has always been concerned with both the sanctification of its members and the church's outreach to the world.

Covenant theology has been enshrined in the Westminster Confession of Faith of 1646, with its focus on the sovereign grace of God worked out in a covenant of works and a covenant of grace. But this, together with the decree of election, has never been the sole emphasis of covenant thought. There has always been the equally significant eschatological dimension, which involves the gathering of the nations in accord with the promise of God to Abraham that he would be not only the father of a nation, but a means of blessing to the nations:

7. Eddie Gibbs and Ryan K. Bolger, "Postmodern Forms of the Church," in *Evangelical, Ecumenical, and Anabaptist Missiologies in Conversation*, ed. James R. Krabill, Walter Sawatsky, and Charles E. Van Engen (Maryknoll, NY: Orbis Books, 2006), 184–95.

8. Ronald J. Sider, *The Scandal of the Evangelical Conscience: Why Are Christians Living Just Like the Rest of the World?* (Grand Rapids: Baker Books, 2005).

Now the LORD said to Abram, "Go from your country and your kindred and your father's house to the land that I will show you. And I will make of you a great nation, and I will bless you and make your name great, so that you will be a blessing. I will bless those who bless you, and him who dishonors you I will curse, and in you all the families of the earth shall be blessed." (Gen. 12:1–3)

The missional vision of the Reformed church flows from its covenantal identity. This has always been expressed by worship and witness, discipleship and outreach. They were seen as inseparable. The creation itself is covenantal in character, as the first two chapters of Genesis make clear. The mandates of God to the whole of humanity provide us with a picture of the calling of the kingdom of God and also constitute our calling. They include fellowship with God, building community with others, marriage as a basis for society, and dominion over creation. Even after the fall, the Lord maintained his purposes unchanged and continued a covenant relationship with his people.

As Craig Van Gelder has written, "To be in covenant relationship is to become recipients of God's gracious favor. To be in covenant is also to be God's guarantee to the world that His redemptive purposes extend towards the Good News being proclaimed to all lost persons with all of His creation being within His purpose." His conclusion is that "not to be in mission is to deny a fundamental part of the essential nature of the covenant." He then goes through the Old Testament, showing the mission focus of each revealed covenant. The Abrahamic covenant (Gen. 12) displays the reality of an "all nations" perspective. The Mosaic covenant (Ex. 19–20) displays the call to sanctified living. The Davidic covenant (2 Sam. 7) outlines the eternal reign of God over all creation. The new covenant (Jer. 31) focuses on the power to live as God's people.[9]

Much missional writing seems to ignore preaching, even displaying a disdain for it, seemingly because it is dismissed as ill equipped to meet the missional demands of a post-Christian culture. Guder

9. Craig Van Gelder, "From Corporate Church to Missional Church: The Challenge Facing Congregations Today," *Review and Expositor* 101 (2004): 425–50.

argues that preaching, as it is understood in the traditional church context, is different from the New Testament use of the word, having been restricted to the inside of the church and addressed only to the faithful.[10] Yet preaching lies at the heart of the church's mandate and is the appointed means of the Lord's blessing. We have seen that the very idea of covenant includes the assumption of proclamation, and that the covenant paradigm determines the "what" as well as the "how" of our proclamation.

What follows are seven propositions about what it means to be missional within a covenantal construct, particularly with regard to preaching.

Covenantal Missional Preaching

Covenantal Missional Preaching Calls for a Preacher

A number of missional church proponents are skeptical about the place of preaching and the need for a preacher, and sometimes denigrate preaching as "speaching."[11] Doug Pagitt, the pastor of an emergent church, advocates, on behalf of "missional thinking," what he calls "progressional dialogue," which involves in-depth conversation and weekly open dialogue with participants.[12] He sees preaching no longer as proclamation, but rather as the conversations of the congregation building one another's lives. He further argues that traditional preaching on anything other than an occasional basis does "relational violence" and is detrimental to authentic community.

Covenantal preaching, however, requires a preacher to announce the terms of the covenant. Reformed thought has always made it clear that because ministry and missions originate in the mind and purpose of God, he has delegated the power of his own commission to his faithful laborers, has exercised his right of appointment in the choice of his own instruments, and so has called men to the ministry by grace through the Holy Spirit and the instrumentality of the

10. Guder, *The Missional Church*, 135.
11. Doug Pagitt, *Preaching Re-Imagined* (Grand Rapids: Zondervan, 2005).
12. Pagitt, *Preaching Re-Imagined*, 25–26.

church. Preachers are to announce the message of the gospel entrusted to them.

While congregational participation in worship is a clear biblical principle, Scripture nowhere suggests that such participation involve all members of the community preaching to one another. The covenant community knows there is a need to cultivate in-depth relationships that are both godly and biblical; it understands that those relationships are directed by the Scriptures and emerge from a common unity of faith and obedience to the terms of the covenant. At the same time, it understands that God has appointed certain men to announce the gospel for the renewal of broken covenants.

Covenantal Missional Preaching Is Trinitarian and Christocentric

When God establishes a covenant, he does so, not to set forth abstract propositions, but as his chosen means of self-revelation. In covenant proclamation, the first priority is the recognition of a sovereign God, who has revealed himself in the Trinity. He is active both in creation and in redemption, and has accomplished his will through the perfect life of obedience and the substitutionary, sacrificial death of Jesus Christ. This work is then made effective through the ministry of the Holy Spirit.

Indeed, in its mysterious workings, the Trinity has the element of covenant attached to it. Geerhardus Vos says that the implicit biblical understanding of a pretemporal covenant between the persons of the Trinity provides a "center of gravity" for Reformed thinking:

> In the dogma of the counsel of peace, then, the doctrine of the covenant has found its genuinely theological rest point. Only when it becomes plain how it is rooted, not in something that did not come into existence until creation, but in God's being itself, only then has this rest point been reached and only then can the covenant be thought of theologically.[13]

13. Geerhardus Vos, "The Doctrine of the Covenant in Reformed Theology," in *Redemptive History and Biblical Interpretation: The Shorter Writings of Geerhardus Vos*,

Because the covenant originates in the interpersonal relationships of the Trinity, albeit for the purpose of redemption, this personal bond, which joins the three persons of the Godhead in a community of life, presents the mandate to call men and women into relationship with God, because it stands as the revealed life in which man was created to participate. This is seen in the prayer of Jesus:

> I do not ask for these only, but also for those who will believe in me through their word, that they may all be one, just as you, Father, are in me, and I in you, that they also may be in us, so that the world may believe that you have sent me. (John 17:20–21)

The oneness of which Jesus speaks is more than ontological oneness and more than simply purposeful; instead, it speaks of another bond that may be said to be covenantal. Thus, missional preaching, far from being simply a pragmatic call to faith, has a definite design for a personal relationship with God.

Covenantal preaching is not just Trinitarian, but Christocentric—both in its hermeneutic and in its ultimate subject matter. Christocentric preaching draws out what it means that God is our Father for Jesus' sake, and it draws out that God the Holy Spirit, for Jesus' sake, renews and strengthens saints in the concrete issues of real life. Christocentric preaching lays before God's people today how he has walked with his sinful people in the past, and so gives due attention to the work of the Father, the Son, and the Holy Spirit. Such preaching sets before God's people how the triune God still walks with sinners today.

Covenantal Missional Preaching Proclaims a Clear Gospel

The nature of the gospel itself is informed by the covenant declarations of God that unfold the building blocks of God's saving purpose. It reveals God's law and his love. His righteousness is allied to his mercy—his law with his love. He demands a perfect righteousness and will judge all who are guilty. Yet, at the same time, he emphasizes

---

ed. Richard B. Gaffin, Jr. (Phillipsburg, NJ: Presbyterian and Reformed, 1980), 247.

that he hates the death of a sinner. God demands that all debts be paid, and he wants his people to be free of condemnation.

To meet this seeming contradiction, the second person of the Trinity comes as the substitute for sinners, living the life that God demands and dying as the substitute in our place in payment for our sins. The person of Jesus Christ, sinless in himself, fulfilled the law's demand for perfect obedience and faced the rejection and punishment of God as our substitute. Thus, law and love are fulfilled in his substitution. And when by faith the sinner is united to Christ, there is a twofold transfer by imputation. Our sins are imputed to Christ, and his righteousness is imputed to us. Paul makes this clear as the very nature of the gospel, which is the outworking of the covenant love of God and his determination to save people for himself, when he writes: "For our sake he made him to be sin who knew no sin, so that in him we might become the righteousness of God" (2 Cor. 5:21).

It is crucial to understand the doctrine of imputation in order to live a transformed life. It enables believers to understand how they can be both saints and sinners at the same time. The doctrine brings assurance that Christians are placed beyond probation, and that those in Christ are, at the same time, both sinful and completely righteous.

The gospel must be expounded in its fullness. Law and grace are inextricably linked in understanding the gospel. To declare the demands of God's holiness and law, without a clear presentation of the work of Christ and the imputation of his righteousness, necessarily produces a distorted gospel proclamation. It will produce discouraged, guilt-ridden people who recognize their own depravity without the conscience-cleansing power of the work of Christ. Alternatively, the proclamation of the free grace of God, without the preaching of the law, will trivialize the pardon that God gives. Central to this proclamation is the reality of the conviction of sin, the accomplishment of Christ's death, and the life-changing power of the indwelling Holy Spirit.

Doctrine and application must go together, so that it is not simply the emotions that are stirred, or the intellect addressed, but rather that what Scripture calls "the heart" is moved. The goal of any sermon is to promote "godly affections," such as humility, love, and zeal. Such preaching necessarily will have warmth and strength, being both tough and tender. The covenant itself displays the heart of God, where his mercy and justice, his wrath and love, all meet. Strength without warmth becomes cold and dismal; warmth without strength issues in sentimentality.

Covenantal Missional Preaching Emphasizes Sanctification and Worship

Because the covenant is communal, it focuses attention on the corporate growth of individuals within the life of the body of Christ. The covenant is addressed by God to his people, and as Sovereign he dictates the covenant, designed to prepare them to live out the life of faith in the midst of the world. The covenantal emphasis on the use of God's law as a guide to sanctification becomes a clear demand of preaching, with an emphasis on remembrance. This emphasis is repeated throughout the Old Testament. Hughes Old sees it as an essential facet of Deuteronomic preaching (Deut. 4:9–14), but it is not confined there. It becomes a theme of the Old Testament, where the forgetfulness of God's people is answered by an active rehearsal of the past.[14] This covenantal theme, then, informs the general "missional" emphasis of preparing God's people for their work in the world. It reiterates the historical nature of revelation, setting it in context, while reminding all hearers of the sovereign acts and demands of God.

The remembrance is first and foremost that of a holy and sovereign God who has created and promised re-creation. Anchoring proclamation in the deliberate act of God in creation and the continued faithfulness of God, who does not abandon that which he has made, but offering eschatological hope of restoration, enables those burdened by guilt and sin, demoralized and marginalized, to see the future in the control of a suzerain who cares for his servants.

This stands in contrast to those, such as George Hunsberger, who

---

14. Old, *Reading and Preaching of the Scriptures*, 1:26.

argue that the *kerygma* has nothing to do with preaching in the context of a worship service.[15] Instead, he says, "the church as community, the church's message, and the church's worship are all cast in the most public of language."[16] Covenantal preaching concentrates on the gospel arising from the missional hermeneutic that the covenant inspires. The church is thus seen as a community deliberately called out by God to stand in the particular context in which they are placed, to live out their witness in faithfulness. At the same time, the covenant makes it clear that the church is both organism and organization: it is both human and divine. Without understanding this reality, we reduce the church to an optional extra in the life of the individual. We not only imperil the mission of the church, but we ultimately imperil the very gospel entrusted to her.

Covenantal Missional Preaching, Proclamation of Spiritual Truths, and Authenticity of Life

The covenant has content, and as such it demands that preaching have theological content emerging from the Scripture that reveals God and the fullness of his purposes. It makes it clear that there is no dichotomy between propositions that are true and authenticity of life. Christian preaching trusts in the presence and ministry of the Holy Spirit to give it transforming power as well as edifying information. It encourages and directs Christian living as it expounds the Scriptures, which are the oracles of God. This has been likened to the two wings of an airplane: communication of the gospel and Christian behavior are both essential for authentic witness.

Intellectual understanding of the gospel alone is insufficient, for it does not guarantee spiritual life and can lead to a dead orthodoxy. Living orthodoxy is found where the Holy Spirit opens the heart and imparts a vision of the true God and the actual human condition. This changes the whole living of life.

The nature of the covenant makes it clear that the demands of

15. George R. Hunsberger, *Bearing the Witness of the Spirit* (Grand Rapids: Eerdmans, 1998), 19.

16. George R. Hunsberger, "Birthing Mission Faithfulness," *International Review of Christian Mission* 92 (2006): 145–53.

the law make up the life of righteousness. The gospel assures us that only in Christ can it be said that God's demands are met—by Christ, whose perfect life has fulfilled the law and whose substitutionary death has atoned for our sin. The first foundation for gospel transformation is sound doctrine, because the gospel is truth. Unless that truth is fully intact and expounded, it cannot be fully grasped, and only then can it have its renewing effect. Scriptural truth is the normal instrument by which the Holy Spirit regenerates the human heart:

> Having purified your souls by your obedience to the truth for a sincere brotherly love, love one another earnestly from a pure heart, since you have been born again, not of perishable seed but of imperishable, through the living and abiding word of God. (1 Peter 1:22–23)

In this passage, representative of many like it, we are reminded that the corporate marks of renewal are a direct result of the gospel in life. The "truth" has its own motivating power under the Holy Spirit. It moves us to freedom of worship, as we now have access to God through the righteousness of the great High Priest. It motivates us to witness in the world, as we see how Jesus the Christ came to save, and it calls us to generosity to the needy as we recognize our own sinfulness. The application of the truth of the gospel to human hearts impels ministry and worship. It is not simply a missional hermeneutic, which would simply be law, but the uniting of the truth and the ministry of the Holy Spirit that produce a concern for the world.

Without the unity of truth and authentic life, and a willingness to see the church as both organism and organization, we run the danger of producing programs without the presence of the Spirit. The integration of life and works is a significant element in covenantal thought.

Covenantal Missional Preaching Confronts the Church and the World

Missional preaching has a significant calling to "disturb" the church and its comfortable existence with the challenge of taking the gospel to the world. It is reflected in what Lee Wyatt has called "abductive preaching," which he advocates as being the best suited for the missional church. By this is meant the use of several forms of proclamation. The first he terms parabolic or storytelling. This is an effective means of reaching secularized and sometimes hostile individuals, and suggests that joke telling, cartoons, and other media modes are suited to engage those who are apathetic to spiritual things. A second form he terms "midrashic preaching," which he sees as challenging the "perceptions, assumptions and expectations of both church and world which are grounded in commitments to principles and powers other than the sovereign love of Yahweh." A third form, called "iconic preaching," leaves listeners with verbal images of Jesus Christ, which will go with the listener to build an identity in Christ. A fourth form he calls "poetic preaching," which he believes has the "capacity to dream and evoke visions on behalf of God's people."[17]

In covenant preaching, which is deductive as it demands the unfolding of revealed truth, there is also a concern to confront both individual and corporate idolatry. Our idols are often unrecognized and create a "delusional field" about them because we have deified them. In the life of an individual, this leads to placing something above Christ. In community, it is often the enculturation of the church in which we become identified with the godless culture of the surrounding world.

The remembrance of God and of the exclusivity of his demand for obedience is found as the covenant is recalled. Preaching must have the goal of calling individuals and communities to real and authentic obedience. It involves a rejection of sociological civil religion in which the state simply co-opts the forms of Christian worship as a means of providing a religious benediction to an otherwise secular event, as is witnessed in multifaith prayer breakfasts. The announcement of God's actions is a call to loyalty and continuous conversion. It is a call to repentance.

Repentance becomes the call to grace and transformation. Gospel

17. Lee A. Wyatt, "Preaching to Postmodern People," in *Confident Witness—Changing World*, ed. Craig Van Gelder (Grand Rapids: Eerdmans, 1999), 155–70.

repentance calls individuals and communities to repent, not only of sin, but also of righteousness, and to see the utter unacceptability of our own deeds, even our best deeds, resting instead in the finished work of Christ. By resting there, we can be completely accepted as righteous in him, so that his record becomes ours and his blessings and rewards become ours also. This not only confronts and converts nominal Christians, but also serves to bring vitality and assurance to true believers. It brings with it spiritual life, freedom, and boldness in confrontation with the world, and it is the source of assurance.

Because the gospel is not based on works and deeds, but rather on the action of Christ, there is no fear of losing identity. Our repentance does not indicate a fear of rejection, but rather is born out of a knowledge that we have wounded the One who has loved us and whom we also love. It is not the legalistic sense of breaking the rules of God that motivates us, but the sense that we have broken the heart of the One who has loved truly and best. While the gospel is moral and the call is to morality, the call to live moral lives flows not from command but from love, as the apostle Paul makes clear:

> For the grace of God has appeared, bringing salvation for all people, training us to renounce ungodliness and worldly passions, and to live self-controlled, upright, and godly lives in the present age. (Titus 2:11–12)

Here we are taught that obedience does not flow simply from a moral demand that is often inadequate to bring about true transformation. It is a response to the grace of God and the logic of the gospel. Titus teaches us to say "no" to immorality, but does so by reasoning with us, rather than commanding us. It exposes the true idol of the heart that contests with Christ for mastery over life, and it calls us from disobedience, assuring us of forgiveness as it invites us to trust acceptance in Christ. As we experience gospel repentance, our comfort and healing become intrinsic in the process.

In a post-Christian and secularized world, Christians must offer a witness that is a personal and moral response to a personal and loving God, instead of a simple intellectual adherence to a set of propositions. While authentic Christian witness is always a response to the self-revelation of God and must affirm propositional truths, there is another dimension of life that must also be practiced. This approach to truth through compelling lives may better touch the lives of postmodern people who have abandoned abstract notions of truth.

Covenantal Missional Preaching Stimulates Evangelism

Covenantal preaching understands the nature of the covenants as including an outreach element that finds its final fulfillment in the direct command of the Son of God, who authorizes and empowers the new community of faith to take the gospel to all nations in the power of the Holy Spirit. Preaching equips the people of God for this evangelistic task. It reminds them of the corporate nature of the task and of the power of the Holy Spirit to bring gifts to every member. Each member is to be engaged in the task that takes place beyond the boundaries of a church facility, but it is still the church as the body of Christ, equipped by the Spirit with gifts that are used in many contexts, that is active outside the traditional worship service.

Unbelievers are attracted by conversions and the reality of worship and community seen in the life of the body. As believers are observed using their gifts and demonstrating a burden in prayer for others outside of their religious community or ethnic grouping, the impact upon nonbelieving observers will be positive and attractive. Such communal involvement in worship, service, and outreach becomes an effective means of crossing cultural divides.

The boundaries of our society are traversed as the Spirit of God empowers believers, equipping them through the proclamation of the gospel and using them. Guder writes:

> The message of the reign of God, the gospel, is always communicated with the thought constructs and practices prevalent within the cultural setting of the church in a specific time and place. But when truly shaped by the Holy Spirit, this message also points beyond the present culture's thought forms and customs to the distinctive culture of God's reign proclaimed by Jesus. For this reason the church is always bicultural, conversant in the language and

customs of the surrounding culture, and living towards the language and ethics of the gospel.[18]

Conclusion

The theology of the covenant gives a sense of definition and direction to the God-given task of proclaiming his gospel. It gives to the church a renewed sense of mission in the face of the increasing secularization of society. While emphasizing the urgency of the evangelistic task, it affirms preaching as the God-given means of accomplishing this task and confronts the methodological pragmatism that often dismisses it as an outdated evangelistic tool.

18. Guder, *The Missional Church*, 114.

9

Tithing as a Covenantal Strategy for Mission

In Whan Kim

Abstract

As Lord of the covenant, God progressively established the biblical tithing institution in the history of redemption as a permanent support for his people who participate in his mission. The tithing institution of ancient Near Eastern culture was transformed and adopted as a covenantal institution to regulate the life of his people when God made the covenant at Sinai. Under the old covenant, it was part of the ceremonial system that was preparatory and was fulfilled by Jesus when he offered himself on the cross. The people of God under the new covenant do not keep the tithing institution as a form and type, as did the old covenant people. Since Jesus came, not to abolish but to fulfill the law, they dynamically adopt the principle, purpose, and practice of tithing. The apostle Paul enacted systematic giving for the church of God as a strategy to meet the church's financial needs when he carried out the commission of the risen Lord (the gospel mandate). The features of the tithing institution under the old covenant were transformed with apostolic authority, in accordance with the nature of the new age. The Pauline method of giving is a final and permanent biblical tithing institution for the new covenant people in accordance with the promise of the new heaven and the new earth. The Korean Protestant churches in modern times show that the biblical tithing institution is a powerful means for supporting the church in the mission of God. This biblical institution enables churches to become self-supporting in mission and to grow to maturity in Jesus Christ, effectively fulfilling his commission.

Introduction

Christopher J. H. Wright defines mission as "our committed participation as God's people, at God's invitation and command, in God's own mission within the history of God's world for the redemption of God's creation."[1] This definition depicts the God of mission, the people of mission, and the arena of mission in the Bible. He rightly argues that mission fundamentally originates in God the Creator, in that God established a covenant relationship with his people and called them to participate in his mission, so that his purpose in creation might be fulfilled for his glory.

When God, the covenant Lord, gave man and woman, created in his image, the mission to multiply and subdue the earth, he also gave them material support. As Creator, God knew the nature of man, and that without these means he could not fulfill his mission. From this perspective, God's mission-giving act cannot be separated from his supporting activities. God made a covenant with human beings so that they might participate in the mission of God, and he gave them the supporting means for fulfilling it. We will investigate the nature and function of the tithing institution in the Pentateuch and the rest of Scripture to demonstrate that it is covenantal and to be used by the people of God as a means to fulfill their mission. We will further explore the tithing institution in the administration of the new covenant in the form of giving that the apostle Paul instituted for the church as a support system to accomplish her God-given mission. Finally, the tithing institution is an effective and dynamic means to accomplish the mission of the church today, as illustrated by a case study of the practice of tithing in the Korean Protestant churches.

---

1. Christopher J. H. Wright, *The Mission of God: Unlocking the Bible's Grand Narrative* (Downers Grove, IL: IVP Academic, 2006), 23.

The Tithing Institution in the Old
Covenant Administration

The Origin of the Tithing Institution

The Reformed faith holds traditionally to a unique view: that God created the heavens and the earth for his own glory, to be his eternal temple and kingdom. To establish his glory firmly and eternally, God demonstrates his rule over all things. God the Creator has revealed himself as a missionary God since the beginning of creation. However, instead of fulfilling his mission alone, he created man and woman in his image and likeness, and sovereignly made a covenant with them, giving them the responsibility to multiply and subdue the earth in order to accomplish his purpose (Gen. 1:26–28). God made creation his eternal glorious temple and kingdom.[2] We may call this the *creation mandate*, under the covenant of creation.[3] In the marriage bond, God called man and woman to participate in his mission and appointed them to be his missionaries from the beginning.

When God instituted this mandate, he gave human beings the material he created as a means to fulfill his calling. God is not a bystander, but an active supporter who supplies what is necessary to carry out the given mission. He made the material world subservient to man. In this way, God the Creator and the Lord of the covenant instituted not only the creation mandate, but also the support system

2. Meredith G. Kline argues that this was the purpose of God in creating the heavens and the earth, and man and woman. See *Kingdom Prologue: Genesis Foundations for a Covenantal Worldview* (Eugene, OR: Wipf & Stock, 2006). John H. Walton in this connection argues that the main focus of the creation narrative is not to present how the created things originated, but how they began to function for the inauguration of the temple of God when God created the heavens and the earth. See *The Lost World of Genesis One* (Downers Grove, IL: IVP, 2009).

3. The Reformed faith traditionally calls it the cultural mandate. However, *creation mandate* would be a more apt term, since the mandate embraces all the activities in the whole realm of human life, including not only bearing children through marital life, but also multiplying animals and plants. The traditional designation *cultural mandate* limits the holistic mandate to the cultural activity of human life and fails to embrace the full scope of covenantal responsibilities. Further, this mandate was given by the Lord of creation and the covenant to the man and woman under the covenant at the time of creation.

for them to successfully fulfill the mission. As vice-regents of the covenant Lord, human beings were enabled to exercise lordship over the material world. They could freely use the God-given material for food to sustain their life and as a means to multiply and subdue the earth, so as to spread God's lordship in every sphere of life in the created world, the temple and kingdom of God.

However, man broke the relationship, disobeying the covenant stipulation in rebellion against the Lord. Consequently, the Lord put both man and the world under the covenant curse, and the supporting system no longer functioned normally. Man became totally depraved and incapable of exercising lordship. Nevertheless, God sovereignly bound himself to his fallen creature, and made a new, redemptive covenant in order to redeem fallen man and creation, so that the original purpose for creation might be fulfilled. In essence, God ordered them again to continue the creation mandate under the curse and to use the created material as supportive means. In this way, God continued to be their sustainer.

In the process of redemptive history in Scripture, tithing was first introduced at the time of Abraham, who voluntarily rendered a tithe to Melchizedek, the priest of Yahweh, who brought him into the land of Canaan and became his covenant Lord. The tithe was an expression of his faith that God had given him the victory in war. It is not known how and where Abraham learned about tithing. There is no biblical evidence that God either created the tithing institution or ordered Abraham or his covenant people to render him a tithe prior to this. We do know from extrabiblical sources that tithing was widely imposed as a tax by royalty or cultic authorities in the nations of the ancient Near Eastern world, and even by the people in the ancient Asian world, such as the Chinese and the Koreans.[4] An analysis of biblical references in the Pentateuch, the foundation of all biblical

---

4. See Arthur V. Babbs, *The Law of the Tithe as Set Forth in the Old Testament: Illustrated, Explained and Enforced from Biblical and Extra-Biblical Sources* (New York: Fleming H. Revell, 1912); Henry Lansdell, *The Sacred Tenth or Studies in Tenth-Giving Ancient and Modern* (Grand Rapids: Baker, 1955); In Whan Kim, "An Analysis and Evaluation of the Practice of the Korean Protestant Church from the Perspective of the Biblical Tithe Law" (PhD diss., University of Wales, 2000).

law, shows that Yahweh, as covenant Lord, adopted and transformed the tithe system of the ancient world as a means by which his people might recognize him as the true owner of creation and learn to participate in their God-given mission. However, it is not known when or who initiated this tithe system, or what kind of process was behind its formation as a fixed practice.

As a voluntary expression of faith, the tithe became a covenantal obligation when Jacob made a vow to give a tithe of the blessings of God in return for God's faithfulness to the covenant commitment given at Bethel (Gen. 28:10–22). Jacob was one of the patriarchs from whom the people of Israel originated, and he represented his descendants before the covenant Lord. Hence, his vow was not personal, but representative for his descendants, and laid a foundation for the Lord of the covenant to stipulate tithing as a covenant institution for his people in subsequent redemptive history.

Tithing as an Official Covenant Institution

When Yahweh redeemed the descendants of Abraham from Egyptian bondage, he made a covenant with them at Mount Sinai. God made them his possession and appointed them to be to him "a kingdom of priests and a holy nation" (Ex. 19:6) for the corrupted and cursed world. In this way, he called them to participate in his mission to carry out his redemptive purpose for the world. God gave them a body of laws when he made the covenant with them at Sinai. He stipulated the tithe law as one of the ceremonial or cultic laws that governed the ritual life of his people in the land of Canaan, and sanctified the tithe as his own. He also sanctioned it with blessings and curses. In this stipulation, each family of the people of God, living in the land of Canaan that God conquered and gave them as an inheritance, was to take a tithe from the crops and animals and render it to God. The Levites and the priests were exempted because God gave them no land, but instead he gave them the tithe as their wages for living. God gave the tithe of the people to the Levites and gave a tithe from Levites to the priests. The priests alone were exempted from tithing, since they represented God.

God commanded that tithes must be exact and holy, as all tithe offerings were his own possession. Therefore, God appointed the Levites, the holy priestly tribe chosen to administer the cultic system, to collect and take charge of the tithe and to safeguard its sanctity. He gave the Levites and priests his tithe as their wages for their holy service. He enacted the tithe to be used as one supportive means among many—such as firstfruits offerings, wave offerings, and cereal offerings—for those who carried out his mission work.

In this way, the tithing institution—which was introduced into redemptive history as an expression of Abraham's faith, allegiance, and voluntary commitment to Yahweh, his covenant suzerain—became an official covenantal institution, a fixed order to govern the life of his people in the land of Canaan. It came with a divine sanction of blessing and curse, so that they might use it to fulfill the mission that the Lord imposed upon them when the covenant was enacted at Sinai. Exegetical study of the biblical references to the tithe in the Pentateuch demonstrates that three functions are embedded in this institution.[5]

First, it is *covenantal.* When the people of God obey the law and take a tithe from their earnings in the land, it demonstrates that the real owner is Yahweh, their covenant Lord. Hence, the sincere and faithful practice of tithing is a living expression of the covenant relationship between the offering and the Lord, deepening the relationship between God and his people, teaching them to fear Yahweh, and engraving his sovereign ownership on their land, possessions, and lives. None of the Israelites, except the priests who represented God, were exempt. It was a compulsory obligation for all.

Second, it is *cultic* or *ceremonial.* The covenant Lord, Yahweh, as the owner of the tithe, wrote the tithe law into the system of cultic or ceremonial law, indicating it to be one of many sacrificial offerings, together with burnt offerings and sacrifices, special gifts, votive offerings, freewill offerings, and firstlings of herd and flock. It was regarded as one of the heave offerings to God, cultic or ceremonial in nature. God stipulated that the annual tithe be brought to the central temple

---

5. For detailed exegesis and discussion, see Kim, "An Analysis and Evaluation," 123–84.

in Jerusalem, to be used for cultic purposes, to sanctify and maintain worship in his theocratic kingdom. The tithe was to be used for the maintenance of the temple, for the wages of priests and Levites, and for the festal meals of the cultic feasts. God further stipulated the sanctity and administration of tithes to make this institution ceremonial. Therefore, it was essential for the people of God to meet the requirements of its form, method, and use, and to observe tithing law strictly. Even slight alteration or negligence was regarded as violating the holiness of God.

Third, it is *theocratic*. God stipulated the tithe be used for the welfare of the people in the theocratic kingdom. During the three festivals of Passover, Harvest, and Tabernacles, when the people gathered at the temple of God to worship, he permitted them to use his own tithe for festal meals. At this festal table, both poor and rich, high and low social classes, cultic officers and lay people, men and women, and servants and their masters, sat together in the presence of their covenant Lord, and God shared his tithe for their blessing. In this way, the tithe identified all the people of God as equal, and strengthened the unity of the covenant community. The triennial tithe was to be brought to a designated place instead of to the temple, and to be used by travelers, widows, orphans, and Levites who had no wealth. This use of the tithe enhanced the welfare of the theocratic kingdom, so that the grace of the covenant Lord permeated the life of the different social classes and so that all might benefit equally and live in happiness.

We can call this system the *Pentateuch tithing institution*. It was foundational, corresponding to the nature and function of the Pentateuch in canonical Christian Scripture.

Tithing in the Old Testament

An analysis of the biblical references to tithing in the rest of the Old Testament reveals that the fundamental nature and function of the Pentateuchal institution was not altered by addition or deletion, but maintained throughout the history of the people of God in the land of Canaan.

However, the Israelites were not faithful in keeping the tithe law and often neglected to practice it. And when they did tithe, they often did so with a wrong motivation, showing reverence to God formally, but not in substance. Their lavish and frequent offerings of tithes in the time of Amos were insincere (Amos 4:4), and in Malachi's day negligence of tithing was the object of God's covenant lawsuit and condemnation. From the perspective of the prophetic writings, God regarded his people's departure from his ordinances as a departure from the covenant relationship with him. Consequently, Malachi brought up the issue of the tithe in answering their question as to how they could return to God (Mal. 3:6–12). His call to tithe scrupulously was an appeal to recover the broken covenant relationship. God considered it to be robbery when his people did not give him tithes and offerings according to the regulations. Malachi's message was proclaimed during the absence of Nehemiah, who led the reconstruction of the city wall of Jerusalem, the city of God, in which the temple was rebuilt, during the postexilic period. The people habitually neglected the tithes and other offerings for the temple. The robbery of God's possession, as Malachi put it, was a sin against him, and he urged them to repent and resume observance of the ordinance sincerely, and to make his storehouse full. He guaranteed blessings to those who would do this, and curses to those who would not. To make the promise sure, he even put himself under a human test (Mal. 3:10–12). In this way, God reconfirmed that keeping the tithing law was a matter of life and death for his people, and that it was God's system of support for those engaged in his mission.

This form of robbery was intensified by the Pharisees under the guise of strictly observing the sanctity and scrupulousness of tithing from the postexilic time onward.[6] Their regulations required tithing beyond the stipulations of the law. In this way, the people actually paid less than the tithe they had to pay according to the Old Testament ordinances. This was highly skillful theft. During his earthly ministry, Jesus confronted the Pharisaic attitude toward tithing. They strictly observed it and regulated when, what, and how to

6. Kim, "An Analysis and Evaluation," 217.

tithe, diversifying the kinds of tithes. They were also boastful of the strict observation of their own regulations, even though in the eyes of Jesus they were a distortion of the laws of the Pentateuch, and did not conform to what it stipulated. Jesus rebuked their hypocritical practices and emphasized conformity to the Pentateuch tithing institution in its substantial principle and purpose.

However, this does not mean that during his earthly ministry Jesus ordained the continuation of the Pentateuch tithe institution under the new covenant. He fulfilled the old covenant in terms of obedience to its laws as the second Adam, and its eschatological culmination did not occur until his death and resurrection. Jesus lived under the old covenant, and the Pentateuch institution was still effective during his earthly ministry. This was, however, preparatory, provisional, typological, and temporary, and awaited the coming of the Messiah in whom its reality was to be found. It foreshadowed the reality to appear when Jesus fulfilled the covenants in their entirety through his obedience, and ushered in the new eschatological era.

Fulfillment in the Redemptive Ministry of Christ

Jesus fulfilled and finalized the previous covenants and introduced a new, living, and eternal covenant. The covenants were completed in the person, life, death, and ministry of the Messiah, the incarnate God, through his once-for-all obedience to their requirements as the second Adam. Jesus accomplished the divine purpose of redemption, renewing the fallen creation, fulfilling its divine purpose, and glorifying the Creator.

As the one mediator, Jesus abolished the civil laws of the old theocratic kingdom and the external form and procedure of the ceremonial laws. Only the substantial principle, purpose, and function embedded in the ordinances of the older covenants continued under the new covenant. The tithe law is no exception. Jesus offered himself to God, the owner of creation, as the once-for-all tithe, representing not only the elect of God, but also their possessions, and he redeemed them. The offering of a tenth, a symbol of the whole, and people's bringing it to the temple became meaningless. The land of Canaan and the theocratic kingdom were universalized in Jesus. A material building is no longer the temple of God, since Jesus himself, the incarnate God, is the temple. The tabernacle/temple is not erected by man, but by Jesus, living in the redeemed people of God. The priestly tribe and system have been abolished; in Christ, all are priests of Jesus, the great high priest. He laid the foundation for the redemption of the elect of God and established the eschatological kingdom, promised by God the Creator and Redeemer. No one is to be judged anymore by what one eats or drinks, or with regard to observance of a religious festival, new moon, or Sabbath day (Col. 2:16). As the apostle Paul declared, the old creation has gone, and the new has been inaugurated here and now in Christ (the "already"). Nevertheless, the old age has not entirely passed away, and the new age will not come in its fullness until the return of Christ (the "not yet"). There is a tension between the two ages, which are not strictly consecutive, but overlapping; spiritual warfare is ongoing in this age between Jesus, as the risen Lord, and Satan, the defeated evil power. God has given Jesus the kingdom established through his finished work, so that he may bind and cast out the evil power and its followers from the new heaven and the new earth, bringing consummation when he comes again to this earth. At the end time, he will hand over the consummated kingdom to God. It is his mission.

How is the eschatological mission of the cosmic exalted Lord, who reigns over his kingdom at the right hand of God's throne, accomplished? By him alone or through his people? He associates his people with his mission under the new covenant, commissioning them to witness from Jerusalem to the end of the world (Acts 1:8) and charging them to preach the gospel, to make disciples of all nations, to baptize in the name of the Father, Son, and Holy Spirit, and to teach them to obey everything he has commanded. His own commitment is to be with them to the end of the age, investing them with his heavenly authority and empowering them with his Spirit (Matt. 28:19–20).

The core of this commission, given at the ascension, can be summed up in two commands: to make and multiply disciples (to fill the earth with children of parents, but also with children of God) and to subdue the earth—what God the Creator commanded the first man and woman to do, under the covenant of creation. It is closely associated with the first mandate to multiply the people of God on earth, reintroducing the terms of the creational commission. The second is closely associated with the mandate to subdue the earth, since Jesus' words are those of the King of the kings, invested with the authority of the heavenly Father. The royal words proclaimed by his disciples call all nations to be subject to him, transforming their lives and culture, and participating in subduing the earth for his kingdom. Jesus Christ's commission is the renewal and reinstallation of the original creation mandate in accordance with the nature of the order of the new creation. Through Christ's finished work of redemption, the goal of the covenant of creation has been reached, and the new creation, the renewal and glorification of the creation, has come. However, its consummation awaits the second coming of the risen Lord and Redeemer. In the interim, his new covenant people participate in the mission of the Lord. We can call the original mandate the *creation mandate* and the reinstituted mandate the *redemption mandate*.[7] There is continuity and discontinuity between the two. In the creation mandate, the marriage institution is the means of multiplying human life; developing culture and its sanctity are the means of subduing the earth. However, in the redemption mandate, in addition to these, gospel preaching is the means of multiplying the people of God and subduing the earth.

7. The creation mandate is traditionally called the cultural mandate, while the redemption mandate is commonly called the Great Commission. Ralph F. Boersma calls the Great Commission the gospel mandate: "The Cultural Mandate and the Gospel Mandate: A Historical and Biblical Study" (ThM thesis, Westminster Theological Seminary, Philadelphia, 1974). However, the designation of the cultural mandate cannot embrace both the responsibilities to multiply on the earth and to subdue it under the covenant of creation. It is only related to the latter. For this reason, a new designation is needed for the mandate. If the unity between the creation mandate and the Great Commission and between creation and redemption is accepted, the designation *redemption mandate* for the Great Commission demonstrates the unity between the two. For the argument on behalf of the unity between the creation mandate and the Great Commission, see Norman Shepherd, "The Covenant Context for Evangelism," in *The New Testament Student and Theology*, ed. John H. Skilton (Nutley, NJ: Presbyterian and Reformed, 1976), 51–75.

Jesus called his people to him and covenanted with them as the temple of God, his body and kingdom, the church. The corporate community of his people is his agent to implement his mission of multiplying redeemed people. To carry it out, a support system is needed for those who are entrusted with mission, in conformity with the new age that Jesus ushered in.

If the requirement of the ceremonial law was accomplished by Christ's thorough obedience and its external forms lost their reason for existence, then its substance, including the tithe law in its nature, function, and purpose, continues, since Jesus came not to abolish but to fulfill the law. The external forms are discontinued in the new age, but the Lord commands his people to practice and teach even "the least of these commandments" of the law (Matt. 5:19) definitely and dynamically. The law's external forms are transformed into a new order for the people of God under the new covenant; the Pentateuch tithing institution is no exception in this regard: its external form is renewed in a way appropriate to the nature of the new age.

The Pauline Strategy of Systematic Tithing

In the post-resurrection era, the risen Lord called servants to participate in his mission, the apostle Paul being the most prominent of these. He undertook three missionary journeys, aware of the fact that the Lord had set him apart as the apostle to the Gentiles. A prominent ex-Pharisee, Paul fully understood the mystery of Christ, since he encountered the risen Lord on the road to Damascus. Later he planted churches wherever he visited, and appointed many servants for these communities. He began his missionary work in a self-supporting way, covering his living and other expenses from his income as a tentmaker. His gospel preaching was so successful that, as time passed, his income could not meet the financial needs in planting new churches in various locations, supporting the teachers he appointed, assisting the poor, and relieving people who suffered from famine and other disasters. So he requested that the churches he planted support him. Their financial support was also much needed when the mother church in Jerusalem suffered famine. This also signified the unity between the mother church, which consisted mainly of Jewish Christians, and the Pauline churches, with mainly Gentile Christians. Paul was aware of the circumstantial importance of the collection project, and with his apostolic authority enacted a financial system for the missional responsibilities of the people of God under the new covenant. He exhorted them to participate in his apostolic mission by giving their resources to support teachers and relieve the burdens of the saints and the poor, imposing financial obligations for the sake of God's kingdom. He finally set up systematic giving as a fixed financial support system for the churches to carry out the God-given mission in administering the kingdom of God (1 Cor. 16:1–2).

Although Paul did not use the term *tithe* or any related words, various expressions are found in his writings, such as *logeia* (1 Cor. 16:1, 2), *apolotes* (Rom. 12:8; 2 Cor. 1:12; 8:2; 9:11, 13), *charis* (1 Cor. 16:3; 2 Cor. 8:4ff.), *koinonia* (Rom. 15:26; 2 Cor. 8:4), *diakonia* (Rom. 15:31; 2 Cor. 8:4), and *eulogia* (2 Cor. 9:5). Each of these words reflects aspects of the contribution, and they collectively expound his teaching on the financial obligations that Christians should bear for the church and the needy. However, when he set up systematic giving, he alluded to the nature and function of the Pentateuch tithing institution; he applies it in the new age as a support system for the administration of the kingdom of God until Jesus comes again. Although no fixed amount is set, every Christian is to participate in the collection project, regardless of his or her financial resources (2 Cor. 8:2). Under the new covenant, tithing is to be regular, on the first day of the week, the Lord's day, the new Sabbath. The offering is to be systematic, proportional to and in keeping with income, as well as sacrificial, with open-ended generosity, voluntary, in an act of free will and cheerful giving, and without a reluctant spirit or compulsion. Its purpose is to support teachers, provide relief for the saints and the poor, support mission, and spread God's blessings among his people, promoting the welfare of the kingdom. The blessing of God is promised to those who participate in this systematic giving cheerfully.

In the context of the eschatological age, as he learned from the revelation of God, Paul appropriated Pentateuchal tithing with apostolic authority as the means by which Jesus supports his church in mission, carrying out the redemption mandate.[8] Pauline systematic giving is the *biblical tithing institution*—the final, permanent institution in which the spirit and thrust of the Pentateuch institution continue as the support system for those who participate in mission in the eschatological age. Paul used this giving strategy effectively to carry out the redemption mandate. He could plant more churches, deepen the unity between the mother church and other churches, and tighten the bond of love among them. In this way, he set up a model for subsequent generations, demonstrating that appropriate use of his systematic giving system, the biblical tithing institution, is the means that the risen Lord provides for his servants who participate in his mission.

Herbert E. Blair, an American missionary in Korea, who initiated the practice of tithing in the early days of the Korean Protestant churches, compared Pauline systematic giving with the Mosaic tithing system and found that the foundational principles and features of the Mosaic system were clearly reflected in Paul's. He made the case that tithing was embodied in Pauline giving, which he called Paul's Christian tithe.[9]

A Case Study of the Korean Protestant Church

The Korean Protestant churches have a reputation for unprecedented church growth in the history of world missions. There is no doubt among scholars, missionaries, and pastors in Korea that this rapid growth was a fruit of the consistent and systematic application of the "Nevius Method." The application of the biblical tithing institution was the main strategic tool that made this method successful.

8. Keith F. Nickle lists numerous contemporary contributory practices as the background of Paul's collection project for the poor, and argues that Paul "borrowed most heavily for the organization of his collection from the Jewish Temple tax." However, Nickel does not consider the possibility that Paul might have borrowed the substance of the tithe institution from the Old Testament, which he cherished as a Pharisee. See Keith F. Nickle, *The Collection: A Study in Paul's Strategy*, SBT (London: SCM, 1966), 74–99.

9. Herbert E. Blair, *Paul: A Christian Financier* (Seoul: Christian Literature Society of Korea, 1937), 6.

The Nevius Method was a mission policy originated by John Livingston Nevius, a resident missionary in Cheffoo, China, from the Presbyterian Church of the United States of America, in the late nineteenth and the early twentieth centuries. It has been adopted by the Korean Protestant churches since 1896. It consists mainly of three "self" policies—self-support, self-government, and self-propagation—interwoven to make an organic unity centered on self-support. The self-support policy proposes that the indigenous church take care of all the financial responsibilities pertaining to ministry and administration, such as the construction of buildings, salary for pastors and staff, evangelism, and charitable works including medical, educational, and other social action. This policy limited dependence upon foreign mission funds as much as possible. The self-government policy specifies that nationals administer the church; self-propagation means evangelizing fellow countryfolk by their own means. These self-supporting policies in Korea can be illustrated by a detailed report of the strategies of a local mission station in 1912:

1. If a church is to be self-supporting, it should be so from the beginning.
2. Poverty has nothing to do with the question of self-support.
3. No chapels or churches are to be built with foreign funds.
4. No native evangelists or pastors are to be on foreign pay. Why deny the means of grace that puts fiber and sinew into the church and gives it its greatest blessing?[10]

The Nevius Method employed the typical Korean-style Bible study class or conference training system to nourish a spirit of biblical stewardship and produce faithful pastoral and lay leadership.[11] The Bible

10. Harry A. Rhodes, *History of the Korea Mission, Presbyterian Church U.S.A. 1884–1934*, vol. 1 (Seoul: Chosen Mission of the Presbyterian Church U.S.A., 1934), 397.

11. Charles Allen Clark, *The Korean Church and the Nevius Methods* (New York: Fleming H. Revell, 1930), 87. The Korean practice is not like Western-style evangelical revival meetings or intellectual Bible classes. It is a combination of fervent prayer meeting at dawn, exegetical Bible study in the morning, evangelism and

class functioned as a melting pot, and contributed to deepening the participants' biblical knowledge and biblical stewardship. It aimed at building up strong, indigenous, self-supportive Protestant churches in the Korean peninsula. Early missionaries from various Western countries were consistent and systematic in applying the Nevius Method, following the tearful advice of Nevius himself, who had experienced failures due to the inconsistent application of his method to his mission field in China.

Missionaries in Korea found the Nevius Method successful beyond expectation. According to a report on giving, read by Charles Allen Clark, a veteran American missionary in Korea, on the twenty-fifth anniversary of Korean Protestant mission work in 1909, giving in the Korean churches was "nearly 70% *more per member than the church in America gives*. If hospital receipts were not included as they may very well have been, without them the Koreans have given 43% more per member than the church in America has given."[12] This report is astonishing, considering the historical situation in which it was read. In 1909, the year when Japan occupied and annexed Korea by force, Korea was one of the poorest illiterate countries in the world. The Japanese imperial government then confiscated all the possessions of Koreans and persecuted the churches. Despite these circumstances, the churches did not cease to carry out the self-support policy and continued to grow, despite the Japanese persecution.

Tithing emerged in the Korean Protestant churches as an essential and effective strategy for carrying out the self-support policy in difficult circumstances. At first, in the early stage of self-support,

---

helping of neighbors to practice Christian love in the afternoon, and evangelical revival meetings in the evening for six consecutive days. The first such class was held in 1891. After that, it received enthusiastic responses from Christians, some of whom even walked two hundred miles on foot to get there, paying all their expenses to attend the class when there was no public transportation system in Korea. Meetings were held at first in a central place in the districts, but later almost every local church had weeklong classes or conferences once or twice a year. It overwhelmingly contributed to realizing the plan to be self-supporting.

12. Charles Allen Clark, "Financial Items of Interest," in *Quarto Centennial Papers Read before the Korean Mission of the Presbyterian Church in the U.S.A.* (Pyeng Yang, 1909), 121–24 (italics original).

various means of collection were devised. Although tithing was taught by some native leaders and foreign missionaries, it was not initially accepted by the majority of Korean churches. Herbert E. Blair—who later developed a theology of Christian tithing similar to our biblical tithing institution, and who played a decisive role in establishing an official, systematic strategy to carry out the self-support policy— revealed that he was not successful in establishing a regular system of giving in his own mission district in 1915.[13] As time went on, more native leaders and missionaries began to recognize that the establishment of tithing as a regular giving system was a solution for bringing the self-support policy to fruition. They were also influenced by the contemporary worldwide movement to promote systematic giving. In 1929, the 18th General Assembly of the Presbyterian Church in Korea approved a resolution to support the systematic giving movement. Blair, who was then on furlough in America, prepared for and led the movement at the request of the General Assembly. He first researched the Pauline systematic giving strategy and found it to be the application of the Mosaic tithing institution in the new age ushered in by Jesus Christ. He called it the Christian tithe, which is a voluntary "one tenth or more of one's profit," unlike the compulsory exact Mosaic tithe. He defined stewardship as follows:

> Stewardship is a parabolic reinforcement of the principles ruling Christian responsibility and conduct, pictured in terms of master and servant. As to stewardship of time, such problems as observance of the Lord's day emerge. As to occupation, stewardship may result in creating a Volunteer Band for life service. As to general Christian conduct, stewardship demands that the whole of life be dedicated to God as a living sacrifice. . . . In reference to Christian finance, let us emphasize the fact that stewardship systematic giving as taught by Paul, the inspired founder of the Gentile church, calls for all Christians to regard all wealth as a trust from God, to be used for His glory, and that each Christian every Sunday, in a

13. Herbert E. Blair, *Stewardship in Korea* (Seoul: Christian Literature Society of Korea, 1938), 19–22.

systematic way, as is most convenient, should "lay by him in store" through church collections a tenth or more of his profits, "as he may prosper," for the work of the Kingdom of God.[14]

Blair successfully led the movement with vision and conviction to a great revival in the whole church. He wrote two books, *Paul: A Christian Financier* and *Stewardship in Korea*. At that time, many written materials pertaining to stewardship were introduced by missionaries and Korean leaders, who did some translation and some writing, and these materials were used to train church members. The result was that in the two years from 1933 to 1935 the sum total of offerings per person increased 70 percent, and the number of church members increased 87 percent.[15] Although the movement could not be continued beyond 1938, due to the growing persecution of the Japanese imperial government, it contributed to shaping a habit of stewardship in all areas of life by Korean Christians, and to establishing tithing in the life of the churches. The churches, regardless of denomination, became self-supporting, and have continued to practice tithing actively and engage in the mission of God, expanding and glorifying his kingdom inside and outside the country, although some have failed to maintain the original theology of tithing. This practice enables the Korean churches to maintain their self-supporting status and to send out more missionaries to the world than any other country besides the United States.

Conclusion

In conclusion, we should not hesitate to adopt the biblical tithing institution today as a legitimate and appropriate strategy for establishing churches in the mission field as self-supporting communities,

14. Blair, *Stewardship in Korea*, 3.

15. Taek-boo Chun, "Kehwa Sasang-kwa Kaesinkyo-eui Kyungkook Chemin Woondong" [Enlightened thoughts and the Protestant statecraft movement in the enlightenment times], in *Kyeohoe Chechung-eui Yiron-kwa Siljae* [Theories and practices of church finance], ed. Korean Laymen Association (Seoul: Chunmang-sa, 1985), 145.

in societies that are culturally sophisticated or not, materially poor or wealthy, undergoing persecution or enjoying freedom. When missionaries consistently teach with conviction and encourage biblical stewardship by establishing tithing in accordance with the principle of the biblical tithing institution, mission churches soon become self-supporting churches and grow to the maturity of Jesus Christ, so as to effectively fulfill the redemption mandate.

PART 3

COVENANT THEOLOGY AND GLOBAL MISSION VISION

10

Covenantal Missions and the City

Naas Ferreira

Abstract

In the first urban generation in world history, the post-Christian church must face the new and challenging missiological realities of our time.[1] To do this in a relevant and effective way, the church needs to rediscover the biblical paradigm of covenantal mission. This is the only way in which the church, as God's covenant community, can still be part of his *missio Dei* and also be strategically relevant in the constantly changing context in which we live. This article presents the biblical contours of this paradigm and provides a brief introduction to the realities that need to be urgently addressed.

Introduction

Our world is simultaneously experiencing the convergence of a never-ending wave of people migrating to urban centers and a massive shift of Christianity away from its traditional rootedness in the West. We are daily witnessing waves of multicultural and international migrants moving into our cities. At the same time, the center of Christianity has already shifted from its traditional mooring within Western culture. The biggest challenge of our time is for the

---

1. The first urban generation was called "homo urbanis" by Eugene Rubingh, "Mission in an Urban World," *Evangelical Review of Theology* 11.4 (1987): 370.

traditional Christian church, still stuck in the Christendom paradigm, to wake up to this new post-Christian context and actively engage it.

The real challenge confronting the church today is not the fact that millions of people are streaming into the urban centers of the world, but that the church which has been in the city for many years is actually fleeing the city or shrinking and dying. This is happening, not only in isolated situations, but all over the Western world. The mission field was hitherto far away, but now is coming uncomfortably close, and churches in traditionally Christian lands are dying, in the city and elsewhere. It seems that they were not ready for the new challenges that the city presented.[2]

In order to survive, some churches are adopting the techniques of the sales and marketing world, or alternatively they use the therapeutic language of pop psychology, or invest in the environmentalist ideology of planet saving. Others structure leadership in the traditional patterns of their culture.[3] However, they will not be successful. Stuart Foster is adamant that Old Testament covenant missiology provides both a model and a challenge in this context of change. He claims that Christians who seek to think missiologically about God's world and to act for him in it need to be sure they are shaped by covenant.[4]

The Christian church needs a missiological paradigm that is faithful to the message of the Scriptures, as well as to the context in which people find themselves today. This is also true for tomorrow's theological education.[5] The church needs to rediscover the biblical paradigm of covenantal mission. David Smith clearly formulates the challenge of our time: "At a time when the whole world has become 'one immense city', theology surely risks the complete loss of whatever credibility it still retains if it fails to meet this central challenge of our times."[6]

2. Ray Bakke, *The Urban Christian* (Downers Grove, IL: InterVarsity Press, 1987), 61.

3. Stuart J. Foster, "The Missiology of Old Testament Covenant," *International Bulletin of Missionary Research* 34.4 (2010): 207.

4. Foster, "The Missiology of Old Testament Covenant," 207.

5. See Wonsuk Ma, "The Theological and Missional Formation in the Context of 'New Christianity,'" *The Ecumenical Review* 66.1 (2014): 53–64.

6. David W. Smith, *Seeking a City with Foundations: Theology for an Urban World* (Nottingham: Inter-Varsity Press, 2011), 25.

This article presents the biblical contours of the paradigm of covenantal mission. It will endeavor to integrate it with the biblical essence of an urban theology, and also give a brief introduction to specific realities that urgently need to be addressed.

From the Garden of Creation to the Babel City of Man

The Beginning: God, Covenant, Creation—Life in Shalom

The first pages of biblical revelation confirm that God intended a formalized relationship with his creation, especially with man created in his image. Bob Wielenga puts it clearly: "Creation was an act of God's will, flowing from his being, and an expression of his love, aimed at his covenant goal."[7] In this way, covenant precedes creation.[8] With creation, the history of God's covenant begins.[9] Man was created with a specific purpose in mind. God created man in his image and gave him a creational[10] cultural mandate (Gen. 1:27–28).[11] As the crown (ruler) of God's creation, man was given the ability to unlock the hidden potential invested in creation. Man was destined to serve God by receiving and serving in a creation of abundance. His task was to faithfully develop it to its fullest potential. In this way, God made man the custodian of life in the world he had created. Man's cultural ability and the strength to do the work were also gifts received from

7. Bob Wielenga, "Covenant and Mission: Mission's Covenantal Character," [6], (2001), http://www.academia.edu/12407997/Covenant_and_mission_Missions _covenantal_character.

8. Walter Vogels, quoted by Wright, also sees a covenantal pattern in the pre-fall relationship between God and creation (including humankind), even though the term itself is not used in Genesis 1–2. See Christopher J. H. Wright, *The Mission of God: Unlocking the Bible's Grand Narrative* (Downers Grove, IL: InterVarsity Press, 2001), 326.

9. Bob Wielenga and Adrio König, "Zending: waarom? Verbond als antwoord," *Die Skriflig* 33.2 (1999): 255–71.

10. Bennie J. Van der Walt, *When African and Western Cultures Meet: From Confrontation to Appreciation* (Potchefstroom: Institute for Contemporary Christianity in Africa, 2006), 2.

11. Culture is the *human element* of creation. See Paul de Neui, "Christian *Communitas* in the *Missio Dei*: Living Faithfully in the Tension between Cultural Osmosis and Alienation," *Common Ground Journal* 9.2 (2012): 48–67.

God. His ultimate goal in life was to live and work to the glory of God. Covenant clearly entails duty.[12]

The biblical word that best encapsulates the world and life as God intended it to be, is *shalom*.[13] It is used repeatedly in the Old Testament to describe the ultimate and perfect relational (covenantal) life given to man as a precious gift and a cultural task (duty) in the beginning.[14] The first chapter of Genesis ends with the conclusion that everything was made very good. There can be little doubt that God's purpose for man and all creation, as well as man's God-given ability to fulfill God's purpose, were established and revealed in the beginning. The opening account of creation portrays God working toward a goal, completing it with satisfaction, and resting, content with the result.[15] God aspires to live in a perfect relationship with his creation, including man, through covenant and its practical realization.[16] All of this is part of the *missio Dei*. Mission is the way in which God reaches his goal on earth in cooperation with his people. It is the external foundation of the covenant, while covenant is the internal foundation of mission. This implies that from the beginning God took man as a covenantal partner for the realization of his creational purpose. The way in which God would do this through cooperation could be called mission (*zending*).[17]

The Fall of Man and the Culture of Self-interest

The third chapter of Genesis reveals a sad and tragic fact. The crown of God's creation sinned against his Creator. The results were devastating. The reality of the fall (Gen. 3) impacted negatively on man's ability to create culture and to continue living in shalom. Adam

12. Terrance L. Tiessen, "The Salvation of the Unevangelized in the Light of God's Covenants," *Evangelical Review of Theology* 36.2 (2012): 236.

13. Robert C. Linthicum, *Building a People of Power: Equipping Churches to Transform Their Communities* (Waynesboro, GA: World Vision, 2005), 4.

14. *Shalom* is used a total of 397 times in the Hebrew Bible. It captures the Hebrew vision of human society, the nonhuman world, and even the environment in an integrated and relational whole.

15. Wright, *Mission of God*, 63.

16. A. König, quoted in Wielenga, "Covenant and Mission," [6].

17. Wielenga and König, *Zending: waarom?*, 264.

and Eve, listening to Satan, no longer wanted to be *imago Dei* (image of God), but chose to be *sicut Deus* ("like God": Gen. 3:5). Whereas the original intent was that man should focus in service on God and his perfect will for creation, man now focused exclusively on himself and his own selfish desires. In this way, man totally and willfully distanced himself from God's covenant. Since a culture of self-interest cannot be part of God's perfect world, man had to leave the garden of God. Through sin, man lost shalom, and his culture-making became the self-interest of an egocentric being living in a cursed and broken world (Gen. 3:17). Although man was intended to be a godly blessing to the entire creation, he became a curse after the fall. In a destructive way, he now exploited creation for his selfish interests. This would become the tragic history of mankind. The sin of the first humans became the sin of their offspring and eventually of all humanity. The first human born into this world, Cain, murdered his own brother. He would also be the first builder of a city (Gen. 4:17).

In Genesis 3:9, the loving heart of the one and only Creator, the God of the covenant, is revealed. This single verse connects the eternal counsel of God (Eph. 1:3–4) with the tragedy of fallen man trying to hide from God.[18] It confirms the mission of God and introduces the first glimpses of the gospel of salvation. God does not destroy man, but seeks to save him. God will honor his covenant, and it will continue. The covenant relationship was designed to lead to the peace of shalom—a comprehensive, wholesome well-being extending throughout a now-marred creation.[19] The stark realities of life in a cursed and broken world are clearly communicated to man. Life within a covenantal relationship with God will continue, but it will

---

18. The eternal counsel of God is called the *pactum salutis*. It is defined by Wielenga as God's eternal counsel wherein he made an intra-Trinitarian covenant with the purpose of rescuing the elect. Wielenga, however, is of the opinion that "this theology does not have a prominence in the biblical material" (Wielenga and König, "Zending: waarom?," 258). Flip Buys, however, is adamant that there is no doctrine that gives more motivation and perseverance and all the glory to God in missions than this doctrine of God's eternal counsel of peace ("Pactum Salutis" [unpub. class notes, North-West University, Potchefstroom, 2012]). Cf. John V. Fesko, *The Trinity and the Covenant of Redemption* (Fearn, UK: Christian Focus, 2016).

19. Foster, *Missiology of Old Testament Covenant*, 206.

not be easy. The battle lines of the continued spiritual war between the people of the covenant and the enemies of God are drawn. The promise of salvation and victory, however, is confirmed.

Collective Culture and the City of Man

Culture-making naturally involves seeking and establishing contact and interaction with other human beings. Man was endowed by God with creativity, and the cultural mandate eventually led, in its unfolding and development, to the building of cities.[20] Man's cultural cooperation produced new products and procedures, and led to the first city that was built by Cain (Gen. 4:17). The city constitutes the corporate cultural endeavor of people working and living together. It is far more than structures being built; it is a lifestyle and an intentionally chosen mentality.

When individual culture is flawed by a sinful heart, this will also be reflected in any corporate cultural endeavor. In this way, individual sin will also become corporate sin, and eventually sin is institutionalized. Sin is not only the wrong people do; it also becomes part of the structures that they erect. In this way, the establishment of a city was not only the natural product of man's cultural endeavors; it also became the collective source of opposition to God. The early history of mankind is recorded in the Bible with the sad comment about man's continued wickedness and God's ultimate regret for creating man (Gen. 6). This is not what God intended, and he shows his anger by destroying the world. True to the covenant, he also rescues the family of Noah. According to Wright, the narrative of the covenant that God made with Noah in Genesis 8:15–9:17 is the first explicit reference to covenant making in the biblical text.[21] God is not only committed to his covenant people, but also to the created order and to the preservation of life on the planet. Although we live in a cursed world, we also live on a covenanted earth.[22] God keeps creation functioning for the benefit of the covenant.[23]

20. Rubingh, *Mission in an Urban World*, 372.
21. Wright, *Mission of God*, 326.
22. Wright, *Mission of God*, 326.
23. Wielenga and König, *Zending: waarom?*, 259.

The wickedness of mankind continued after the flood (Gen. 7–10) and the culture of self-interest was willfully demonstrated in building the city of Babel (Gen. 11). In this corporate cultural endeavor, the sin of the first humans in paradise became the sin of humanity. Mankind united in opposition to God and his purpose for man (Gen. 11:6). Babel, continued in the spirit of Babylon, became the biblical symbol of mankind's enmity and cultural opposition to God. In this way, Babylon, introduced in the book of Genesis, became the biblical symbol of a city given over to Satan.[24] It became synonymous with all that is dark and evil in a city.[25] From there on, worldly cultures throughout history are described by the cities that represent their particular culture. The sin of man became the sin of mankind.

God used the confusion of languages at Babel as a means to pursue his original plan of cultural diversity.[26] He destroyed man-made unity that opposed his will. By sending people away to populate the face of the earth, God established different peoples with different cultural expressions. The sad reality of this dispersion is the fact that all cultures throughout the world are at heart infected with the sinful spirit of Babylon. Man's culture of opposition was realized in the formation of the diverse cultures of the world. The culture of opposition to God will eventually dominate the culture of all the cities of the world.

From Ur of the Chaldeans to Jerusalem

A New Beginning—God's Covenantal Purpose Confirmed

When God called Abram, he and his family were part of the dominant culture of Ur of the Chaldeans.[27] Like all the other cultures

24. Robert C. Linthicum, *City of God, City of Satan: A Biblical Theology of the Urban Church* (Grand Rapids: Zondervan, 1991), 24.

25. Linthicum, *City of God, City of Satan*, 24–25. Babylon is painted in Scripture as a bureaucratic, self-serving, and dehumanizing social system with economics geared to benefit its privileged and exploit its poor, with politics of oppression and with a religion that ignores covenant with God and deifies power and wealth. See Isa. 14:5–21; Jer. 50:2–17; 51:6–10; Dan. 3:1–7; Rev. 17:1–6; 18:2–19, 24.

26. Van der Walt, *When African and Western Cultures Meet*, 3.

27. Ur was an ancient city and district in Sumer, southern Mesopotamia. It was situated on a former channel of the Euphrates River in what is now southern Iraq.

formed after the dispersion of Genesis 11, this culture was also infected with the spirit of Babylon. It was a culture opposing God. Although man was not focused on God anymore, the God of the covenant was still focused on man. In his mission of mercy and grace, God again reached out to mankind. Abram's calling was part of a new beginning, not only for him and his family, but also in God's plan of salvation for creation. The original covenant purpose was again confirmed when Abram and his family were called to distance themselves from Ur of the Chaldeans. They were called to leave this city because it represented a way of life dishonoring God. Although God was particularistic in choosing Abram and his descendants, his work was universalistic in that it embraced all peoples.[28] Wright calls the covenant with Abraham the most significant of the biblical covenants from a missiological perspective.[29] The family of Abram had to demonstrate in the midst of the world and its cultures how to be a nation that depends for its identity, security, and very existence on the Creator of the world. The purpose of God's covenant with Abraham was to form a missionary community as an instrument through which God would bless the nations. It was not focused on the development of a community within which God would exclusively do his saving work.[30]

Just as Babel was the cultural embodiment of independence from God, so Israel was to be the embodiment of dependence on God. God's intent for mankind in the beginning would be realized in the

---

One of the oldest cities of Mesopotamia, it was settled sometime in the fourth millennium B.C. In the twenty-fifth century B.C., it was the capital of southern Mesopotamia under its first dynasty. Although it later declined, it again became important around the twenty-second century B.C. It is mentioned in the Bible (as Ur of the Chaldeans) as the early home of Hebrew patriarch Abraham (*ca.* 2000 B.C.). In subsequent centuries, it was captured and destroyed by many groups, including the Elamites and Babylonians. Nebuchadnezzar II restored it in the sixth century B.C. Excavations, especially in the 1920s and 1930s, uncovered remains of great archaeological value. See http://www.answers.com/topic/ur.

28. Roger E. Hedlund, *The Mission of the Church in the World* (Grand Rapids: Baker Book House, 1985), 33.

29. Wright, *Mission of God*, 327.

30. Tiessen, "The Salvation of the Unevangelized," 240.

life of Abraham and his descendants. God started a new *communitas* that eventually, through Israel, as the people of God, would become the New Testament church, the bride of Jesus Christ.[31] This was the start of the people of God as the shalom community, in which shalom would be the hope of Israel and the early church, its vision of what the world would someday be.[32] As God's people, Abraham and his family demonstrated this future reality in their daily life on earth. This was the ecclesiological starting point of God's redemptive work in a broken world.

It is clear from biblical history that Abraham and his son Isaac, in obedience to God's call, never again settled in a city or became part of any popular culture. In their cultural life as pilgrims in their world, God used them to proclaim the kingdom of the one true God in this fallen world. The early history of the patriarchs emphasizes the calling of God's people to be in the world, but not to become a part of it. God wanted them, as his chosen people, and his church of all ages, to grasp his intention for the whole of humanity. As his people, they had to understand the sad reality of the fallen world as it really is; and while living in this reality, they had to be different in their way of life, in order to draw the world toward what God intends it to be.[33] God's covenant community was called to be part of the *missio Dei*. The election of Israel was fundamentally missional, not just soteriological.[34] God's plan for Abraham was continued in the history of the people of Israel and would also become the mission of the New Testament church.

Although the patriarchs never settled in a city, Genesis 14 briefly introduces an important theme that would increasingly dominate biblical revelation about the city, as well as the covenant history of God's

---

31. See de Nieu, "Christian *Communitas* in the *Missio Dei*," 60. *Communitas* is a bond of oneness beyond ordinary community, an actual communion together that does not destroy individuality but brings alive the full gifts of each participant. In this new *communitas*, God wants to demonstrate to the world how he intended life to be.

32. Linthicum, *Building a People of Power*, 4.

33. Linthicum, 4.

34. Wright, *Mission of God*, 263.

people. Abraham met Melchizedek, called the king of Salem[35] and a priest of God Most High. This meeting happened after he rescued Lot from the hands of rival kings. One of these was Amraphel, the king of Babylonia (Gen. 14:1). This introduced the reality of the radical enmity between the two cities (cultures), Jerusalem and Babylon. It is clear from Hebrews 11:8–10, however, that Abraham knew what God expected, and was willing to honor God and obey his command.[36] He truly became the father of all believers.

Egypt, the Cradle of a People: From Chosen Family to Covenant Nation

The covenant history of God's redemptive work follows the contours of human history. Within a concrete historical setting, God prepares the way for the family of Jacob to move to the land of Goshen in Egypt.[37] Although the family of Jacob was originally separated from the people and the culture of Egypt, they were systematically absorbed by the dominant culture of Egypt. Paul de Neui calls this cultural process *osmosis*.[38] In world history, it is always a threat to the people of God. Over time, the family of Jacob became the nation of Israel, but also slaves in Egypt. Not much is revealed about this process of absorption, but the stark and sad reality and its consequences are clear. We can conclude that Egypt as a culture also harbored the spirit of Babylon. It was an instrument in the hand of Satan to destroy God's shalom community by enslaving it to the self-interest culture of Egypt.[39] The spirit of Babylon continued in the culture of Egypt.

---

35. Genesis 14:18—Melchizedek, the king of Salem (later called Jerusalem).

36. Hebrews 11:8–10: "By faith Abraham obeyed when he was called to go out to a place that he was to receive as an inheritance. And he went out, not knowing where he was going. By faith he went to live in the land of promise, as in a foreign land, living in tents with Isaac and Jacob, heirs with him of the same promise. For he was looking forward to the city that has foundations, whose designer and builder is God."

37. The Bible tells us the history of Jacob and Joseph and how God prepared the way for Joseph to be the "king" of Egypt in a time of world famine.

38. See de Nieu, "Christian *Communitas* in the *Missio Dei*," 56. Osmosis is to become absorbed by, become part of, or to be drawn into something else.

39. When Joseph was a leader in Egypt, he served the world in a time of need

God rescued his people from Egypt because he still intended them to be part of his *missio Dei*. Although Egypt represented urban world culture opposing God, God used it as the cradle for the birth and growth of his chosen people. He could not use Israel as his redemptive instrument focused on the rest of the world while they were in bondage as slaves in Egypt. The entire rescue mission, vividly portrayed in the book of Exodus, is a testimony of the kingdom/kingship of God proclaimed to the dominant culture of the time. Everything that happened during this period became known to the other nations. Rescue from Egypt symbolized the way that God saved his people from spiritual oppression and slavery to be his shalom community in the world. He molded a family in the furnace of Egyptian slavery to become a nation he could use to proclaim his kingship throughout the world of that time.

Saved from Egypt and Brought to Jerusalem

God's purpose in rescuing Israel from Egypt was to bring them to Jerusalem. Jerusalem was not primarily a concrete place, but rather a relational culture—a way of life focused on God again—as in the beginning. It was not only a place for Israel to stay, but a beacon of light to be visible throughout the world. That is the reason why the promised land of Canaan was strategic in the world. God established a spiritual Jerusalem in opposition to the spiritual Babylon. Israel's theocentric purpose was, for the sake of the world, to be the recipient and guardian of special revelation, the channel for the Redeemer to enter human history as God's servant and witness to the nations.[40] The history of Israel unveils the continuation of God's involvement with the nations. The God of Israel is the Creator and Lord of the world. For this reason, Israel understands its own history in continuity with the history of the nations, not as a separate history.[41]

On Israel's way to Jerusalem, God revealed his perfect will and

---

(Gen. 41–42), but after his death, the culture of Egypt became self-centered and enslaving for the children of Israel.

40. Hedlund, *Mission of the Church in the World*, 42.

41. David J. Bosch, *Transforming Mission: Paradigm Shifts in Theology of Mission* (Maryknoll, NY: Orbis Books, 1991), 18.

his covenant to his people at Mount Sinai. The Ten Commandments are the embodiment of shalom, life as God intended it to be from the beginning.[42] The cultural application of the law is worked out extensively in the books of Moses. This is the relational culture that God intended for his people as a message of hope. In a world that was and still is darkened by the unholy spirit of Babylon, Jerusalem was destined to be a shining light. The promise of shalom is clearly stated in Leviticus 26:3–6, 12–13:

> If you walk in my statutes and observe my commandments and do them, then I will give you your rains in their season, and the land shall yield its increase, and the trees of the field shall yield their fruit. Your threshing shall last to the time of the grape harvest, and the grape harvest shall last to the time for sowing. And you shall eat your bread to the full and dwell in your land securely. I will give *peace* [shalom] in the land, and you shall lie down, and none shall make you afraid. And I will remove harmful beasts from the land, and the sword shall not go through your land. . . . And I will walk among you and will be your God, and you shall be my people. I am the LORD your God, who brought you out of the land of Egypt, that you should not be their slaves. And I have broken the bars of your yoke and made you walk erect.

Before they entered the promised land, God warned his people about the cultures of the people living in Canaan and the negative influence that they could have on Israel. Israel was about to come into contact with peoples and cultures that were foreign to them. They were about to receive things that they had not worked for and cities to live in.[43]

---

42. Studying the books of Moses, it becomes clear that the Ten Commandments have practical implications for every human relationship. Our relationships to God, other people, and even creation as a whole are governed by the commandments. This is as God intended life to be from the beginning.

43. God gave his people cities as a covenantal gift. They were signs of God's grace in the present, and their walls were signs of God's security for the future. See Harvie Conn and Manuel Ortiz, *Urban Ministry: The Kingdom, the City and the People of God* (Downers Grove, IL: InterVarsity Press, 2001), 111.

They were called to make a decision.[44] God commanded them to rid the land of the heathen peoples and their cultural heritage. In this way, they could be unique among the nations of the world. In applying the practical implications of God's covenant for his people, Jerusalem became the city of God—the city which, as a social system, was called to witness to God's shalom (Pss. 122:6–9; 147:2). It became the spiritual center of the world, a model city living in trust and faith under the lordship of God, the symbol of God's presence and power in the world (Isa. 8:18; Deut. 17:14–20).[45] Jerusalem also became the symbol of a culture focused on revealing God's presence in a nation. Their social existence was to be a true model of the kingdom of God among the nations. Her worship of God had to be clear and uncompromised.[46] In their economic, political, and socio-religious relationships, they would reflect God's shalom. One of the most concise and yet visionary descriptions of the world as God intended it to be is found in Isaiah 65:17–25:[47]

> "For behold, I create new heavens and a new earth, and the former things shall not be remembered or come into mind. But be glad and rejoice forever in that which I create; for behold, I create Jerusalem to be a joy, and her people to be a gladness. I will rejoice in Jerusalem and be glad in my people; no more shall be heard in it the sound of weeping and the cry of distress. No more shall there be in it an infant who lives but a few days, or an old man who does not fill out his days, for the young man shall die a hundred years old, and the sinner a hundred years old shall be accursed. They shall build houses and inhabit them; they shall plant vineyards and eat their fruit. They shall not build and another inhabit; they shall not plant and another eat; for like the days of a tree shall the days of my people be, and my chosen shall long enjoy the work of their hands. They shall not labor in vain or bear children for calamity,

44. Joshua 24:14–15.
45. Linthicum, *City of God, City of Satan*, 25.
46. Hedlund, *Mission of the Church in the World*, 61.
47. Linthicum, *City of God, City of Satan*, 21.

for they shall be the offspring of the blessed of the LORD, and their descendants with them. Before they call I will answer; while they are yet speaking I will hear. The wolf and the lamb shall graze together; the lion shall eat straw like the ox, and dust shall be the serpent's food. They shall not hurt or destroy in all my holy mountain," says the LORD.

In this concrete, realistic, and maybe achievable vision, the city of Jerusalem became the symbol of life as God intended.[48] Israel was special only because she was given a universal concern as a nation. Unlike others that could and would live only for self-interest and self-preservation, Israel would always be a nation for the blessing of all.[49] The characteristic of God's shalom community, as Linthicum interprets Isaiah 65, is

- Decent, safe, sanitary, secure, and affordable housing for everyone (65:21–22).
- Jobs that provide adequate income and bring meaning and focus to people's lives (65:21–22).
- Health care that adequately provides for all people, contributes to longevity, and ends infant mortality (65:20).
- Neighborhoods that are stable, safe, and mutually supportive (65:25).
- Environments that are healthy and are not dangerous to people's health and safely (65:20).
- Wealth relatively and equitably distributed, so that there are no great disparities in income, wealth, position, or status between people (65:21–23).
- People living in peace with each other (65:19, 25).[50]

This was God's will for his shalom covenant community in the concrete historical situation of Israel in Canaan. During the Old

48. Linthicum, *Building a People of Power*, 22.
49. Stephen A. Rhodes, *Where the Nations Meet: The Church in a Multicultural World* (Downers Grove, IL: InterVarsity Press, 1998), 39.
50. Linthicum, *Building a People of Power*, 21–22.

Testament period, God did not leave himself without witness among the peoples of the world.[51]

From Jerusalem to Babylon—the Exile

The Tragedy of a Rebellious People

The tragic conclusion of the Old Testament is that Israel, as God's chosen people, never became the unique covenant people God intended them to be, because they never lived according to his calling. They were constantly reminded of God's purpose, but they persisted in their sin. Over several centuries, God patiently called them to repentance through the prophets, but they were unable to obey his commands. There were moments of glory and praise, but they were unable to develop the permanent relational culture that would make God's covenant a practical reality of life. God's intended Jerusalem continued to be an ideal, but it never became a reality.

Because of their sinful nature, the Israelites were attracted to the culture of self-interest that the surrounding nations displayed. From the moment they entered Canaan, the Israelites were attracted to the cultures of the people living in the land. They did not drive these peoples out, as God commanded. The tragic result was that these people and cultures became a trap for Israel (Judg. 2:2–3). God tested the sincerity of their faith and commitment, and they failed miserably.

The task of religion is to build the values of society around the relationality of life, but by rejecting and disobeying God, Israel's existence deteriorated.[52] They tried to cover it over with a veneer of liturgically correct worship, and it became so commonplace that they didn't know how to be embarrassed any longer by their own actions.[53] The prophet Ezekiel (in chapter 22) traced Israel's profound spiritual shift: Jerusalem's political (vv. 6–7, 25), religious (vv. 8–9, 26), and economic (vv. 12–13, 27) systems had become corrupt.[54] While

---

51. Hedlund, *Mission of the Church in the World*, 65.
52. Linthicum, *Building a People of Power*, 26.
53. Linthicum, *Building a People of Power*, 23.
54. Linthicum, *City of God, City of Satan*, 61.

claiming to be Jerusalem, the city of God, they became Babylon, the city of Satan, and the culture of Babylon manifested itself in the life of Jerusalem.

The people of Israel, chosen by God to be unique, chose to be like the nations. Eventually the exile, of which God had warned them, became a harsh reality. God abandoned Jerusalem when it continued to be Babylon. The nations, which were supposed to be the objects of Israel's witness, became the means of their correction.[55]

The Exile: Not Victims, but Missionaries

The exile was not the abandonment of God's plan of salvation to reach the world through his chosen people, but a confirmation of it, although in a different way. It was a time of great upheaval in the world. Different nations and cultures were competing against each other, and a succession of empires ruled the biblical world. In this world of turmoil, the focus would not be on Israel as a political entity anymore, but on a faithful remnant that God sent into the world to prepare the way for his coming kingdom.[56] Not Jerusalem the place, but the true spirit of Jerusalem in the heart of God's remnant, would carry on God's work. The focus was now on individuals. Jonah was sent to the city of Nineveh, Daniel and his friends were in Babylon, Esther became a queen in Persia, Nehemiah also worked in Persia, and thousands of unknown Jews were scattered among the nations. While the strategy of the spiritual enemy, Babylonian culture, was to eradicate the identity of its conquered peoples and forcefully integrate them into the pagan society, God called his remnant to be and to act differently. They were not to hide or try to flee, to adapt to the new culture, or to listen to false prophets who preached false deliverance. God had a very specific plan for them.

55. Hedlund, *Mission of the Church in the World*, 69.
56. Hedlund, *Mission of the Church in the World*, 105, 108. The doctrine of the remnant particularly evolved during the early ministry of Isaiah. Hedlund calls it "the spiritual Israel of the Old Testament." It is the "progenitor of the church of the New Testament." The remnant was to carry out the function of service among the nations. Israel's mission was to mediate the revelation of God to the nations. What Israel had failed to do, the remnant would carry out.

Jeremiah 29 introduces a group of exiles in Babylon who were eagerly waiting for the time of rescue that the false prophets predicted. They wanted to go back to Jerusalem, the place. God communicated with them in a special letter that Jeremiah the prophet had to deliver. In this letter, his covenantal plan for them, while they were still in exile in Babylon, was revealed. He still planned to use them in his service, exactly where they were at that moment in time. Jeremiah 29:4–7 states:

> Thus says the LORD of hosts, the God of Israel, to all the exiles whom I have sent into exile from Jerusalem to Babylon: Build houses and live in them; plant gardens and eat their produce. Take wives and have sons and daughters; take wives for your sons, and give your daughters in marriage, that they may bear sons and daughters; multiply there, and do not decrease. But seek the welfare of the city where I have sent you into exile, and pray to the LORD on its behalf, for in its welfare you will find your welfare. For thus says the LORD of hosts, the God of Israel: Do not let your prophets and your diviners who are among you deceive you, and do not listen to the dreams that they dream, for it is a lie that they are prophesying to you in my name; I did not send them, declares the LORD.

God would use his chosen shalom community, called to practice a relational culture. The difference is that they were not in Canaan anymore, but living as exiles in Babylon. God wanted them to be a Jerusalem while they were in Babylon. Roger Hedlund concludes: "The cultural adaptations as well as the spiritual purification of the Jews in captivity prepared them for an eventual missionary vocation. Israel has failed to go to the nations in missionary obedience. In the exile the Jews are scattered in the midst of the nations. The missionary vocation is begun."[57]

It is not the nation of Israel as a whole, but the chosen remnant, that is still part of God's plan, even in their relocation. In Jeremiah

---

57. Hedlund, *Mission of the Church in the World*, 108.

29, we see that he gives them a short-term, a medium-term, and a long-term vision. Although their cultural and covenantal mandate was confirmed, God also showed them that they needed to seek the benefit (shalom) of Babylon. They were not called to survive, but to serve, live in the city, love it, and work for its shalom—its economic, social, and spiritual flourishing.[58] The call was not about them, but about their mission. They needed to focus their attention (cultural practice) and even their prayers on the well-being of Babylon. They were called to live in the true spirit of Jerusalem while remaining there. Through their cultural life, they were to work toward the goal of showing the people of Babylon what God's shalom was all about. They had to commit themselves, not only to show it to others, but to make sure that others experienced it themselves. Only if they were seeking God's shalom for Babylon would they be able to experience God's shalom for themselves. In working toward giving it to others, they would also receive it. In this we learn that God makes his covenant *tangible* in every phase of history. There is no historical situation in which the covenant will not receive its form and content from God and in which people will not be God's coworkers in the realization of his purposes for creation.[59]

Throughout this time of worldly turmoil, God prepared for the coming of his kingdom.[60] In different parts of the known world of that time, God's remnant was strategically placed in cities in preparation for the spreading of the gospel in the time of the New Testament. In exile, Israel became a missionary people. The centrifugal mission that is characteristic of the New Testament was preceded by a period of Jewish missionary activity during the intertestamental period. Hedlund maintains that the Christian mission in the New Testament took over and built upon the Jewish message of this time.[61] The

58. Timothy J. Keller, "A New Kind of Urban Christian," *Christianity Today*, May 2006, 36–39.

59. Wielenga and König, *Zending: waarom?*, 261.

60. Jesus built his theology around the concept of "the kingdom of God," by which he meant the living-out of shalom on the earth. The kingdom of God was shalom personified and particularized in the life of God's people.

61. Hedlund, *Mission of the Church in the World*, 108.

establishment of the Roman Empire was God's way of culturally preparing the world for the fullness of time. The spiritual focus of the whole world was again on Jerusalem.

From Jerusalem to the Ends of the Earth

The Fullness of Time—A New Beginning

God promised that he would send someone to prepare the way for the Messiah (Isa. 40:3). John the Baptist was the bridge between Old Testament prophecy and promise and the New Testament realization of God's salvation. He prepared the way by calling the people to radical repentance and conversion. No ethnic claim to be the children of Abraham would suffice (Luke 3:8). The only way to become a spiritual child of Abraham and be part of the kingdom that Jesus Christ was about to establish was by being *born again* through the Holy Spirit (John 3:3).

In the fullness of time, Jesus Christ was born. The *missio Dei* of Genesis 3:9 was fulfilled in the incarnation of God's Son (John 3:16).[62] Jesus' life and ministry confirmed God's plan of transforming a chosen people and using them to reach the world with the message of salvation. It was the continuation and final conclusion of what God started with Abraham and the remnant of Israel. God's shalom community of the Old Testament was continued in the kingdom community of the New—the church. The difference was that it would not be the shadow community waiting for and expecting salvation as something to happen in the future, but the saved and triumphant community experiencing and living out the salvation it received. Jesus preached against the popular and dominant culture of his time that captivated people's lives in sinful slavery, and called all to acknowledge the one true God. Through his life, ministry, death, and resurrection, he inaugurated God's kingdom.[63] In this way, he not only communicated a message, but began a kingdom movement of renewal. Jesus did not come to die solely for our personal sins,

---

62. On the fullness of time, see Galatians 4:4–5.
63. Linthicum, *Building a People of Power*, 61.

but "for both the transformation of people and the transformation of their society so that people and their systems would both embrace authentic relationship with God, exercise a politics of justice, and practice a stewardship of their common wealth so that poverty would be eliminated from the society."[64]

Jesus' salvation has implications for the renewal of the whole of creation. In him the promise of a new heaven and a new earth was registered. Salvation, as Jesus preached, was not "pie in the sky when you die," but to be part of a new community, the church, living in a new way, proclaiming the reality of the kingdom of God that had started already, although it was not yet fully deployed. Wielenga and König warn against the idea of an individualized salvation. They state that personally experienced salvation functions in a covenantal framework in communion with the community and is relevant for all of creation.

Jesus' first focus was on the culture and religion of the Jewish people, which was dominated by different religious sects.[65] From the time of the exile until the coming of Jesus, the Jews still claimed to be the chosen people of God, yet were unprepared for his coming. Religious practice was still in and around the temple, but the spirit of Babylon was in their hearts. At first, masses of people followed Jesus, but eventually the spirit of Babylon turned them against him. At the climax of his ministry, Jesus wept for Jerusalem and turned away from the temple, because the people of Israel were still caught up in the self-serving religion and the culture responsible for the exile many years before. That is why they did not hesitate to connive with the Roman government to kill Jesus. The spirit of Babylon united the Jewish church and the Roman authority. The temple in Jerusalem was destroyed in A.D. 70.

From there on, a "mystery" was about to be revealed. The promise of salvation and the entry into this established kingdom was opened to people from other cultures (Eph. 1:9–11; 3:6). Although

64. Linthicum, *Building a People of Power*, 62.
65. Lucien Legrand, *The Bible on Culture* (Maryknoll, NY: Orbis Books, 2000), 83–96.

Jesus' ministry started within and with the people of Israel, he eventually broadened the scope of his ministry to also include other peoples. The remnant of Israel, becoming part of the remnant of people from other cultures, would eventually form the unique people of the kingdom of God, the church. When Jesus rose from death, he received all power in heaven and on earth, promised to be with his church until the end of time, and sent them in the power of the Spirit to the ends of the earth to proclaim his kingdom to all nations (Matt. 28:19). He then ascended to heaven to initiate the last days.[66] His promise was to equip the church for the important missional task given her.

From Jerusalem to Rome and Beyond—the New Jerusalem

The book of Acts highlights the earthly reality of the heavenly enthronement of Jesus, which is not something just to mentally note, but something to experience practically in the church on earth. Each member of the church individually, and also as a part of the body of Christ corporately, receives gifts from the Holy Spirit. In this way, believers are equipped for kingdom service in the world. This is what happened at Pentecost. Jesus Christ gave his church the necessary gifts to fulfill the global task that he had already given them (Matt. 28 and Acts 1). The newly created language of Pentecost was the language of faith. The message of the gospel was translated into the languages of the world. God was sending his church to the different peoples and cultures that came into existence when he dispersed mankind from Babel. The church was born of the telling of the story of the life, death, and resurrection of Jesus Christ. In listening to and proclaiming the mighty acts of God in Christ, a new *polis* was created, an alternative community.[67] The Spirit of the New Jerusalem was at work in the church to enable her to be Christ's body, proclaiming his

---

66. The last days are the period between the ascension and the return of Jesus Christ. In this period of time, the church is the messenger of God.

67. Rhodes, *Where the Nations Meet*, 71.

kingship by living out the reality of his presence.[68] The first congregation in Jerusalem grew from three thousand to five thousand members in a very short time. The first Christians constituted a counterculture because they not only witnessed verbally to the world, but also lived sacrificially in a new way as a new kingdom community. They were indeed the covenant community of God—not primarily the body of those saved, but a community through whom God pursued his mission in the world.[69]

This first congregation at the start was still Jewish in its attitudes and relationships. A person's cultural orientation is very strong and naturally focused on itself and those of one's own kind. Only through the grace of God is it refocused outward as an instrument for serving God and one's fellow man. This was soon rectified in the first congregation by the appointment of deacons, but also more radically through the persecution by Saul, as God sent believers, as he had ordered earlier, to the ends of the earth.[70] The newly formed church and some individuals still struggled with deeply ingrained cultural issues. Through Peter's "repentance" (Acts 10) and the first council that was held in Jerusalem (Acts 15), God confirmed his vision in their midst. The mystery that Paul spoke about was now a reality. God's message of salvation had to reach the whole world and its entire people. God will have his way with his church, even if it means forceful sending.

Those belonging to this movement were first called Christians at the newly formed multicultural church in Antioch. The missionary journeys of the apostle Paul unfolded God's plan of taking the gospel to the ends of the known world. The book of Acts records the missional movement of the Christian church from Jerusalem to Rome. That makes it clear that the exile of the Jewish people played an

---

68. Linthicum, *Building a People of Power*, 83. Jesus Christ was crucified on a rugged cross between two thieves, on the city's garbage heap, in the kind of place where powers conspire and systems dominate, and the people become powerless victims. That is where he died, and that is what he has died about. And that is where his people should be and what his people should be about.

69. Tiessen, "The Salvation of the Unevangelized," 242.

70. Acts 1:8 had to become Acts 8:1.

important role in the proclamation of the gospel. Wherever the exiled Jewish people went, they built synagogues. When Paul visited new cities during his mission trips, he first brought the gospel to the synagogues, and this brought the gospel to the major cities of the Roman Empire, from which it spread further. The missional strategy of the Christian church was to target major cities in evangelistic campaigns. The book of Acts traces the movement of the gospel from Jerusalem to the imperial capital, Rome.

The New Testament letters describe the struggles of local churches in the practical realization of Jesus' kingdom. It was and still is not easy to be the church of Christ in a world that is hostile to the people of God and which seeks to destroy the faith. The local realities in the major cities of the world are seen in the different letters that make up the New Testament. The process of contextualization is highlighted in these texts and is reflected in the way the message is made relevant today.

In the book of Revelation, Jesus urgently speaks to his church to prepare her for the harsh realities that await in this Babylonian world. Throughout history, Jerusalem has struggled with Babylon, but their struggle will intensify as the end comes closer. The last days before Jesus returns will not be days of comfort and ease for the church, but days of struggle she has to endure. Revelation is a book of comfort for the church and an encouragement to stay focused. Times will be increasingly difficult as the end approaches. He who knows exactly what is going on has promised to be with his church to the end, and he also deals sternly with her if she falls short of the goal. The Lord does not leave his church in the dark, but shows what is happening in the world, encouraging her to endure and stay motivated. Revelation 21–22 makes it clear that the ultimate purpose of redemption is not to escape the material world, but to renew it.[71] God's people should constantly strive to disengage themselves from Babylon and its culture, because it still strives to absorb God's people. But in the end everything is clear: the New Jerusalem will be established by God and will descend from God.

71. Keller, "New Kind of Urban Christian," 39.

Conclusion

In Reformed covenantal theology, the concept of progressive salvation history is decisive and nonnegotiable. The Bible itself gives a paradigm for mission that is embedded in God's covenant. Following the contours of biblical revelation, it becomes clear that God and his creation are mutually implied in a relationship and a history. In this relationship, a covenant is unilaterally initiated by God in which his chosen people are called to actively participate.[72]

God uses the whole of creation as well as the whole of world history to finalize his covenant. Salvation history recorded in Scripture highlights the continued affirmation of God's covenant as it unfolds more clearly through the different ages and stages of world history. This history not only reflects God's continued commitment to his covenant, but also the continued failure of his people to really live as a new covenant community in a broken and sinful world. Despite this, God constantly reaffirms his commitment to see it through. At every historical stage, he uses a remnant from within the covenant community to move his covenant to its predetermined conclusion.

Christendom Is Dead—the Formation
of Global Christianity

After biblical times, Christianity developed within the bounds of Western culture that later became known as *Christendom*.[73] For about five hundred years, the fortunes of the Christian church and the

---

72. Wielenga and König, *Zending waarom?*, 266. Where the covenant is a reality, the people of the covenant come into existence, constituted by God and called to participation. This participation is not based on freedom of choice by individual Christians. It is an essential part of being a covenant people. Without it, the covenant people cease to be people of the covenant.

73. "Christendom" is a concept that embraces all Christian churches that have a distinct historical connection (origin) and current association with the Christian churches in the Western world. Christendom is the name given to the religious culture that has dominated Western society since the fourth century. See Michael Frost, *Exiles: Living Missionally in a Post-Christian Culture* (Peabody, MA: Hendrickson, 2006), 4.

peoples of Europe were intimately entwined. In 1920, Hilaire Belloc stated, "The Church is Europe: and Europe is The Church."[74] The so-called Western church was originally founded in a rural European setting and never really came to grips with the urban realities of a developing and industrializing world. For many decades, Western Christianity had a comfortable and privileged position in society. Eventually, Western culture enslaved and suffocated the Christian church. As in biblical times, the people of God slowly but surely became absorbed by the dominant culture. The results for the church were disastrous. She not only lost her missionary focus, but also became self-serving, consumer-driven, introverted, materialistic, and maintenance oriented. Although not openly hostile toward Christianity, and in some ways still wrongly associated with it, Western culture eventually abandoned Christianity and pushed it from the center of cultural privilege to the margins of irrelevance. This led to the rapid demise of Christendom and the rise of a post-Christian and postmodern world. It is no wonder that the church in the West is considered to be in deep trouble.[75] This is part of the reason why Philip Jenkins is convinced that we are living through one of the transforming moments in the history of religion worldwide.[76] As the Western world is becoming dechristianized, the Christian church is confronted with a profound paradigm shift that announces the end of one world and the birth of another.[77] We are experiencing the beginning of a new world order. In such a time, much of what people used to think and do is redefined.[78]

Migration and Urbanization

We are also living in the midst of the greatest period of migration in human history.[79] The world as we know it is currently experiencing

74. Hilaire Belloc, *Europe and the Faith* (New York: Paulist Press, 1920), ix.

75. Rose Dowsett, "Dry Bones in the West," in *Global Missiology for the 21st Century: The Iguassu Dialogue*, ed. William D. Taylor (Grand Rapids: Baker Academic, 2001), 448.

76. Philip Jenkins, *The Next Christendom: The Coming of Global Christianity* (Oxford: Oxford University Press, 2002), 1.

77. Bosch, *Transforming Mission*, 3.

78. Bosch, *Transforming Mission*, 4.

79. Ray Bakke, "Urbanization and Evangelism: A Global View," *Word and World*

a major population and cultural shift. Globalization is changing the face of society, spearheaded by the process of urbanization. This process has now become unstoppable, and it is estimated that by 2050, over 70 percent of the world's population will be living in cities. According to Harvie Conn, the reality of a world in movement has brought us into the fourth era of modern missions—reaching the cities.[80] The frontier of missions has shifted. "A hundred years ago we sent missionaries to the nations to look for the cities. Today you go to the cities and you find the nations."[81] In the light of God's revelation in Acts 17:26, we should humbly ask the following questions: Why at this time in history are the nations coming to the cities? What is God doing in this massive migration of the world? As the world rapidly changes and Christendom is slowly dying, the Christian church needs to face this new reality with the assurance that God is using this age and stage in world history to finalize his covenant. We need a missiological definition of the city.[82]

The Formation of Global Christianity

The ends of the earth are now gathered in the cities of the world. The so-called unreached have become reachable. God is on a mission and includes his covenant church in this mission. It is not the end of Christianity. It is the end of a period in history in which Christianity was primarily associated with a Western cultural expression. We are now seeing a new and fresh resurgence in the formation of Global Christianity.[83] It is also called the formation of "the Third Church, the Southern Church." Today the largest Christian communities on the planet are to be found in Africa and Latin America.[84] "The period

---

19.3 (Summer 1999): 225.

80. Harvie M. Conn, ed., *Planting and Growing Urban Churches: From Dream to Reality* (Grand Rapids: Baker Books, 1997), 10.

81. Ray Bakke, in Harvie Conn, Manuel Ortiz, and Susan S. Baker, *The Urban Face of Mission: Ministering the Gospel in a Diverse and Changing World* (Phillipsburg, NJ: P&R Publishing, 2002), 38.

82. Bakke, *Urbanization and Evangelism*, 232.

83. This is a very distinct resurgence of Christianity outside its original alliance with Western theological tradition.

84. Jenkins, *Next Christendom*, 2.

since 1792 has seen the Christian center of gravity steadily move away from the West and toward the Southern continents."[85] Although this shift in the center of Christianity is an undeniable fact, the shift is not yet fully complete. According to Walbert Buhlmann, "The Southern Church is the Church of the future as well as the future of the Church."[86]

The Western Church—Refocused, Revitalized, and Covenantally Realigned

The clarion call of this article is focused on the so-called Western church in rapid decline and tragic denial. The church's experience today is mirrored in the experience faced by the exiles in Babylon in biblical times.[87] That is why the church urgently needs to develop a theology of the city—an understanding big enough to see what God is doing in the urbanization of his world and the internationalization of his cities.[88] It should not be a piecemeal, ad hoc, reactive, and problem-oriented endeavor, but a consistent, long-term approach to urban mission that also uncovers the reasons for the church's orientation to its tribal, rural, and suburban settings.[89] It is not enough for Christians to live in the city. As God's covenant people, they are called to be an alternate city,[90] and the church in the West will have to break through its own homogeneity to do so.[91] The Western church needs to recognize that the future of the urban congregation is very closely related to the future of the city, which means that the greatest challenge to world evangelization is urban ministry.[92]

85. Andrew Walls, *The Cross-Cultural Process in Christian History* (Maryknoll, NY: Orbis, 2002), 31.

86. Kwamo Bediako, *Christianity in Africa: The Renewal of a Non-Western Religion* (Maryknoll, NY: Orbis Books, 1995), 128.

87. Frost, *Exiles*, 9.

88. Ray Bakke, *The Urban Christian* (Downers Grove, IL: InterVarsity Press, 1987), 62.

89. Harvie Conn, "The Rural-Urban Myth and World Mission," *Reformed Review* 37.3 (1984): 126.

90. Keller, "New Kind of Urban Christian," 38.

91. Conn, "Rural-Urban Myth," 125.

92. Conn, *Planting and Growing Urban Churches*, 46.

This concluding quotation provides a motivation for rediscovering God's covenantal mission paradigm for the challenge of the urban world:

> The particular splendor of the New Testament church is displayed in the assembling and diversity of people. No longer are the tapestries and temples the significant treasures of the Kingdom, nor cushioned pews or weighty vestments. The treasures are people, and so the lot of the church is cast where people are increasingly in our day, they are in the city. The church has not yet responded well to this imperative.[93]

93. Rubingh, "Mission in an Urban World," 367.

11

The Witness of Reformed Christianity in a Minority Situation: Indonesia

Benyamin F. Intan

"Colonalism
Imperalism

Abstract

The dissemination of religion that relies on the power of arms and is motivated by economic greed will not only fail, but also become counterproductive to religion itself. It has not been easy for Christianity to exist and bear witness in Indonesia, due to the Dutch colonialization for three hundred and fifty years, although it was the Dutch who brought Christianity. How could the Protestant churches that used to be "colonial churches" change and become "ethnic churches" and later on "Indonesian churches"? Only by the grace of God were the Protestant churches able to establish a mission in the country, bearing witness to the gospel and struggling to fulfill its calling. To present a comprehensive picture of this endeavor, this article will discuss the challenges that the Indonesian Protestant churches have faced from the time of the Dutch and Japanese occupations up to the era of independence under the Old Order and the New Order administrations. The discussion will be followed by a critical reflection on the struggle of the Indonesian Protestant churches from the perspective of Reformed theology in a missional minority context.

The Dutch Colonial Era (1602–1942)

Christianity first came to Indonesia in the sixteenth century through Portuguese missionaries who promulgated Roman Catholicism in certain parts of the country. They were followed by Dutch missionaries who introduced Protestantism at the beginning of the seventeenth century.[1] At that time, Islam was at the peak of disseminating its teaching in Indonesia, forcing the Hindu religion to move from Java to the island of Bali.[2] Christianity was present and taking root in such regions as the Moluccas (Maluku) and Timor in the eastern part of Indonesia before Islam spread to them. The Dutch, being enemies of the Portuguese politically, commercially, and religiously, succeeded in crushing Portuguese power in those regions and converting their inhabitants from Catholicism to Protestantism.[3]

Protestantism was propagated through Dutch colonialism in Indonesia in two stages: first, through the Vereenigde Oost-Indische Compagnie (VOC, the United East India Company) in 1602–1799, and second, through the Dutch East Indies in 1800–1942.

The United East India Company, or VOC (1602–1799)

Dutch colonialism in Indonesia through the VOC was mainly motivated by interest in spices found in abundance in the eastern part of the Indonesian archipelago, particularly on the islands of Celebes (Sulawesi) and the Moluccas. At the outset, the contract between the Dutch government and the VOC did not mention Christianity, but after 1623 the VOC became involved in the propagation of Christianity.[4] Christian mission was included in the

1. See Th. Müller-Krüger, *Sedjarah geredja di Indonesia*, 2nd ed. (Jakarta: Badan Penerbit Kristen, 1966).

2. Islam first entered Indonesia around the thirteenth century. When Marco Polo visited Aceh at the end of the thirteenth century, he observed the presence of Islam at some trading centers. See T. B. Simatupang, "Doing Theology in Indonesia Today," *CTC Bulletin* 3:2 (August 1982): 22.

3. T. B. Simatupang, "Dynamics for Creative Maturity," in *Asian Voices in Christian Theology*, ed. Gerald H. Anderson (Maryknoll, NY: Orbis Books, 1976), 91.

4. Karel Steenbrink, "The Arrival of Protestantism and the Consolidation of Christianity in the Moluccas 1605–1800," in *A History of Christianity in Indonesia*,

VOC's organizational structure, first as part of the Department of Trade and Colonies, and later as part of a new department called the Department of Education, Worship, and Industry.[5] The VOC's commercial motive was accordingly inseparable from evangelistic mission, since at that time the Dutch government embraced the principle of *cuius regio eius religio* (whose realm, his religion). Article 36 of the Dutch Statement of Faith stated that the government is obliged to "preserve the holy Church, oppose and eradicate all forms of false religion and idol worship, abolish the kingdom of the antichrist and advance the kingdom of Jesus."[6] Consequently, the unification of the church and the state at that time brought about the establishment of a state church in Indonesia during the VOC era.[7]

The VOC's interest in trade motivated its support for the propagation of Christianity. The conversion of the people from Catholicism to Protestantism was necessary in order to divert their loyalty from the Portuguese to the Dutch. Catholics inhabiting areas previously occupied by the Portuguese were converted to Protestantism, except for those living on the islands of Flores and Solor, in which the VOC had no interest, since no economic significance was attached to those islands.[8] The Reverend Wiltens, one of the first pastors stationed in Maluku, wrote in 1615:

> Nominal Christians benefit the VOC since their becoming Christians enables the VOC to subjugate a large number of people. If territories are subjugated in which the people have been baptized, those territories will then remain under our sovereignty; if this is not the case, they will remain under the power of the Moros (Islam) who are at war with us.[9]

---

ed. Jan Sihar Aritonang and Karel Steenbrink (Leiden, Boston: Brill, 2008), 99–100.

5. Gerry van Klinken, *Minorities, Modernity and the Emerging Nation: Christians in Indonesia, a Biographical Approach* (Leiden: KITLV, 2003), 9–10.

6. Müller-Krüger, *Sedjarah geredja di Indonesia*, 30.

7. Müller-Krüger, *Sedjarah geredja di Indonesia*, 31.

8. John Titaley, "From Abandonment to Blessing: The Theological Presence of Christianity in Indonesia," in *Christian Theology in Asia*, ed. Sebastian C. H. Kim (New York: Cambridge University Press, 2008), 74.

9. Müller-Krüger, *Sedjarah geredja di Indonesia*, 31–32.

The political and economic gain that Dutch colonialism reaped from Protestant mission prompted the VOC to send 254 pastors and 800 Christian counselors from the Netherlands to Indonesia during its administration from 1602 to 1800. Moreover, the VOC bore all the expenditure of the church, including the remuneration of pastors and Christian counselors, the construction of church buildings, and the publication of Christian literature.[10]

Thus the Protestant mission, due to its orientation to political and economic gain, produced nominal Christians. Already in 1615 the Rev. Wiltens complained about "people who are Christians in name only."[11] In turn, nominal Christianity produced syncretism. It is not surprising, therefore, that in the Moluccas a so-called *Ambon religion* appeared that was "a mixture of Christianity . . . and traditional religion."[12] Karel Steenbrink observes,

> The formal conversion to Christianity did not mean a total change in the life and rituals of the new Christians. . . . For many situations in daily life, on the occasion of birth, marriage, burials, harvest, earthquakes or other natural disasters, it was still the traditional religion that often was resorted to.[13]

Operating under the shadow of colonialism, the Protestant mission had no intention of contextualizing theological teaching. The theology taught was fraught with a Western-oriented way of thinking. "Thought patterns brought by European missionaries or by the western church," as John M. Prior and Alle Hoekema have put it, "were considered normative. Missionaries were often afraid of heterodox thinking by indigenous believers and suppressed their ideas."[14] In other words, the Protestant mission rejected various

---

10. Müller-Krüger, *Sedjarah geredja di Indonesia*, 31.
11. Müller-Krüger, *Sedjarah geredja di Indonesia*, 31.
12. Steenbrink, "The Arrival of Protestantism," 109.
13. Steenbrink, "The Arrival of Protestantism," 108.
14. John M. Prior and Alle Hoekema, "Theological Thinking by Indonesian Christians, 1850–2000," in *A History of Christianity in Indonesia*, ed. Aritonang and Steenbrink, 749.

attempts at "indigenous theologizing."[15] It is not surprising that until the year 1800, although Christianity had been present in Indonesia for about two hundred years, it had not been owned by the churches in Indonesia. Th. Müller-Krüger calls Indonesian Christianity of the time "the Church of people under age."[16]

So strong was the influence of Dutch colonialism on mission that it inculcated Christians with a pietistic theology, which emphasized a "personalistic, spiritualistic, otherworldly, and futuristic understanding of Christian faith and life."[17] Pietistic theology focuses mainly on personal piety and faith experience, but neglects concerns for social justice.[18] For this reason, the Protestant mission displayed an indifferent attitude toward the actions of Dutch colonialism that unmistakably violated human rights.

Thus the Protestant mission, guided by the power and interests of the VOC, was not only ineffective, but also counterproductive to Christian mission itself. By remaining silent in the face of the ruthlessness of Dutch colonialism, evangelism became a stumbling block to those who embraced Christian faith, particularly when it was carried out with an orientation to political and economic gain for the colonial government. In this situation, the Protestant mission was in fact committing suicide. Converts to Protestantism were not true Christians, but nominal ones. Nominal Christianity had in turn brought about not only a syncretism of beliefs, but also hypocrisy, which was dangerous to the Christian faith.

Its dependence on, and affiliation with, colonialist power caused the Protestant mission to lose its faithfulness to the Christian faith. By rejecting "indigenous theologizing," it denied the essence of theology

---

15. Prior and Hoekema, "Theological Thinking," 749.

16. Theodore Müller-Krüger, ed., *Indonesia Raja* (Bad Salzuflen: MBK, 1966), 99, quoted in Simatupang, "Dynamics for Creative Maturity," 91.

17. Simatupang, "Dynamics for Creative Maturity," 94. Cf. Frank L. Cooley's description of Moluccan Christianity in "Das Gesicht der ältesten evangelischen Kirche in Asien," in Müller-Krüger, *Indonesia Raja*, 117–30, quoted in Simatupang, "Dynamics for Creative Maturity," 115.

18. T. B. Simatupang, "Christian Presence in War, Revolution and Development: The Indonesian Case," *Ecumenical Review* 37.1 (January 1985): 79.

itself. Theology should be understood, as T. B. Simatupang has put it, "as the self-conscious reflective response to God's continuing action in Christ in the midst of the concrete situation of the church's life, of man, and of society."[19] In sum, theology should become what Müller-Krüger calls "*theologia in loco*."[20] The third World Missionary Conference in Tambaram (1938) articulates this *theologia in loco*:

> It is inadequate to express Christian truth in words and concepts satisfactory only to western theologians. Rather, the gospel must be proclaimed in terms and expressions that make its summons intelligible in the context of life as actually lived.[21]

Furthermore, by inculcating a pietistic theology that emphasizes only love for God through spiritual conversion, but neglects justice, the Protestant mission failed to carry out a wholistic *missio Dei*. In God, love and justice are inseparable, as Psalm 89:14 says: "Righteousness and justice are the foundation of your throne; steadfast love and faithfulness go before you." Interestingly, Simatupang notes an incident that happened when Thomas Matulessy, also known as Pattimura (1783–1817), later honored as a national hero, led an insurgence against the Dutch in Saparua. As he was hunted down by Dutch soldiers and fled from Saparua, he managed to leave open a Bible on the pulpit of the church at Psalm 17, which begins with this ringing opening sentence, "Hear a just cause, O LORD; attend to my cry!"[22] He thereby intended to convey that he was fighting for justice—not only to the invading Dutch commander, but also to the local church that remained indifferent toward injustice.

After the VOC went bankrupt on December 31, 1799, the Dutch

19. Simatupang, "Dynamics for Creative Maturity," 87.

20. See Th. Müller-Krüger, "Theologia in loco," in *Basilea: Walter Freitag zum 60 Geburtstag*, ed. Jan Hermelink and Jochen Margull (Stuttgart: Evangelischer Missionsverlag, 1959), 313–25, quoted in Simatupang, "Dynamics for Creative Maturity," 116.

21. John Bolt, James D. Bratt, and Paul J. Visser, eds., *The J. H. Bavinck Reader* (Grand Rapids: Eerdmans, 2013), 117.

22. Simatupang, "Doing Theology in Indonesia Today," 23.

government took over all its territories and placed them under the authority of the Dutch East Indies while continuing the work of the Christian mission.[23]

The Dutch East Indies (1800–1942)

Governing Indonesia from the beginning of the nineteenth century, the Dutch East Indies, following its predecessor, adopted a state church policy. However, there was a fundamental difference between the two. During the VOC era, the state church was one of the departments of the VOC and therefore remained under colonial power and depended fully on it. But in the era of the Dutch East Indies, the state church was more independent and self-reliant in carrying out the Protestant mission. By the decree of King William I, the Dutch East Indies established the state church under the name "the Protestant Church of the Netherlands Indies," in which various Protestant denominations, including the Lutheran church, came together. The self-reliance of the Protestant Church was reflected in its openness and freedom to invite various missionary societies from Europe to assist local churches.[24] From 1800 to 1900, fifteen missionary societies started working in the Netherlands Indies.[25]

The independence of the Protestant Church was reflected in its mission to create independent local ethnic churches by pioneering the formation of what Simatupang calls "protochurches."[26] At the end of the nineteenth century, the Protestant Church opened itself to "indigenous theologizing" by allowing Indonesian Christians to be involved in ecclesial offices as assistant pastor or evangelist, and then as pastor.[27] Although Indonesian Christians holding ecclesial offices remained subordinate in position to the European missionaries,[28]

23. See Th. van den End, "1800–2005: A National Overview: The Colonial Era: 1800–1900," in *A History of Christianity in Indonesia*, ed. Aritonang and Steenbrink, 137–40.

24. Titaley, "From Abandonment to Blessing," 75.

25. Van den End, "The Colonial Era: 1800–1900," 141.

26. Simatupang, "Dynamics for Creative Maturity," 92.

27. Prior and Hoekema, "Theological Thinking," 751.

28. Simatupang, "Dynamics for Creative Maturity," 92.

their presence—involving what Simatupang calls "proto-theological awareness"[29]—was significant for establishing local ethnic churches in the Netherlands Indies that were self-reliant. The self-reliance of local ethnic churches in the twentieth century was seen when the Minahasa Evangelical Christian Church (*Gereja Masehi Injili Minahasa*) was founded in 1934 in North Celebes, the Protestant Church of Moluccas (*Gereja Protestan Maluku*) in 1935, and the Timor Evangelical Christian Church (*Gereja Masehi Injili Timor*) in 1947. Other ethnic churches, such as the Chinese-speaking churches, the Javanese churches, the Borneo Evangelical Church (*Gereja Kalimantan Evangelis*), and the Batak Protestant Christian Church (*Gereja Kristen Batak Protestan*) were also founded during this period.[30]

Nevertheless, the colonial government represented by the Dutch East Indies limited the independence and self-reliance of the Protestant Church. The Protestant Church refused help from the colonial government for evangelistic work, but the government bore all the operational costs of the church. This situation caused concern among the missionary societies.[31] Although the colonial government was not involved in evangelistic mission, missionary societies were concerned that in social services, for example, the Dutch East Indies would exert its influence. Therefore, missionary societies took the initiative in founding various social services like hospitals, schools, and orphanages, even though they would later receive assistance from the Protestant Church and the colonial government.[32] The attachment of the Protestant Church to the Dutch East Indies to some extent reflected the Dutch political situation at the time, in which church and state were unified.

Another problem that caused concern among the missionary societies was the large number of Protestant Church ministers who adopted liberal theology that basically neglected mission work.[33] This situation resulted from the fact that the Protestant Church was created

29. Simatupang, "Dynamics for Creative Maturity," 92.
30. Titaley, "From Abandonment to Blessing," 75.
31. Van den End, "The Colonial Era: 1800–1900," 159.
32. Titaley, "From Abandonment to Blessing," 75.
33. Van den End, "The Colonial Era: 1800–1900," 159.

by the colonial government out of many denominations. Since many of its ministers adopted liberal theology, the Protestant Church functioned to a large extent, according to Th. van den End, as "a government agency for the fulfilment of the religious needs of its Protestant subjects. As such, it was not supposed to do any missionary work." He adds, "Even if the government had allowed it to do so, the leadership of the church would not have felt an inner urge towards mission."[34] So it was the missionary societies that were most engaged in evangelism and founding churches. The German Rheinische Missionsgesellschaft, for example, pioneered mission work in South Borneo as early as 1835, and began working in North Sumatra among the Batak tribe in 1862 and founded churches there.[35] Similarly, the Zending der Gereformeerde Kerken (ZGKN), the mission of the Dutch Reformed Church founded by Abraham Kuyper, pioneered mission work and founded a church on the island of Sumba.[36]

The majority of European missionaries engaged in the Protestant mission shared the mind-set of the colonial government, which van den End calls "a hard-core racism," according to which "other races were simply unable to ascend to the level reached by Europeans, and would die out or forever remain in an inferior position."[37] Even Müller-Krüger, the first dean of the Hoogere Theologische School (HTS),[38] to some extent adopted this mind-set, in which local inhabitants of the Netherlands Indies, unlike their Western counterparts, were regarded as being incapable of providing a foundation for clear, independent theological thinking.[39] Even Hendrik Kraemer,

34. Van den End, "The Colonial Era: 1800–1900," 138.
35. Van den End, "The Colonial Era: 1800–1900," 141.
36. Th. van den End, "1800–2005: A National Overview: The Last Decades of the Colonial Era: 1900–1942," in *A History of Christianity in Indonesia*, ed. Aritonang and Steenbrink, 167.
37. Van den End, "The Colonial Era: 1800–1900," 145.
38. HTS was established in Bogor in 1934 and was moved two years later to Jakarta. In 1954, the name of the school was changed to Sekolah Tinggi Teologia (STT, Higher Theological School). See Prior and Hoekema, "Theological Thinking," 757.
39. See Th. Müller-Krüger, "Theologische opleiding in Indië," *De Opwekker* 82 (1937): 317–34, quoted in Prior and Hoekema, "Theological Thinking," 758.

a missionary in the Netherlands Indies and a prominent figure in world mission, thought that "western peoples had more talents in the field of the creative transfer of knowledge and science than . . . had the Javanese."[40] Thus, it is not surprising that the leadership and key persons of the churches in the Netherlands Indies and the HTS were dominated by European missionaries.

In opposition to the discriminatory attitude of the colonial government and the missionaries who regarded the local inhabitants of the Netherlands Indies as "primitive" people, Todoeng Soetan Goenoeng Moelia, while pursuing doctoral study at Leiden University, wrote a dissertation in 1933 entitled *Het primitieve denken in de moderne wetenschap* (Primitive thinking in modern science).[41] In his dissertation, supervised by Ph. Kohnstamm, Moelia rejected the view of anthropologist Lucien Lévy-Bruhl, who maintained that "the 'primitive' was somehow ontologically discontinuous with the 'modern.'"[42] For Moelia, the primitive mind is aware of causality and logic and is able to reach intellectual conclusions in the same way the modern mind does, provided it is given an opportunity for study and experience for improving knowledge.[43] Moelia's dissertation was well received in Dutch academic circles. Kraemer wrote a review of it in the journal *De Opwekker* and described it as "extraordinary."[44]

Discriminatory thinking toward the people of the Netherlands Indies greatly influenced the success of mission work. As missionaries considered them as "lagging behind" and their culture "inferior, as is their religion,"[45] they conducted mission work in one direction only and refused to learn from the religion and culture of those receiving the gospel. Hence, their mission not only failed, but was embarrassing and

40. Prior and Hoekema, "Theological Thinking," 762.

41. T. S. G. Moelia, *Het primitieve denken in de moderne wetenschap* (Groningen, Den Haag, Batavia: Wolters, 1933), quoted in Klinken, *Minorities, Modernity and the Emerging Nation*, 262. After Indonesian independence, T. S. G. Moelia was appointed as Minister of Education. He founded the Christian University of Indonesia and pioneered the publication of the *Indonesian Encyclopedia*.

42. Klinken, *Minorities, Modernity and the Emerging Nation*, 70.

43. Prior and Hoekema, "Theological Thinking," 762.

44. Simatupang, "Dynamics for Creative Maturity," 115.

45. Van den End, "The Colonial Era: 1800–1900," 145.

became a laughingstock.[46] In the meantime, Albert C. Kruyt, in his mission work among the Batak Karo people, and Pieter Middelkoop, among the Timorese, had studied the religion and culture of the local people before they evangelized them, with the purpose of knowing their religion and culture as well as understanding their way of thinking in order to ensure the effectiveness of gospel transmission.[47] As a result, Kruyt's and Middelkoop's method of evangelizing was tremendously successful.[48]

Overall, Protestant mission during the Dutch East Indies era was better than it was during the VOC era. By inviting European missionary societies to the Netherlands Indies, the Protestant Church, in spite of its limited independence and self-reliance, played an important role in pioneering mission work and founding indigenous ethnic churches through the work of the missionary societies. The presence of missionary societies played a strategic role in preserving the purity of the Christian mission, not only from the danger of the colonial government's vested interests, but also from the influence of liberal theology, which was held by a majority of the ministers in the Protestant Church.

The racism of the European missionary societies in the Netherlands Indies reflected the Western worldview of the time. Europeans considered themselves superior to the nations they conquered. The presence of "hard-core racism" showed the influence of their European contemporaries on the missionary societies.[49] In this case, Christianity, using Ernst Troeltsch's terminology, was not what "dominates the world," but was instead "dominated by the world."[50] In his magnum opus, *Christ and Culture*, H. Richard Niebuhr argues that presenting Christ as the transformer of culture, as in the work of Augustine and John Calvin, is the best option for Christians when dealing with culture. On this view, since culture is under the judgment of God and his sovereign rule, "the Christian must carry on cultural work in obedience

46. Van den End, "The Colonial Era: 1800–1900," 148.
47. Van den End, "The Last Decades of the Colonial Era: 1900–1942," 172.
48. Van den End, "The Colonial Era: 1800–1900," 148.
49. Van den End, "The Colonial Era: 1800–1900," 145.
50. Ernst Troeltsch, *The Social Teaching of the Christian Churches*, trans. Olive Wyon (Louisville, KY: Westminster / John Knox Press, 1992), 1:342.

to the Lord."[51] When relating Jesus' teaching on the salt and the light of the world (Matt. 5:13–16) to Christian mission, John Stott asserts that "Christians can influence and change non-Christian society."[52] And Christ reminds us of his power, as John 1:5 says: "The light shines in the darkness, and the darkness has not overcome it."

Christian mission requires an understanding of the religion and culture of the people who are the target of mission. This understanding is important, not only to enhance the effectiveness of evangelism, but also to lead those evangelized to genuine conversion. The Protestant mission during the Dutch East Indies era believed that genuine conversion could not be achieved without conversion in the hearts of Christian individuals. Aside from the work of the Holy Spirit, in order for the heart to be converted, it is important that the gospel be communicated in the mother tongue of the recipients.[53] So without translating the gospel message, genuine conversion would be impossible. And without understanding the religion and culture of those evangelized, translation work would be impossible as well. Lamin Sanneh, professor of missions and world Christianity at Yale Divinity School, confirms this in his book *Translating the Message: The Missionary Impact on Culture.*[54]

Dutch colonialism in the Netherlands Indies ended with the Japanese occupation in 1942, as part of the Japanese campaign to establish an East Asian commonwealth.[55]

The Japanese Occupation (1942–45)

The three-and-a-half-year Japanese occupation was a blessing in disguise for the development of churches in Indonesia. In order to

---

51. H. Richard Niebuhr, *Christ and Culture* (New York: Harper & Brothers, 1956), 191.

52. John Stott, *The Living Church: Convictions of a Lifelong Pastor* (Downers Grove, IL: IVP Books, 2007), 133.

53. Van den End, "The Colonial Era: 1800–1900," 147.

54. See Lamin Sanneh, *Translating the Message: The Missionary Impact on Culture* (Maryknoll, NY: Orbis Books, 1990).

55. Titaley, "From Abandonment to Blessing," 76.

pursue their agenda of establishing "the Greater Asia Co-prosperity Sphere,"[56] the Japanese colonial administration expelled the Dutch colonialists and replaced the European leadership of the churches with local Christians. Simon Marantika, for example, was appointed as Chairman of the Synod of the Protestant Church of Maluku in 1942.[57] The change of leadership to locals made Christians realize their responsibility to the faith they embraced.[58] In other words, under the Japanese occupation, the Indonesian churches experienced a "moratorium" in the sense that all forms of contact, including aid, between the churches and their European mission boards were completely severed.[59] This experience, in spite of the ensuing difficulties, actually became a blessing for the churches as it increased their fighting spirit in preparing them for self-reliance later on.

During the Japanese occupation, Japanese ministers played an important role in the continuation of Christian missions in Indonesia. On several occasions, the church and Christian mission organizations in Japan sent ministers to Indonesia to assist local churches. The ministers were assigned to several areas in Borneo, North Celebes, South Celebes, and the Moluccas. Their duties included not only "providing funds" and "ordaining Indonesians as ministers," but also "organizing courses for church workers" and "visiting the congregations."[60] With support from Japanese ministers, the Indonesian churches tried as much as possible to survive without European aid. When a transition of power from the Dutch to the Japanese took place in several places, the Muslims took advantage of the situation and intimidated or even persecuted Christians. At that time, a number of Indonesian Christians and European missionaries were killed.[61] The presence of

56. Van den End, "1800–2005: A National Overview: Indonesian Christianity during the Japanese Occupation, 1942–1945," in *A History of Christianity in Indonesia*, ed. Aritonang and Steenbrink, 179.

57. Van den End, "Indonesian Christianity during the Japanese Occupation, 1942–1945," 182.

58. Titaley, "From Abandonment to Blessing," 76.

59. Simatupang, "Christian Presence in War," 81.

60. Van den End, "Indonesian Christianity during the Japanese Occupation, 1942–1945," 184.

61. Van den End, "Indonesian Christianity during the Japanese Occupation,

the Japanese ministers was also intended to protect Christians and to end their persecution by Muslims, as witnessed by the case of Rev. Shusho Miyahira in Makassar, South Celebes.[62]

Here we cannot help but note the immensity of God's providential care for the Indonesian church. Who would have thought that the Christian church in Japan, where Christianity was once banned and Christians were a minority group numbering merely half a million in 1940,[63] could display such deep solidarity with the Indonesian church? Showing solidarity as members of the body of Christ required sacrifice. Van den End notes that the church and mission organizations in Japan sent ten Japanese ministers to Indonesia, but only six arrived safely in January 1944, after their ship was torpedoed by an American submarine. But they were not dismayed by the experience, and in the same year sent another nine ministers to Indonesia.[64]

The main challenge for the Indonesian churches during that time was to prepare themselves for independence and self-reliance, to become what Simatupang calls "protochurches."[65] He writes,

> With the Japanese occupation, the Western dominance over Indonesia came to an end. But the church in the meantime had become strongly rooted in the nation. Historically, the church in Indonesia was planted and matured under the umbrella of Western expansion. During the Japanese occupation the churches proved able to continue their existence after that historical external umbrella was removed. In a way, the Japanese occupation prepared the churches for the next period, the period of national independence, by infusing into the minds of the leaders of the churches the hard lesson that being the church means living under God in the midst of the

---

1942–1945," 179–80.

62. Van den End, "Indonesian Christianity during the Japanese Occupation, 1942–1945," 184.

63. Van den End, "Indonesian Christianity during the Japanese Occupation, 1942–1945," 180.

64. Van den End, "Indonesian Christianity during the Japanese Occupation, 1942–1945," 184.

65. Simatupang, "Dynamics for Creative Maturity," 94.

realities of the day without any ties, if necessary, with churches outside the country.[66]

After Japan was defeated and the Second World War ended, the Indonesian churches had to deal once again with their European counterparts. However, this time they did not treat their fellow European pastors as masters, but as equals. Becoming a self-reliant church reached its peak at the proclamation of Indonesian independence in 1945.

Independent Indonesia (1945–98)

During the period of Indonesian independence, the Protestant churches underwent a drastic change: they no longer depended on overseas mission organizations, but became independent and self-reliant, with a national profile. The main struggle of the Protestant churches during the independent era was how to get involved in the nationalist movement. Different from the Catholic churches, which participated in the nationalist movement almost without obstruction, the Protestant churches faced a great challenge. In what way could Protestant churches, which were basically ethnic churches, such as the Protestant Church of the Moluccas, Minahasa Evangelical Christian Church, and the Batak Protestant Christian Church, become Indonesian churches that viewed "the whole of Indonesia" as "one field for the common calling of all churches to witness and service"?[67] In May 1950, Protestant church leaders decided to found Dewan Gereja-Gereja di Indonesia (the DGI, the Council of Churches in Indonesia), with the intention of founding the Gereja Kristen yang Esa di Indonesia (the Single Christian Church in Indonesia). One motivation for the DGI, says Simatupang, was "national consciousness, in the sense that the ethnic churches were seen as being called to grow into one church in order to express together the Christian presence in the nation."[68]

The Protestant Christians played a strategic role in achieving a

---

66. Simatupang, "Dynamics for Creative Maturity," 99.
67. Simatupang, "Dynamics for Creative Maturity," 108.
68. Simatupang, "Doing Theology in Indonesia Today," 25.

united Indonesia. From May 29 to June 1, 1945, Badan Penyelidik Usaha Persiapan Kemerdekaan Indonesia (BPUPKI, the Investigating Committee for Preparatory Work for Indonesian Independence) met to discuss the formation of Indonesia's ideological basis of state (*Weltanschauung*). The discussion reached a deadlock due to the ideological confrontation between *golongan Islam* (the Muslim nationalists group), who wanted Islam to be the ideological basis of the state, and *golongan kebangsaan* (the secular nationalists group), who wanted Indonesia to be a secular state in which religion would be separated from the state.[69] Sukarno's address to the meeting about *Pancasila* on June 1, 1945, was well received by both parties and succeeded in breaking the deadlock.[70]

However, on June 22, 1945, *Pancasila* was reformulated in a document known as the Jakarta Charter (Piagam Jakarta). In this document, the first principle of *Pancasila*, the principle of Lordship, was reformulated by adding the clause "*with the obligation to carry out the Islamic law (Shari'ah) to its adherents*" after "Lordship." Although it had been repeatedly asserted that the clause would apply only to Indonesian Muslims and not to other religious groups, it soon attracted rigorous objections, especially from the Christian side. Latuharhary, a strong Protestant figure and member of BPUPKI, expressed his

69. The Muslim and secular nationalists may be described as follows: "'Secular nationalists' [are] a group of Indonesian political leaders—Muslims, Catholics, Protestants, Hindus or others—who firmly rejected religion as the basis of the state, even though they were not personally secularists, nor lacking in religious sentiments, tendencies and affiliations. They simply chose not to use religion as a political ideology or as a political system, but rather restricted it to their personal lives. In contrast, . . . 'Muslim nationalists' [are] that group of Muslim leaders, who deeply committed to their faith, believed that Islam should be used as the basis of the state. They believed that religion and state cannot be separated since there is no separation of worldly matters and other-worldly affairs in the teachings of Islam" (Faisal Ismail, "Islam, Politics and Ideology in Indonesia: A Study of the Process of Muslim Acceptance of the *Pancasila*" [PhD diss., McGill University, 1995], 4–5).

70. Derived from Sanskrit and Pali, the word *pancasila* means "five principles"— *panca* (five) and *sila* (principles). The five principles of *Pancasila* are: one Lordship, a just and civilized humanity, the unity of Indonesia, democracy guided by the spirit of wisdom in deliberation and representation, and social justice for all the people of Indonesia.

objection by stating that the phrase "could have considerable consequences regarding other religions, and moreover could lead to difficulties in connection with the *adat-istiadat* (common law)."[71] In line with Latuharhary, other secular nationalists such as Wongsonegoro and Hoesein Djajadiningrat also opposed the phrase, thinking that it "may well create fanaticism, because it seems that Muslims would be forced to keep *shari'ah*."[72]

On August 18, 1945, one day after the Proclamation of Independence, in the first meeting of Panitia Persiapan Kemerdekaan Indonesia (PPKI, the Preparatory Committee for Indonesian Independence), the Jakarta Charter was abrogated.[73] Shortly before the opening of PPKI's formal meeting, Muhammad Hatta, who later became the first Vice President of Indonesia, proposed changes to the draft of the preamble of the Constitution. Hatta had been informed by a Japanese navy officer that in the eyes of Christians, the clause "with the obligation to carry out the Islamic law (*shari'ah*) to its adherents" was "discriminatory against all minority groups," since it served only part of the Indonesian people.[74] If this phrase remained, Christians living predominantly in the eastern parts of Indonesia would not join the Republic. In short, their agreement resulted in the removal of the Islamic clause from the preamble and the body of the Constitution.

The effort of the Protestant Church to change from an ethnic church to an "Indonesian church" proceeded through the church's opposition to the Jakarta Charter in order to create a unified Indonesia. In other words, it determined that the church's mission should not be limited to serving its own interests, but should involve efforts to become a blessing for all people. The Protestant leader W. J. Rumambi, who was later appointed as a minister in Sukarno's Dwikora II cabinet, expressed it this way:

71. B. J. Boland, *The Struggle of Islam in Modern Indonesia* (The Hague: Martinus Nijhoff, 1971), 28.

72. Boland, *Struggle of Islam*, 29.

73. PPKI was founded on August 7, 1945, to replace BPUPKI and was led by Sukarno and Muhammad Hatta as its chairman and vice chairman, respectively.

74. Deliar Noer, *Partai Islam di Pentas Nasional, 1945–1965* (Jakarta: Pustaka Utama Grafiti, 1987), 40.

We view it [*Pancasila*] according to our confidence as Christians. We do it because we are also responsible for the salvation and the happiness of Indonesia. That responsibility is firstly to our Lord and then to our fellows. . . . Our task as Christians in Indonesia in the political field is to join to attempt to secure the welfare, peace, justice and orderliness for the whole people of Indonesia and not only for the Christians, by words as well as by actions, based on the salvation plan of our Lord as evident in our Holy Scriptures; Jesus Christ is the Saviour of the world and the Saviour of Indonesia as well. That is our confidence.[75]

Following independence, Sukarno became the first President of Indonesia, and his administration is known as "the Old Order."

The Old Order (1945–66)

During the Sukarno administration, the challenge faced by the Protestant churches still revolved around the Jakarta Charter. In order to compensate Muslim nationalists for their legislative "loss" of the Jakarta Charter, on January 3, 1946, a special Ministry of Religion was established in the executive branch of the Old Order government, in spite of criticisms raised. Latuharhary from the Protestant side argued that this ministry "might give rise to feelings of offence and dislike" and suggested that "religious affairs be handled by the Ministry of Education."[76] One sharp judgment came from J. W. M. Bakker, a Catholic writer, who thought that this ministry from the beginning turned out to be "a bulwark of Islam and an outpost for an Islamic State."[77]

The Ministry of Religion was initially intended to administer the affairs of Islam only. Although it was later expanded by providing sections for non-Muslim religions—Protestant, Catholic, and

75. Jan S. Aritonang, "1800–2005: A National Overview: Independent Indonesia (1945–2005)," in *A History of Christianity in Indonesia*, ed. Aritonang and Steenbrink, 198.
76. Aritonang, "Independent Indonesia (1945–2005)," 190.
77. J. W. M. Bakker, "De godsdienstvrijheid in de Indonesische grondwetten," *Missiewerk* 4 (1956): 215, quoted in Boland, *Struggle of Islam*, 106.

Hindu-Buddhist—the ministry's existence, as Clifford Geertz has put it, "is for all intents and purposes a *santri* [devout Islam] affair from top to bottom."[78] It has been used by *santri* Muslims to promote their agendas. With the purpose of forcing *abangan* (nominal) Muslims[79] to recommit to the Islamic religion, *santri* Muslims attempted to use the Ministry of Religion to prohibit the practice of the religion of the *abangan*, known as *kebatinan* (mysticism).[80] In 1952, the ministry proposed a minimum definition of religion, which included three necessary elements, namely, "a prophet, a holy book, and international recognition." This effort, however, did not succeed, due to opposition from the Balinese Hindus.[81] In 1961, the Ministry again advanced a definition of religion with the same purpose of denying mysticism as one of Indonesia's recognized religions. The definition of religion proposed contained the following necessary elements: "a holy scripture, a prophet, the absolute lordship of *Tuhan Yang Maha Esa* [God], and a system of law for its followers."[82] Based on this definition of religion, for political reasons, Sukarno then issued Presidential Ordinance no.1/1965, which decreed that there were six officially recognized religions, namely Islam, Protestantism, Catholicism, Hinduism, Buddhism, and Confucianism.[83]

78. Clifford Geertz, *The Religion of Java* (Chicago: University of Chicago Press, 1976), 200. The *santri* are Muslims who follow the Islamic orthodox teaching and practices more strictly and carefully. See Benyamin F. Intan, *"Public Religion" and the Pancasila-Based State of Indonesia: An Ethical and Sociological Analysis* (New York: Peter Lang, 2006), 36.

79. Nominal or *abangan* Muslims know very little about Islam, but still consider themselves Muslim. Their religion is actually based on a mixture of different religions, including Islam, Hindu-Buddhism, and animism. See Intan, *"Public Religion" and the Pancasila-based State of Indonesia,* 36.

80. *Kebatinan* is the indigenous religion of the Javanese, mostly in Central Java, who practice mystical beliefs based on a mixture of different religions including Hinduism, Buddhism, Islam, and animism. Cf. Howard M. Federspiel, *A Dictionary of Indonesian Islam* (Athens, OH: Ohio University Center for International Studies, 1995), 124.

81. Niels Mulder, *Mysticism and Everyday Life in Contemporary Java: Cultural Persistence and Change* (Singapore: Singapore University Press, 1978), 4.

82. Mulder, *Mysticism and Everyday Life in Contemporary Java,* 6.

83. Mulder, *Mysticism and Everyday Life in Contemporary Java,* 6.

Regrettably, Christians displayed an inconsistent and ambiguous attitude in its response to the government decisions. They had initially rejected the Jakarta Charter and the presence of the Ministry of Religion due to their discriminative nature. However, they remained silent as religion was redefined in such a way as to lead President Sukarno to officially recognize six religions, including Protestantism. This response by Christians seemed to have been motivated by the position that Christianity now enjoyed as one of the official religions. Still, for whatever reason, Christians should have critically evaluated the redefinition of religion, as this policy tended to be discriminatory and could have provided opportunities for the state to interfere in the internal affairs of religion.

In what follows, we will discuss whether this inconsistent and ambiguous attitude of Christianity toward the government laws regarding religion continued in the next administration, known as "the New Order" under President Suharto.

The New Order (1966–98)

In 1965, General Suharto, supported by various elements of the nation, succeeded in suppressing the attempt of the Communist Party (PKI)—commonly called the G-30-S/PKI or Gestapu/PKI—to overthrow the Indonesian government. After that, the leadership of the nation transferred from Sukarno to Suharto. In the aftermath of the aborted coup, traditionalist Muslims (*Nahdlatul Ulama*, NU) and modernist Muslims (*Muhammadiyah*), with support from the army, were actively engaged in anti-Communist retaliation.[84] Their youth groups went from village to village, arresting and executing suspected Communists. For most of them, the fight against the Communists could be considered "an aspect of the *djihād*, the 'Holy War' against the enemies of Islam, God's foes."[85] Consequently, within months at least half a million Indonesians were killed, and hundreds of

---

84. Greg Barton, "Islam and Politics in the New Indonesia," in *Islam in Asia: Changing Political Realities*, ed. Jason F. Isaacson and Colin Rubenstein (New Brunswick, London: Transaction Publishers, 2002), 8.

85. Boland, *Struggle of Islam*, 145.

thousands of others were jailed and persecuted.[86] Most of these victims were *abangan* Muslims who had turned Communist.

In this dangerous situation, it became important for everyone to be affiliated with a recognized religion; otherwise, one could easily be suspected of being a Communist. As mentioned before, the issuance of Presidential Ordinance no.1/1965 explained that the term "religion" in Article 29 of the 1945 Constitution referred to the officially acknowledged religions of Islam, Protestantism, Catholicism, Hinduism, Buddhism, and Confucianism. However, due to the involvement of Chinese Communists in the aborted coup, in 1966 the Majelis Permusyawaratan Rakyat Sementara (MPRS, Provisional People's Representative Council) issued its Decision no. XXVII, in which Confucianism was removed from the list of acknowledged religions, as it was regarded as a Chinese religion and belief. It is important to note that in seeking protection, many of the *abangan* Muslims who previously supported the PKI or a PKI-affiliated front organization, did not recommit themselves to Islam. Instead, they converted to Christianity. "The slaughter of the suspected 'communist' *abangan* in 1965–66, and the pressure to show that one had become an obedient Muslim," as Niels Mulder put it, "boomeranged on Islam."[87] In early 1969, the World Council of Churches reported that from 1965 to 1968, 2.5 million *abangan* Muslims had converted to Christianity.

The struggle of the Protestant churches at the beginning of the New Order focused mainly on the consequences of the conversion of *abangan* Muslims to Christianity. In response to this change of religion, Muslims urged the government to hold a Musyawarah Antar Umat Beragama (Inter-Religious Consultation) between Muslim and Christian leaders with the Minister of Religion as moderator. The consultation was held on November 30, 1967. Favoring the Islamic group, the consultation envisaged a joint statement focused on two major points: (1) Every religious group ought to restrict its religious

---

86. Benedict R. O'G. Anderson, *Language and Power: Exploring Political Cultures in Indonesia* (Ithaca, London: Cornell University Press, 1990), 6.

87. Mulder, *Mysticism and Everyday Life*, 6.

activities to its own circle. (2) No religious group should try to convert anyone who already has a religion.[88] Both the DGI (the Council of Churches in Indonesia) and the Majelis Agung Wali Gereja Indonesia (MAWI, the Supreme Council of Indonesian Bishops) refused to sign the joint statement, since the prohibition to convert anyone from one religion to another, as T. B. Simatupang, who represented the DGI, asserted, contradicts the very message of the Bible, which is to spread the gospel to all mankind (Mark 16:15).[89] However, both councils agreed that mission work had to refrain from "all kinds of improper methods of propaganda such as persuading, seducing, forcing and offering gifts."[90] The consultation eventually ended without producing a statement that would have prohibited a religious organization from introducing another religion to a person who had already embraced a religion.[91]

The Muslims' response in this case did not stop here. Since so many *abangan* Muslims had become Christians, they now urged the government to limit the building of places of worship. On September 13, 1969, the Minister of Religion, together with the Minister of Internal Affairs, issued Surat Keputusan Bersama (SKB, Joint Decision) No.1/BER/MDN-MAG/1969, regarding the building of places of worship, in which it was stated that the building of every place of worship would require permission from the Head of the Local Government (Article 1), and prior to issuing the permission, the official in charge could request the opinion of representatives of local religious organizations and spiritual leaders (Article 3).[92] Although this decree was intended to apply to all religious groups, in reality it was enforced only to regulate the building of worship places of non-Muslims, particularly Christians. This decree and especially Article 3 has made it difficult, if not impossible, for non-Muslims and

88. Boland, *Struggle of Islam*, 231.

89. T. B. Simatupang, *The Fallacy of a Myth* (Jakarta: Pustaka Sinar Harapan, 1995), 199.

90. Aritonang, "Independent Indonesia (1945–2005)," 208.

91. Simatupang, *Fallacy of a Myth*, 199–200.

92. Weinata Sairin, ed., *Himpunan Peraturan di Bidang Keagamaan* (Jakarta: BPK Gunung Mulia, 1996), 3–6.

Christians in particular to build places of worship in a community where Muslims are a majority.

After 1965, Christianity experienced tremendous growth, especially numerically. Apart from the role of Indonesian evangelists, such as Petrus Octavianus, Stephen Tong, and Chris Marantika, many overseas mission agencies were working in Indonesia, especially those of evangelical and Pentecostal affiliation.[93] The rapid growth of the churches caused concern on the part of the Muslims, who again urged the Ministry of Religion to issue Ministerial Decision no. 70/1978 on "the Guidelines for Evangelism," where section (a) of Article 2 states that religious evangelism aimed at people who already have a religion is not permitted by any means.[94] Although the decree did not indicate which religions were involved, it was obviously targeted at Christian evangelists. Moreover, in order to tighten the state's control of evangelistic activities, the Minister of Religion issued Ministerial Decision no. 77/1978 concerning "Foreign Aid to Religious Institutions in Indonesia." In its implementation, this decree banned foreign missionaries from coming to Indonesia (Article 3, section 1). Any foreign aid in the form of workers, materials, or finance can be implemented only after receiving approval from, and passing through, the Minister of Religion (Article 2).[95]

The DGI and the MAWI responded to these decrees by questioning the Ministry of Religion's decision to promulgate them before discussing them with all religious groups, if indeed the Ministry was meant to serve all religions. They submitted strong objections to the Minister of Religion, Vice President Adam Malik, and even to President Suharto, asking that the regulations be revoked. Their primary reason was that the regulations were contrary to Article 29 of the Constitution, which guarantees religious freedom. Moreover, Article 29 of the Constitution was to be applied by the legislature in cooperation with the executive arm of the government, namely, Dewan Perwakilan Rakyat (DPR, People's Representative Council)

---

93. Aritonang, "Independent Indonesia (1945–2005)," 203, 208.

94. Simatupang, *Fallacy of a Myth*, 202.

95. Simatupang, *Fallacy of a Myth*, 204–5.

and the President, and not by ministerial regulations with guidance from the President. Based on these considerations, the regulations had, in their opinion, no legal basis at all.[96] The *Sinar Harapan* daily, representing the Christians' voice, expressed a Christian view in its editorial:

> We do not have to become an expert on the comparative study of religion in order to know that every major religion cannot accept becoming a religion which is not universal. . . . This means that the freedom for propagating religion to all persons is an intrinsic part of the universality of religion.[97]

In response to the concerns of the DGI and the MAWI, the government later issued Joint Decision of the Minister of Religion and the Minister for Home Affairs no. 1/1979 concerning "the Guidelines for Evangelism and Foreign Aid to Religious Institutions in Indonesia," which reinforced the Ministerial Decision no. 70/1978, but without section (a) of Article 2, and made the application of the Ministerial Decision no. 77/1978 less restrictive.[98]

Another major challenge for the Christian church during the New Order was the implementation of the *azas tunggal Pancasila* (*Pancasila* as the only basis), ideologically and philosophically, for the life of society, nation, and state. Initially, through the ratification of Undang-Undang (UU) No. 3/1985, the obligation to adhere to the *azas tunggal Pancasila* was limited to political parties. However, after the Parliament ratified UU No. 8/1985 a few months later, adherence to the *azas tunggal Pancasila* was required of all social and collective organizations, including religious organizations. To this obligation, all religious organizations, particularly Muslim and Christian, responded by renouncing it. Sjafruddin Prawiranegara, a prominent Muslim leader and former Prime Minister, wrote in response:

96. Ramlan Surbakti, "Interrelation between Religious and Political Power under New Order Indonesia" (PhD diss., Northern Illinois University, 1991), 153.

97. *Sinar Harapan*, 1978, cited in Surbakti, "Interrelation between Religious and Political Power," 354.

98. See Sairin, ed., *Himpunan Peraturan*, 63–68.

We Muslims can wholeheartedly accept [*Pancasila*] as the basis or principle of the state, but as Muslims, it is impossible for us to accept it as the [only basis] for our lives. It's impossible for the Quran and Hadith to be exchanged for the 1945 Constitution based on *Pancasila*.[99]

Hence, for Muslims, *Pancasila* is to be understood only as the basis of the state, but never as the basis for social life.

Like their Muslim counterparts, Christians typically apply the term *azas tunggal* only to Christ or the Bible; thus, it is impossible to apply it to an ideology of the state. Munawir Sjadzali, the Minister of Religion at that time, recalled what one Christian pastor told him that even "if the sky should fall down," he "would not accept the [*azas tunggal Pancasila*]."[100] This government policy caused some Christians, who used to be strong defenders of *Pancasila*, to become its opponents. This was the reason why, in mid-1985, some Christian students in Central Java "were no longer willing to take part in the numerous and often pseudo-religious nationalistic ceremonies at school, such as bowing before the flag and saluting it."[101]

In response to this government policy, delegations to the tenth General Assembly of the DGI in October 1984 in Ambon discussed the fundamental question whether the DGI is a church—a communion of believers in Christ—or a social organization. They came to the conclusion that the DGI is a church organization, and accordingly changed its name from DGI (*Council* of Churches in Indonesia) to *Communion* of Churches in Indonesia (Persekutuan Gereja-gereja di Indonesia, PGI). According to Article 3 of its Statute, the PGI as a communion of believers "has its foundation (*dasar*) in Jesus Christ,

99. Sjarifuddin Prawiranegara, "Guidelines for Islamic Propagation in Indonesia," *Indonesia Reports—Culture and Society Supplement* 12 (October 1985): 6.

100. Douglas Ramage, *Politics in Indonesia: Democracy, Islam, and the Ideology of Tolerance* (New York: Routledge, 1995), 37.

101. K. A. Steenbrink, "Indonesia: A Christian Minority in a Strong Position," in *Missiology, an Ecumenical Introduction: Texts and Contexts of Global Christianity*, ed. A. Camps, F. J. Verstraelen, L. A. Hoedemaker, and M. R. Spindler (Grand Rapids: Eerdmans, 1995), 91.

Lord and Savior, in agreement with God's Word in the Bible [1 Cor. 3:11]." Further, Article 5 of the PGI's Statute states that as part of Indonesian society, the PGI "in light of the foundation described in Article 3, fully accepts its responsibility to recognize, realize and promote *Pancasila* as 'the only basis' (*azas tunggal*) for social, national and [state] life in Indonesia."[102] Although the Assembly may not distinguish clearly between "foundation" (*dasar*) and "the only basis" (*azas tunggal*), it had at least secured "the theological basis."[103]

The problem was that the acceptance formulation includes 1 Corinthians 3:11, which says that "there is no foundation other than the one that has been laid, Jesus Christ." After the adoption of *Pancasila* as the *only basis* was sanctioned at the Assembly, certain opinions were voiced within government circles that the government's idea of *Pancasila* as the only basis seemed different from the church's idea. In order to avoid the problem of having a "double" basis instead of one, the PGI later changed its Statute by using biblical texts other than 1 Corinthians 3:11—texts that do not contain the word "foundation"' (*dasar*). In this way, the problem of the acceptance of *Pancasila* as the *only basis* by PGI was considered resolved.[104]

Another challenge that churches had to face during the New Order was the ratification of UU No. 7/1989 concerning the establishment of Islamic religious courts to deal with marriage, inheritance, and endowment. This bill affirmed the independence and equality of Islamic courts in relation to civil courts. This means that Islamic judges are equal to other judges in other courts in terms of position, rights, and facilities given by the state. More than that, there is still a possibility, at least in theory, for an Islamic judge to be appointed by the President to serve as head of the Supreme Court.[105]

Arguing against this law, Abdurrahman Wahid, who was at the time chairman of the NU, the largest traditionalist Islamic organization, maintained that there should be only "one law code for all

---

102. Steenbrink, "Indonesia," 91.
103. Steenbrink, "Indonesia," 91.
104. Simatupang, *Fallacy of a Myth*, 187.
105. Ismail, "Islam, Politics and Ideology in Indonesia," 290–93.

Indonesian citizens."[106] Like Wahid, the famous human rights lawyer Adnan Buyung Nasution (himself a Muslim) rejected such a regulation by reiterating that all Indonesians should be equal before the law, based on the sole criterion of "sameness of citizenship," not of religious faith.[107] In agreement with Wahid and Nasution, Eka Darmaputera, a prominent Protestant theologian, saw the promulgation of Islamic-oriented religious court and education laws as evidence of government regulation serving one particular faith only. For him, law and government policy should apply equally to all Indonesian citizens. Due to these developments, he was worried that the nation would no longer appear "inclusive and non-discriminatory."[108]

When the Islamic courts bill was formally submitted to the DPR by the government for approval, the Protestants voiced strong opposition through the PGI. They presented three objections:

1. In line with the "Insights of the Indonesian Archipelago" (*Wawasan Nusantara*), only one national law should be applied to serve national interests;
2. The bill on Islamic religious courts was beyond the DPR jurisdiction, since it was the responsibility of the entire nation to lay down a basic framework in the legal field; and
3. The bill was in "contradiction" to the *Pancasila* and the 1945 constitution in a true sense.[109]

Through their magazine *Hidup* (Life), Catholics charged that the bill on religious courts was "an attempt to revive the Jakarta Charter," since the bill was "discriminatory towards non-Muslim groups in the legal domain."[110]

Last but not least, during the New Order era, the churches also encountered challenging maneuvers from the Ikatan Cendekiawan Muslim Indonesia (ICMI, Association of Indonesian Muslim

106. Ramage, *Politics in Indonesia*, 87.
107. Ramage, *Politics in Indonesia*, 87.
108. Ramage, *Politics in Indonesia*, 174.
109. Ismail, "Islam, Politics and Ideology in Indonesia," 293–94.
110. Ismail, "Islam, Politics and Ideology in Indonesia," 294.

Intellectuals), which Suharto founded in December 1990. Comprising a large number of government officials and leading fundamentalist Islamic intellectuals, the ICMI was established not only as an ally to short-circuit Suharto's potential opposition—especially the military generals who were maneuvering against him—but also as a tool to attract certain Islamic groups to Suharto's side prior to the general election of 1992 and the presidential election of 1993.[111]

This emerging closeness between Islam and the state received much criticism from *abangan* Muslims as well as non-Muslims. Eka Darmaputera, for example, argued that this alliance between political power and religion would put national unity in danger. He described this direct interference of religion in the realm of the state as follows:

> Slowly but surely, the judiciary system, the substance of our leg-islation, the policies of our government, the recruitment and the promotion system of our bureaucracy, etc., are all tailored in such a way to serve the political interest of one particular religious group only.[112]

The most ardent critique of ICMI, however, came from Wahid, who was at the time chairman of the NU. He argued that in order to satisfy his own short-term political imperatives, Suharto had offered an opportunity to the dangerously sectarian Muslim leaders to legiti-mize their intolerant, and ultimately anti-*Pancasilaist*, Islamic political views. Wahid repeatedly warned the President that playing with fun-damentalist fire could lead to "sectarian violence like that in Algeria," which could result in disintegration.[113]

111. R. William Liddle, "Media Dakwah Scripturalism: One Form of Islamic Political Thought and Action in New Order Indonesia," in *Leadership and Culture in Indonesian Politics* (Sydney: Asian Studies Association of Australia, in association with Allen & Unwin, 1996), 283.

112. Eka Darmaputera, "The Search for a New Place and a New Role of Reli-gion within the Democratic Order of Post-Soeharto Indonesia: Hopes and Dan-gers" (paper presented at the Third Annual Abraham Kuyper Award, Princeton, NJ, December 1, 1999), 20.

113. Robert W. Hefner, *Civil Islam: Muslims and Democratization in Indonesia* (Princeton: Princeton University Press, 2000), 163.

Wahid was right that the use of religion to co-opt Suharto's potential opposition could lead to sectarianism, disunity, and possibly even disintegration. From 1995 to 1997, "ethno-religious" riots broke out in East Java and West Java, areas regarded as strongholds of Wahid's NU, causing hundreds of churches and scores of Chinese shops to be burned and destroyed. The riots, led by "a small dirty-tricks bureau operating out of ICMI" and involving Wahid's NU members, were intended to discredit him by showing that he could not control his own members and that his vision of a tolerant Islam had little support among his followers.[114] In the Situbondo incident on October 10, 1996, known as "Black Thursday," twenty-four churches were demolished and burned by three thousand people. A pastor of Gereja Pentakosta Pusat Surabaya (GPPS, the Pentecostal Church of Surabaya), together with his wife, child, nephew, and an evangelist of the church, all died when their church in Situbondo was burned that day.[115] In response to this state-approved violence, during late 1997 and early 1998 Wahid and the NU leadership, in collaboration with Christians, created a network of activists to guard against violence. For example, to prevent further terror in East Java, the NU's youth activists organized peace patrols around Christian churches. Although repeated acts of provocation occurred, there were no eruptions of sectarian violence.[116]

Summary

A number of conclusions are now in order.

First, the church did well in welcoming the conversion of *abangan* Muslims to Christianity. This in itself brought a blessing to the church, despite the price it had to pay in encountering Muslim maneuvers due to the change in religion. On the other hand, in this situation

114. Robert W. Hefner, "Islam and Nation in the Post-Suharto Era," in *The Politics of Post-Suharto Indonesia*, ed. Adam Schwarz and Jonathan Paris (New York: Council on Foreign Relations Press, 1999), 56–57.

115. See Aritonang, "Independent Indonesia (1945–2005)," 218.

116. Robert W. Hefner, "Profiles in Pluralism: Religion and Politics in Indonesia," in *Religion on the International News Agenda*, ed. Mark Silk (Hartford, CT: Greenberg Center, 2000), 94.

the church also needed to beware and be alert by asking whether the conversion of the *abangan* Muslims was genuine or, rather, motivated by their need to seek protection from the church "as far as it is not Islam." When discussing this matter in his book, *Indonesian Revival: Why Two Million Came to Christ*, Avery Willis mentions three main factors that caused the conversion of *abangan* Muslims to Christianity—namely, spiritual need, government, and protection.[117] Thus, the church had to beware of the motivation behind the conversion. If there were motives other than spiritual need, the conversion would no longer be genuine and could result in the rise of syncretism and hypocrisy, reproved by all religions.

Second, while uncompromising in their obedience to the divine call to preach the gospel to all mankind, the churches also rejected "all kinds of improper methods of propaganda such as persuading, seducing, forcing and offering gifts." This is important for preserving sincerity in conversion. It should be noted, however, that evangelism accompanied by social action does not belong to the "improper methods" category stated above, as the 1974 Lausanne Conference emphasizes—namely, that evangelism cannot be separated from social action. The Conference formulated three kinds of relationships between evangelism and social action:

- *The first relationship* is when social action is considered "*a means to evangelism*." In this relationship, "evangelism and the winning of converts," as John Stott puts it, "are the primary ends in view, but social action is a useful preliminary, an effective means to these ends."[118] The negative side of this relationship is that it easily creates hypocrisy and hence the terms "rice Christians" and "rice evangelists."[119]
- *The second relationship* is when social action functions as "*a manifestation of evangelism*." In this case, Stott maintains

117. Avery T. Willis, Jr., *Indonesian Revival: Why Two Million Came to Christ* (South Pasadena, CA: William Carey Library, 1977), 12–13.

118. John R. W. Stott, *Christian Mission in the Modern World* (Downers Grove, IL: InterVarsity Press, 1975), 26.

119. Stott, *Christian Mission*, 26.

that "social action becomes the 'sacrament' of evangelism, for it makes the message significantly visible."[120] Johannes H. Bavinck, in his magnum opus, *An Introduction to the Science of Missions*, holds this view. "Medical assistance and education," says Bavinck, are more than "a legitimate and necessary means of creating an opportunity for preaching," for "if these services are motivated by the proper love and compassion, then they cease to be simply preparation, and at that very moment become preaching."[121] Bavinck points out that in the preaching of Jesus, his words and deeds are constantly intermingled, as John 5:36 says: "The very works that I am doing, bear witness about me that the Father has sent me."[122]

- *The third relationship* is when social action becomes "*a partner of evangelism.*" Stott explains this approach:

> As partners the two belong to each other and yet are independent of each other. Each stands on its own feet in its own right alongside the other. Neither is a means to the other, or even a manifestation of the other. For each is an end in itself. Both are expressions of unfeigned love. As the National Evangelical Anglican Congress at Keele put it in 1967, "Evangelism and compassionate service belong together in the mission of God" (para. 2.20).[123]

Although evangelism and social action are independent from each other, both are also closely linked to each other as part of God's mission. Support for this view comes, for example, from 1 John 3:17–18, "But if anyone has the world's goods and sees his brother in need, yet closes his heart against him, how does God's love abide in him? Little children, let us not love in word or talk but in deed and in truth."

When obliged to choose one among the three options, evangelicals were divided. Leighton Ford, for example, tended to choose the

120. Stott, *Christian Mission*, 26.

121. J. H. Bavinck, *An Introduction to the Science of Missions* (Grand Rapids: Baker Book House, 1961), 113.

122. Bavinck, *Introduction to the Science of Missions*, 113–14.

123. Stott, *Christian Mission*, 27.

first option, while J. Herman Bavinck the second, and John Stott the third. So which position were the Indonesian churches in? We believe that churches do not have to choose between these options. All three are not something to choose from, but rather something to take advantage of, in the following order: (i), (ii), (iii). This means that social action functions first and foremost as a "means" for evangelism. If this fails, then social action becomes a "manifestation" of evangelism. But if this also fails, then social action should function as a "partner" of evangelism.

Third, the challenges that churches in the New Order era had to face were oriented not only to the Muslims' attempt to implement the Jakarta Charter in various forms, such as in the Ministry of Religion and Islamic religious courts, but also to Suharto's efforts to transform *Pancasila* into a pseudo-religion and the various maneuvers of the ICMI with Suharto's support behind it. While facing such challenges, the Protestant churches did not compromise and remained faithful to their beliefs. In facing these challenges together, they cooperated with the Catholic churches and even with the moderate Muslim side to fight against various forms of injustice that threatened to erode the rights of religious freedom.

Conclusion

It was solely by God's grace that Protestant churches are present as a minority in Indonesia. While the Protestant mission during the VOC era and the Protestant Church were unable to do much in the propagation of the gospel, due to their subordination to the Dutch colonial government, nevertheless God guided European missionary societies in carrying out the task of evangelism throughout the Indonesian archipelago. During the Japanese occupation and the era of independent Indonesia, the Protestant churches learned to become the "Indonesian church" (proto-churches) that is self-reliant and released from dependency on the European missionary societies and the Dutch colonial government. In becoming self-sufficient, the churches learned to rely fully on Christ, the Head of the church, who redeemed them with his blood.

God's mission carried out by the Protestant churches in Indonesia involved not only evangelism, but also social action. In his message at the 1974 Lausanne Conference and in his book *Christian Mission in the Modern World*, John Stott distinguishes mission from evangelism. For him the word *mission* cannot "properly be used to cover everything God is doing in the world." He explains further:

> In [his] providence and common grace he is indeed active in all men and all societies, whether they acknowledge him or not. But this is not his "mission." "Mission" concerns his redeemed people, and what he sends *them* into the world to do.[124]

In other words, mission is a comprehensive concept, describing "everything the church is sent into the world to do."[125] Evangelism, on the other hand, is less comprehensive and actually constitutes a component of mission. In short, one can define mission as "evangelism plus social action."[126] Again, it is solely by the grace of God that the minority churches were able to continue evangelizing in a country that has the largest Muslim population in the world. By his guidance, Christianity played a strategic role in social action when it rejected the Jakarta Charter, thereby preventing the disintegration of the nation and creating a united Indonesia. It is important to note that when Christians engaged in social action, they worked in cooperation even with Muslims to bring about social justice.

As mentioned above, aside from the work of the Holy Spirit, the success of mission work depends strongly on the *theologia in loco* and *translating the message*. It is therefore important for missionaries not only to have a cognitive understanding of the culture of the people they serve, but also to have a deep knowledge of their religious life. As Abraham Kuyper, the Dutch Reformed theologian who held the office of Prime Minister of the Netherlands (1901–5), once stated,

124. Stott, *Christian Mission*, 19.
125. Stott, *Christian Mission*, 30.
126. Stott, *Christian Mission*, 15–30.

In missions, it is not enough for you simply to profess Christ, to learn the language of an unfamiliar people, and to dedicate yourself personally to preaching the gospel in that strange tongue; what is even more essential than daily bread in this regard is that you possess a living rapport with the religious thought-world of the people that you would like to convert, and ultimately that you discover that point of connection that makes you one with them.[127]

Carrying out God's mission sometimes makes enemies. Christians who live consistently in obedience to God's word and do not compromise with sin, will most likely have a lot of enemies. In Matthew 5:44, when Jesus says, "Love your enemies," he assumes that all Christians have enemies. In its original language, "your" is an objective, not a subjective, genitive. This means that your enemy is not someone you hate, but someone who hates you. Here "you" is the object of the enemy and not the subject.

Consequently, when churches carry out God's work in obedience to his will, they cannot escape from challenges and suffering. Jesus sends Christians into the world like "sheep in the midst of wolves" (Matt. 10:16). To become Jesus' followers is not an easy task. Churches have to "deny [themselves] and take up [their] cross" (Matt. 16:24). Nonetheless, they should not be discouraged. Paul reminds us that "the sufferings of this present time are not worth comparing with the glory that is to be revealed to us" (Rom. 8:18). And even more important are Christ's promises to his church: "I will build my church, and the gates of hell shall not prevail against it" (Matt. 16:18), and "I am with you always, to the end of the age" (Matt. 28:20). For his sake, as long as Christ entrusts this minority group of Christians to carry out his mission, the churches in Indonesia should implement the tasks of their calling faithfully and gladly. May the Lord give all of us strength and help his church in Indonesia.

---

127. Abraham Kuyper, *Encyclopaedie der heilige godgeleerdheid* (Amsterdam: J. A. Wormser, 1894), 3:448–49, quoted in Bolt, Bratt, and Visser, eds., *The J. H. Bavinck Reader*, 117.

12

The Missional Minority in Post-Christian Europe

Paul Wells

Abstract

A cloud of spiritual depression hangs over Christians and church life in Europe, laws are rapidly changing, and some are feeling the heat of Christianophobia. Institutional Christianity inspires no confidence, something succinctly expressed by novelist Julian Barnes: "How peculiarly repellent were the perversions of an institutional religion once it began its irreversible decline. The sooner the edifice was swept away the better."[1] Some hanker after the past that perhaps never was, others pin their hopes on revival, and yet others project a golden future because of a new evangelicalism that is, unlike the old orthodoxy, alive and often kicking. Roman Catholics talk about reevangelizing Europe, seemingly taking for granted that time when it was evangelized. How can the church react today and embrace its new position and face this challenge as a missional minority?[2]

---

1. From Julian Barnes's novel *Arthur & George* (London: Vintage Books, 2006).

2. An earlier version of this article was published in Italian: "Essere una minoranza: Sfide e opportunità," *Studi di teologia* 40 (2008): 159–81.

Minority Profiles

Exaggeration of fears and hopes is only human. The church in Korea or the United States seems large by European standards, but it is still a minority in those areas.[3] Many of us in Europe would settle for that kind of minority, if we could. One thing seems certain: Europe and the national entities that compose it are not in any respect Christian, and this is taken to be a bad thing by many confessing believers. We may well be sad, and we should be, about the aimlessness of the lost around us, but this does not mean that it is legitimate to attach the adjective "Christian" to a nation or group of nations and think that this corresponds or corresponded to a spiritual reality. When "Christian" is used to qualify groups or institutions other than the church, the legitimacy of such usage is open to question.

Minorities are notoriously difficult to define, and we are not going to attempt it where others have not passed muster. It is frequently taken for granted that when the word *ethnic, religious,* or *cultural* is added to *minority,* the meaning becomes self-evident, but it is not necessarily so. What is perhaps more interesting is what minorities can do. More often than not, they seem to exercise group pressure on opinion through individuals, either heroes or victims—and sometimes both.

Asking questions about minorities is the same as asking questions about identity and also about marginality: what is it that distinguishes a group from the generality, what danger does it constitute, or what contributions can it make to global society? One of the features of late modern societies is the proliferation of such minorities and the unprecedented influence they exercise because of information technology.[4] Groups militating for ecological ends, for equal rights, particularly in gender issues, for religious causes,

---

3. Steve Bruce, *Secularization: In Defence of an Unfashionable Theory* (Oxford: Oxford University Press, 2011), chap. 8, on the American exception, which he considers "unexceptional" and destined not to last—a thesis hotly contested in some quarters.

4. Manuel Castells, *The Rise of the Network Society: The Information Age: Economy, Society, and Culture* (Oxford: Blackwell, 2000).

or simply acting in civil disobedience, use their minority status effectively to advance their cause, enlarge their constituency, and, in many cases, gain global sympathy and recognition. Recently the agenda of gender equality and massive immigration have become the focus of debate about minorities.[5] It seems that while majorities administer the present on the basis of integration and compromise, minority groups use muscle to innovate and change the social landscape for their own good and, no doubt, from their perspective, for the sake of humanity at large.

A generation ago, it was suggested that there are majority periods in the development of societies when things depend on the greater number and when the status quo is well in place. In minority periods, individuals or groups manage to set the tempo, creating events and deciding the course of things.[6] Late modernity seems to be such a time of rapid change, when pressure groups dictate policy, provided they know how to do it. This is obviously a great challenge and opportunity for the Christian minority in our societies, one that needs to be taken seriously.

The Paradoxical Situation in Europe

In modern Europe, Christian belief—we will ask what that is later—is caught between a rock and a hard place. Christianity has institutional representation, a history, external trappings of past glory, a rooting in the cultural soil of nations, and public visibility. It seems to have all the advantages that accrue from majority status and public recognition. The incense of Christian Europe hangs heavy in the air of the European Union. However, in spite of these apparent advantages, it also finds itself in an increasingly minority situation. Christianity seems to be a spent force, a leftover from the past, rather than a dynamic, future-oriented movement. It is irrelevant to whole swathes of society, above all the young, intellectually

5. Hakan Ovunc Ongur, *Minorities of Europeanization: The New Others of European Social Identity* (Lanham, MD: Lexington Books, 2015).

6. Serge Moscovici, *Psychologie des minorités actives* (Paris: PUF, 1982), 9ff. Translation of *Social Influence and Social Change* (London: Academic Press, 1976).

nonviable to the best minds, the butt of the media, and generally overcome by inertia. It shows few of the features that attract people to participate actively and invest personally. Innovation is the last thing that people would expect from the church. It is like a battery that has lost its charge.

The paradox of a former majority that is now in fact a minority is a major problem for Christian faith in Europe today. Many illustrations could be given of this fact. For instance, theological institutions seem to train people as though they will be speaking to a majority Christian constituency characterized by stable congregations. Little training is given about how to speak to Christianity's despisers or how to evangelize in this setting. It may be doubted whether very many of those teaching have ever faced up to this kind of situation.

While Christianity has an apparently majority status in Europe and is called upon to be a feature of the establishment and of stability in society, its constituency is in fact lightweight. It is *de facto* a minority, but finds it difficult to act like one in order to take advantage of its minority status. The problem is aggravated by the fact that many Christian institutions still seem to think of themselves as a majority and assume they have a place in the sun, even though others have understood for a long time that that is not the case. They think they are playing at home before a friendly crowd, but really they are playing away. Roman Catholic leaders in France still call it the elder daughter of the church and refer to the Roman communion as the "the church of France."

The sooner Christianity stops acting like a majority and accepts minority status and attitudes, the better it will be. This means accepting marginality and the need to accept a new perspective for Christian mission.[7] There are several reasons for saying this, and we will develop some of them briefly in the following pages.[8]

---

7. Stuart Murray, *Church after Christendom* (Carlisle: Paternoster, 2004), chap. 5.

8. Stuart Murray, *Post-Christendom: Church Mission in a Strange New World* (Carlisle: Paternoster, 1998), chap. 7.

A Variegated Christian Identity

"It is agreeable to be admired and loved by those who are like us. It is even better to be loved and admired by those who are different from us."[9] Those are fine words indeed, but surely something not applicable to Christians today, apart from rare exceptions like Mother Theresa, the Abbé Pierre, or the charismatic John Paul II. One reason is that Christianity in Europe *forfeited* the right to be loved a good while ago. At the end of the First World War, Winston Churchill jotted on a sheet of War Office paper:

> All the horrors of the ages were brought together and not only armies but whole populations were thrust into the midst of them. . . . When it was all over, Torture and Cannibalism were the only two expedients the civilised, scientific, Christian States had been able to deny themselves: and they were of doubtful utility.[10]

So climaxed centuries of bloody history that belied all that New Testament Christianity and its founder stood for. The idea of Christian Europe had been exposed once and for all, it might seem, but the myth strangely lived on and is still swallowed hook, line, and sinker by Islamic groups and people from the Third World. However, those within the house know that it has little resemblance to the house built on the Rock.

Europe is "Christian" in the same way that instant coffee is coffee. It bears but a fleeting resemblance to the original substance, and comes in many brands. If we only had instant coffee, we might well ask if there were any such thing as real coffee. Similarly, we might well doubt that there is any objective reality called Christian Europe in a historical or geographical sense.[11] Certainly the notion that Europe is

---

9. Moscovici, *Psychologie des minorités actives*, 230.

10. Quoted by Paul Johnson, *A History of the Modern World* (London: Weidenfeld and Nicolson, 1983), 13–14.

11. Edgar Morin, *Penser l'Europe* (Paris: Gallimard, 1987); Jean-Paul Willaime, *Europe et religions: Les enjeux du XXIe siècle* (Paris: Fayard, 2004), chap. 1; Grace Davie, *Europe: The Exceptional Case: Parameters of Faith in the Modern World*

Christian can be hardly more of a reason for excluding Turkey from the EU than the claim that the United States is WASP would be a reason for excluding Hispanics from it.[12]

Christianity does not define Europe, even though "christiani-tude," a term coined by French sociologist Émile Poujat, indicating a cultural spin-off from certain Christian values, might be pressed into service.[13] Then we could speak of the symbiosis of Christianity, Enlightenment, and the effects of the French Revolution producing a hybrid entity that places some value on human rights, freedom of conscience, tolerance, and justice. It is a memory that mutates, as the title of Grace Davie's book aptly puts it.[14] Secularization theorists see this identity becoming only more hybrid.[15]

Moreover, when we consider the nature of the christianitude that is the religious reality in Europe, we are not faced with a minority, but a patchwork. There is no definable Christian minority as such in Europe. Roman Catholic, Orthodox, Anglican, Reformed, Lutheran, evangelical, and charismatic groups might all be ingredients to beat into a minority mix and pour into a mold. However, even in Catholicism there is an enormous difference between its Spanish, Polish, and French variants. Appearances of unity often belie reality; one invariably ends up with the question: which Christianity?

It is interesting to note that when sociologists get to work, they deal in broad questions like belief in God, belief in the afterlife, and frequency of worship, which anyone with vague religious inclinations can latch on to. Niceties like those that enter into the Nicene Creed

---

(London: Darton, Longman & Todd, 2002); Grace Davie and Danielle Her-vieu-Léger, eds., *Identités religieuses en Europe* (Paris: La Découverte, 1996).

12. Felice Dassetto, "Musulmans de l'Europe des douze: Entre un espace vécu et une stratégie d'implantation," in *Religions et transformations de l'Europe*, ed. Gilbert Vincent and Jean-Paul Willaime (Strasbourg: Presses Universitaires, 1993), 153–63.

13. Émile Poulat, "Le Catholicisme comme culture," in Poulat, *Modernistica: Horizons, physionomies, débats* (Paris: Nouvelles Editions Latines, 1982), chap. 3; cf. also Poujat, "L'Europe religieuse des états," in *Religions et transformations de l'Europe*, ed. Vincent and Willaime, 407–19.

14. Grace Davie, *Religion in Modern Europe: A Memory Mutates* (Oxford: Oxford University Press, 2000).

15. Bruce, *Secularization*, chap. 5.

lie somewhere over the horizon of the belief demanded of believing citizens, who may be Christian by name, but hardly by nature. Twenty-five years ago, the European average for church attendance was 29 percent at least once a week, which seems high, and 40 percent never; 70 percent believed in God (but only 45 percent in Sweden, where Protestant identity is dominant).[16] Today Protestants are said to constitute only 20 percent of the 455 million inhabitants of the EU countries.[17] Church attendance is diminishing rapidly.[18]

The church father Origen thought that Christians in his day were very few in number. Later Eusebius stated they were "the most numerous of peoples." Adolf von Harnack estimated that at the start of the fourth century, Christians were still less than half of the population.[19] None of this gets very far, as it bypasses the question of who defines what a Christian is. Just now, the way "Christian" is defined is evolving, as is the way people define it to themselves.[20] While the majority are no longer Christian in any meaningful way, what it means to be British, German, etc., may include a reference to a Christian heritage, particularly where a state church is still in place.[21]

However, the power of the church itself has eroded and the influence of the clergy is barely evident. The status of religion itself has undergone a metamorphosis. There is what French sociologist Jean-Paul Willaime has called a certain "homogenisation of the religious attitudes of western Europeans." This he sums up with words such as

16. Davie, *Religion in Modern Europe*, 9–10. The statistics are from 1992. See also Willaime, *Europe et religions*, 19, 52–72.

17. Christopher Sinclair, "La minorité protestante en Europe," in *Minorités religieuses dans l'espace européen*, ed. Jean-Pierre Bastian and Francis Messner (Paris: Presses Universitaires de France, 2007) 209.

18. Bruce, *Secularization*, 10. In the United Kingdom, a 2014 YouGov survey found 10 percent saying religion is "very important" to their own lives, 19 percent "fairly important," 24 percent "not very important," and 44 percent "not important at all."

19. Adolf von Harnack, *Mission et expansion du christianisme dans les trios premiers siècles* (Paris: Cerf, 2004), 746.

20. Grace Davie, Paul Heelas, and Linda Woodhead, eds., *Predicting Religion: Christian, Secular and Alternative Cultures* (Aldershot: Ashgate, 2003).

21. Steve Bruce, "The Demise of Christianity in Britain," in *Predicting Religion*, ed. Davie, Heelas, and Woodhead, 53–63.

"do it yourself experience, entertainment, participation, and indifferentism"—or, to put it in a nutshell, "pastiche spirituality."[22] None of these descriptions draw a line between Christianity and some New Age practices.

In the past, majorities were right and there was no question about it.[23] Belonging and conformity went together, but conformity is no longer a condition of social acceptance. Religion in this context becomes a matter that is irrelevant, a private affair, so that freedom of religion is no longer an issue.[24] As institutions, churches are caught in a no-man's land between the globalization that religion offers, where the most exotic can exercise the greatest attraction, and the primacy of individual preference based on subjectivity and choice in the imperious present. In this respect, the Christian churches are no exception to what happens in ultramodern society to other institutions previously invested with symbolic authority: family, school, political parties, or the agents of law and order.[25]

So the situation at the start of the twentieth-first century in Europe seems not wholly dissimilar to that of religion in the Roman world at the time of the planting of Christianity. When religion was formally and publicly practiced, it was for the social good and without any great conviction, whereas private *superstitiones* flourished unchecked, as long as they did not offend public order.[26] Recently, when the congregation at the celebration of the tenth anniversary of Princess Diana's death listened to prayers and sang hymns, did they

22. Willaime, *Europe et religions*, 67; cf. David F. Wells, *Above All Earthly Pow'rs* (Grand Rapids: Eerdmans, 2005), chap. 3 on "pastiche spirituality"; Bruce, *Secularization*, chap. 4 on religion outside the churches.

23. Bastian and Messner, eds., *Minorités religieuses dans l'espace européen*, 63–94.

24. The exception is perhaps in Eastern Europe, where Protestant minorities are subject to pressures from the majority. Cf. Peter G. Danchin and Elizabeth A. Cole, eds., *Protecting the Human Rights of Religious Minorities in Eastern Europe* (New York: Columbia University Press, 2002); Neil Addison, *Religious Discrimination and the Hatred Law* (Abingdon: Routledge-Cavendish, 2006).

25. Willaime, *Europe et religions*, 61ff. and chap. 4.

26. Michael Green, *Evangelism in the Early Church* (Grand Rapids: Eerdmans, 1970), 34–37; Harnack, *Mission*, 43–45. On religion in the ancient city, see Larry Siedentop, *Inventing the Individual: The Origins of Western Liberalism* (London: Penguin / Random House, 2015), 21–28.

believe in the God being invoked any more than their Roman counterparts did when engaged in pagan worship? One may well doubt it.

Europe is a heterogeneous entity—historically, politically, geographically, and religiously—and for this reason it is anomalous to speak of Christian Europe.

The Christian Problem

The situation we have described is one in which Jane and John may believe without belonging. Church planters tell us that new churches bring in people like them, hitherto unconnected.[27] They may also belong without believing, no matter where they darken the door on a Sunday morning. Neither of these situations really tallies with a biblical norm, at least not in New Testament terms, which presents another scenario, one in which believing *and* belonging is the template. In this lies the problem, because if belonging is visible, believing is not, or at least not directly so.[28]

This is the heart of the matter. In sociological terms, the status of religious groups shows a great diversity in present-day Europe, with Catholic Poland or Orthodox Romania at one end of the scale and secular France or Germany at the other. However, the forms of belonging, either to a virtual majority in one case and to an almost invisible minority in the other, have little to do with what being a Christian fundamentally means. The problem for social description is that "Christian" is no more definable in sociological terms than "conversion" is in psychological terms. In both cases there is something about what religious experience claims to be that escapes analysis, and that something is the transcendent element that can be humanly described only as mysterious or irrational. I am not suggesting that there are more Christians in Europe than we might think—there might in fact be fewer—but God only knows.

Transcendence, as Charles Taylor remarked, can be seen either as a

27. Stuart Murray, *Church Planting: Laying Foundations* (Carlisle: Paternoster, 1998), 42–43.

28. See Murray, *Church after Christendom*, chap. 1 on belonging, believing, and behaving.

threat to our greatest good or as an answer to our need for fulfillment of the good.[29] The transcendent aspect of Christian faith refers to *origins* in two ways, and must always be seen in the correct order. *First*, origins in the historical sense are concerned with the Word becoming flesh and we beholding his glory, full of grace and truth (John 1:14). Christianity is defined above all as flowing from this point; what is Christian is related to the truth laid down in incarnational revelation. Being a Communist is not defined by what some Communist party might say or do today, but by Marx, Engels, and the *Communist Manifesto*, with Lenin tagging along as apostle. Similarly, Christianity is not defined by what such and such a church might say or do today, but in terms of its original truth and the apostolic witness to it.

Second, origins in the personal sense are concerned with reception of this truth, which is a work of transcendence. Not by chance did the founder of Christianity teach the necessity of the new birth to enter the kingdom and become one of his followers. Being a Christian implies a personal relationship with Christ himself that results from our spiritual origin. "Unless one is born of water and the Spirit, he cannot enter the kingdom of God" (John 3:5). Belonging to the kingdom, an invisible one for the present, because it is not of this world (John 18:36), depends on being brought into this relationship with Christ by new birth, which in contrast with physical filiation, is a spiritual act of God giving new life (John 3:6). New birth is synonymous in the New Testament with being raised to newness of life from death (Eph. 2:6), to becoming a new creation in Christ in a way similar to the creational light shining in darkness (2 Cor. 4:6).

In a transcendent sense, Christianity refers to an identity related to the founder and perfecter of faith (Heb. 12:2) and initiation into his spiritual body, sonship, love, and hope. These facts lie beyond the scope of the descriptive, statistical, and quantitative analysis of sociology, which has no tools to evaluate their presence and reality. This form of spiritual believing in and belonging to Christ is an act of God, and this is what defines what being a Christian is.

29. Charles Taylor, *A Secular Age* (Cambridge, MA: Belknap Press, 2007), 548–49, on "the imminent frame."

Social analysis can only examine the husk, which may be bigger or smaller, but never the kernel. For those who look at the Christian faith from its transcendent perspective, this kernel is all-important as the presence of new life in Christ. People are neither educated nor born into true faith; neither national origin nor ecclesial belonging can make for true Christianity. Nations or entities like Europe do not become Christian; only disciples who are baptized and instructed do so. The Great Commission of Matthew 28:20 speaks of *all* authority, *all* nations, and *all* the days to the end of the world, not in a tangible, but in an eschatological sense:

> Because of the gospel of the cross a new future has been opened, and the progress of this preaching may be made the measure of the progress of the time of salvation and of the expectation of the consummation of all things.[30]

There is doubtless a Christian minority in Europe today, believers in Christ known to God, but this minority is invisible and may well be silent. Perhaps true followers of Christ have always been in the minority. Even during the height of Christendom, it must have been problematic for true Christians to differentiate their faith from the leaven around them. Has following Christ ever been a bed of roses, and has confessing his name ever been easy? It certainly does not seem that the Master himself anticipated it to be so (John 16:33).

A Minority with a Complex Identity

European nations that were once sending out missionaries are now being targeted by religions whose epicenter is not historically in Europe.[31] Jean-Paul Willaime, the author of this opinion, does not seem to include in his statement Christian missionary activity, giving the impression that as far as Europe is concerned, little is needed, as

---

30. Herman N. Ridderbos, *The Coming of the Kingdom* (Philadelphia: Presbyterian & Reformed, 1969), 174.

31. Willaime, *Europe et religions*, 90.

Christianity is well established. This, however, is precisely what is *not* true in the light of the preceding comments. No spiritually forward movement of Christianity befitting the expectation of the *eschaton* is presently discernable on our continent, at least not in a way comparable to other areas of the globe, such as Latin America or Asia. What Europe needs is prophetic missionary activity.

Islam no doubt sees things in a similar perspective, and its adherents living in Europe are invited to claim the land of unbelief as a *dar al-islam*. When in 1989 the Ayatollah Khomeini placed Salman Rushdie, a British citizen, under a *fatwah*, Islamic jurisdiction was being effectively extended to a new territory. The rule of the Muslim Brotherhood, founded in the 1920s, is "The Quran is our constitution." The preaching of radical imams challenges Muslims to be Islamic Europeans and not European Muslims. The appeal takes the line: "If you are European, British, French, before you are a Muslim, you are not a real Muslim. True Islamic faith demands that one be Muslim first and foremost, before being a citizen, a man or woman, etc."[32] The policy of modern radical Islam is based on persistent opposition to all that is infidel, an attitude developed in the struggle against the Shah and in the action of the Taliban in Afghanistan, to say nothing of the recent Islamic State (ISIS) and Boko Haram.[33]

The Islamic minority seems at present to have many advantages for the propagation of its faith. It can bounce off Western degeneracy, count on people groups, support alienated immigrants, and propose a coherent message and dynamic actions appealing to just causes, such as the right to wear a hijab on a French beach.[34] By comparison, Christianity seems hidebound by tradition, out of sync with the modern world on questions like gender equality, about which it cannot agree, and incapable of institutional renewal.

32. See the analyses of Gilles Kepel in *The War for Muslim Minds* (London: Belknap Press, 2004) chap. 7, and *The Roots of Radical Islam* (London: Saqi Press, 2006).

33. See the chapter on the subject of Islamic extremism and oppositional policies in Ryszard Kapuscinski, *Shah of Shahs* (London: Penguin Books, 2006).

34. A good, though popular description of how Islam profits from adversity against the backdrop of terrorist activity in France, is Andrew Hussey, *The French Intifada: The Long War between France and Its Arabs* (London: Granta Publications, 2015).

If the fundamental reality of Christian identity is being born anew into Christ's kingdom, it is difficult not to sympathize with Islamic radicalism. There is a sense in which we must say "Christ before all else" and that this is implied by the nature of faith. Those who were first called Christians at Antioch (Acts 11:26) were a minority in a pagan society and stood out because of their attachment to Christ, aided and abetted by Jewish opposition. Barnabas saw the grace of God at work and "exhorted them all to remain faithful to the Lord with steadfast purpose" (v. 23). These Christians obviously put Jesus above all, and because of this "a great many people were added to the Lord" (v. 24). There are no doubt situations like that, in the world today, where putting Jesus before other sociocultural realities will lead to sacrifices and maybe even persecution. In principle, Christians must say "Christ before" other realities because of their deep spiritual identity.   *Essential*

However, the either-or choice must be made in extraordinary situations. We do not overtly have to make it very often in Europe, no doubt because of the success of Christian teaching and its impact on our legal system, even though it is now diminishing.[35] Christian identity is complex and does not interpret the world dualistically in terms of black and white. It does not normally ask us to make a choice between being Christian or being French and European, because the salvation it proposes does not cut against creation, but rather redeems it.

In Galatians 3:28, the apostle Paul states: "There is neither Jew nor Greek, there is neither slave nor free, there is no male and female, for you are all one in Christ Jesus." This is the case because all who are "baptized into Christ have put on Christ" and so are "sons of God,

---

35. Harold J. Berman, *Law and Revolution,* vol. 2, *The Impact of the Protestant Reformations on the Western Legal Traditions* (Cambridge, MA: Belknap Press, 2003), 16–17. Berman describes the process: The Western legal tradition was founded on Christian belief in a God-given law. Until 1914, "it continued to be widely believed in the West that the ultimate sources of authentic positive law are divine law, especially the Ten Commandments, natural law discovered by reason and conscience, and historical tradition expressed in sources such as Magna Carta." A century later, after two world wars and the Soviet revolution, this consensus has vanished and is being replaced by humanistic secularism.

through faith" (vv. 26–27). This makes for a complex identity, due to the fact that believers are still Jews and Greeks, men and women, bosses and workers. Christian identity is put on "over" our human constitutions and heritages, and serves to renew and transform them. What is required of Christians is that their new status in Christ recondition the realities that make up their identity and become relevant to all of their existence. For children of God in Christ, all of life is different, and no compartments can be erected to allow the believer a quiet life in which business as normal is separated from faith. All of life falls under the perspective of the kingdom.

When faith is dispossessed of its implications for life, it invariably loses its cutting edge. Christians then become rather like those "pietistic" orthodox Muslims who live their faith in the land of unbelief, enclosed in a spiritual ghetto. Adaptation to Western culture and cooperation with the system is the European Muslim attitude much berated by the radicals.

The Reformed faith does not invite us to deny our identity, but to fulfill it—with as many life-expressions as possible. One does not have to belong to a majority to succeed in this calling, but one does have to have conviction, dedication, and sacrifice. Christians and churches in Europe have worried too much about status, numbers, influence, and sometimes affluence, and too little about essentials like regeneration. They have slipped through the doorway of temptation to adaptation, cooperation, and compromise, and have become bastions of the bourgeoisie. In the process, the vision has been lost, the light has gone, and the salt has lost its savor and perhaps its Savior as well. What the Christian minority in Europe needs above all is a faith-and-life radicalism that challenges believers to live consistently and differently in the way that its Reformed expression has been advocated by its best proponents.

Jesus' Minority Teaching

The preferential option expressed in the gospel with regard to the poor has generated a considerable flow of ink and molded missional policies. Similar attention could be given to the minority and marginal status of Christian believers and the concrete realities of the life of Jesus himself.[36]

It cannot be ignored that much of the vivid teaching of our Lord relates to minorities and minority situations. The text that jumps to mind and has sometimes been incorrectly called upon to justify small-ness and "theologies of the little flock" is Luke 12:32, "Fear not, little flock, for it is your Father's good pleasure to give you the kingdom." The context of this exhortation is anxiety in the face of temporal pres-sures and the attraction of things "the nations of the world seek after" to alleviate such cares. What is in view is not primarily the smallness of the flock, but the wonder of the kingdom that the Father gives to an insignificant minority:

> Although the faithful, especially as compared with the great nations of the world, are few in number and, as regards their own power, like a small flock of defenceless sheep, they should nevertheless have no fear, for their heavenly Father, because it is His good pleasure to do so, has given the kingdom to those who seek it. In principle they already possess it and share in its blessing; but at the end of the age they will receive it in fullness.[37]

In continuity with the Old Testament, the flock is the people belonging to God: there is one flock and one shepherd-ruler who appoints under-shepherds to "feed his lambs" (John 10:16; 21:15). The flock is God's eschatological people, purchased with the life of the shepherd of the sheep, united in him to receive the promise of the kingdom.[38] It may be small, but belonging to God, it has a great future. So it is not size that counts, but God's good pleasure and his promise, which, in covenantal terms, is the reward held out to faith-fulness. Reflection on these perspectives is a timely antidote to the modern obsession with size and the erroneous idea that mega is better.

36. Murray, *Post-Christendom*, 310–17.
37. Norval Geldenhuys, *Commentary on Luke*, NICNT (Grand Rapids: Eerd-mans, 1951), 359.
38. Paul Minnear, *Images of the Church in the New Testament* (Philadelphia: West-minster, 1960), 84–89.

It is striking how many of the parables reflect on minority situations, care for individuals, growth, and final fulfillment. In a sense, and quite naturally so, they were tailor-made for a minority that was destined to grow spiritually in its own imperceptible way.[39] Think of the mustard seed, the wheat and the tares, the leaven, the net and the fishes, the lost sheep, the lost drachma, the workers of the final hour, and the sower's seed. Other parables place minorities in a good light, such as the publican and the Pharisee, the good Samaritan, the rich man and Lazarus, the unjust judge, etc.

The secret of the kingdom is its amazing finale that belies situations deemed to be going nowhere. That inauspicious origins are no reason for despair was a guiding principle directing the life of the Master, who must have lived with discouragement and "the contradiction of sinners" every day. The grain of wheat falling on the ground, dying, but bearing much fruit is emblematic (John 12:24). However, there is an awkward question that cannot be avoided. If the mission of the sower is to sow the Word, was not three-quarters of it unproductive—a consideration that might well justify pessimism? That is hardly the focus of the story. If it is true that the preaching of the gospel is often fruitless (Matt. 7:13ff.; 22:14), then the parable of the sower

> points to the wonderful germinal force of the seed together with the failures. . . . It consists in the revelation that the eschatological all-conquering coming of God into the world goes the way of the seed. . . . In spite of Satan's power, of the hardness of hearts, of the cares of the world and the delusion of riches, the crop is prepared by God's powerful word and the work of Christ.[40]

Far from being discouraging, the focus of the Lord's teaching is on the contrast between apparent insignificance in worldly terms and the miraculous outcome that epitomizes God's way with the world. Against the background of the Old Testament, the minority plays a part in the fulfillment of God's promises and the remnant anticipates

---

39. Tom Sine, *The Mustard Seed Conspiracy* (Dallas: Word, 1981).
40. Ridderbos, *Coming of the Kingdom*, 131–32.

the fullness of salvation.[41] The accent is on God's grace and judgment in the fulfillment of the divine purpose. This provides the backdrop to the gathering of the apostolic church, which shames the wise and the strong and "brings to nothing things that are" because the source of its life is Christ Jesus (1 Cor. 1:26–31).

The conclusion to Jesus' teaching on the sower and the purpose of parables in Luke's gospel is the illustration of the lamp on the stand and the exhortation, "Take care then how you hear, for to the one who has, more will be given, and from the one who has not, even what he thinks that he has will be taken away" (Luke 8:16–18). Here the world's "haves" and "have-nots" are reversed, because the having is related to the word in the heart, the secret of the seed that bears fruit. This is a reminder of the importance of not only hearing the word, but also doing it.[42] What constitutes the vitality of a minority, and particularly this one, is the nature of its behavior. It is a source of influence, independent of social status, money, or even dynamic leadership.[43] In fact, the only real impact a minority may have tends to lie in its behavior.[44] This is a sobering thought for the church in Europe today because, as Marcello Pero, an Italian politician, wrote, "The apostasy of Christianity is exposing the entire West to the risk of a grave cultural and political crisis, and perhaps even to a collapse of civilization."[45]

Christian identity is defined in terms of origin and the Christian community expresses this reality spiritually in newness of life. The

41. Rom. 9:27; 11:5; Isa. 10:22; 1 Kings 19:18.

42. Cf. Craig Blomberg, *Contagious Holiness: Jesus' Meals with Sinners* (Downers Grove, IL: InterVarsity Press; Nottingham: Apollos, 2005).

43. This is the case for minorities in general. Cf. Moscovici, *Psychologie des minorités actives*, 164.

44. Ernst Troeltsch describes the impact of the Christian behavior of the early church in *The Social Teaching of the Christian Churches* (Chicago: University of Chicago Press, 1981), 1:115–50. See also Jürgen Zangenberg and Michael Labahn, eds., *Christians as a Religious Minority in a Multicultural City: Modes of Interaction and Identity Formation in Early Imperial Rome* (Edinburgh: T. & T. Clark, 2004); Green, *Evangelism in the Early Church*, 45ff.

45. Marcello Pera, *Why We Should Call Ourselves Christians: The Religious Roots of Free Societies* (New York: Encounter Books, 2008), 62.

key to the influence of Christian witness in society does not lie in accompanying or adapting to the world's progress, or in making its teaching acceptable to current trends, but in its new lifestyle as a hospitable minority.[46]

Advantages of Being a Minority

Minorities have many possibilities for action when and if they assume their status and plan and act accordingly.[47] The present time in Europe is marked by a redistribution of social roles, and minorities do rather well in advancing their causes. If, on the one hand, the situation bears witness to a decomposition of former authorities under the corrosive effects of ultramodern secularization, there is a resurgent religious hunger of a different kind with Buddhist groups, Muslims, and some evangelical groupings profiting from it, to say nothing of a multitude of sects descending like locusts. The common denominator of these movements seems to lie in the fact that they are nonconformist and militant, and present something different that corresponds to a need.[48]

In his classic analysis of the psychology of active minorities, Serge Moscovici describes how minorities, which in the past used to be termed "deviant," exercise influence on majorities. Several of his ideas are relevant to this study. Active minorities are ones that progress by entering into conflict with accepted norms, rather than just seeking to adapt to the status quo. When they do this, they become agents of transformation and grow because of their influence.[49] This point alone gives rise to a question about how the Christian churches have tended to act when faced with modernism, conforming to new ideas

---

46. Paul Wells, "Hospitality and Ministry in Trinitarian Perspective," in *Triniteit en kerk: Festschrift Arie Baars*, ed. G. C. den Hertog, H. R. Keurhorst, and H. G . L. Peels (Heerenveen: Groen, 2014), 174–84.

47. Y. Bizeul, "Définition sociologique: Minorité *versus* majorité," in *Minorités religieuses dans l'espace européen*, ed. Bastian and Messner, 95–104.

48. Willaime, *Europe et religions*, 249ff.

49. Moscovici, *Psychologie des minorités actives*, 14f. Cf. Serge Moscovici, Gabriel Mugny, and Eddy Van Avermaet, eds., *Perspectives on Minority Influence* (Cambridge: Cambridge University Press, 1985), part 1 in particular.

only after a defeatist rearguard action against them and only when they are accepted by the majority in society. Numerous ethical issues that have caused divisions, such as blasphemy laws, abortion, homosexuality, and women's ministry, provide all too obvious illustrations. The churches have given the impression of being the outdated establishment, rather than having something to say.

Being a minority is not, in and of itself, a way to influence, and Moscovici points to several crucial factors. Existing and being active as a minority are fundamental, he says. In a practical sense, having something to say—a precise position and coherent point of view—transforms a passive minority into an influential group. That it disagrees with what is taken for granted—the "orthodoxy" of the majority—matters little. When people are asked to believe something new, they must be made to doubt what they have hitherto accepted as normal. This implies that a minority functions well when it accepts a conflicting position that differentiates it from global attitudes. The goal of a minority will sometimes involve enlarging the gap between what the majority thinks and the "heterodoxy" it proposes.[50] This serves to underline the originality and value of its position.

Ecological groups have excelled at this kind of activity, making people doubt that science always knows best, to the point of getting them to spend more money for green products.[51] Christian churches and groups of Christians have obviously not had similar success in influencing opinion, on this continent at least. There are many reasons for this. On too many subjects there is no apparent Christian position, at least for the unchurched majority in society. Theologians like John A. T. Robinson, Don Cupitt, Harry Kuitert, and Hans Küng have gained repute because of their Christian heterodoxy, but they have only been saying what pagans have said for a long time. In other words, they have simply conformed to the majority while appearing very innovative and radical. In fact, they show that the church is going the way of the world. A useful subject of reflection

---

50. Moscovici, *Psychologie des minorités actives*, 104ff., 210ff.

51. Harold B. Gerard, "When and How the Minority Prevails," in *Perspectives on Minority Influence*, ed. Moscovici, Mugny, and Van Avermaet, 171–86.

could well be how the early church Christian minority, with its clear-cut separation from the world, managed to exercise influence and grow by standing apart from the mainstream in a situation of opposition and persecution.[52]

Consistency and firmness of behavior and belief stand high on Moscovici's list of priorities for active minorities.[53] They do not make minorities attractive, but that is not necessary to get a hearing. Conviction and firmness create the impression of the rightness or justness of the cause. It doesn't matter if a group is not loved, as it can be admired for the moral qualities it exhibits. A consistent attitude is one that conveys the confidence of a group in its beliefs and creates the impression of being right. What it offers is worthwhile, to the point where it is prepared to go out on a limb to defend its position. This signaling of virtue suggests that a group counts for something and that what it stands for is probably more than meets the eye. When minority groups rise to the visible surface, it is often the result of a long effort to win people's trust, and the fact they have managed to do this is sometimes a cause for surprise. Are we not impressed by the success of the Mormons or Jehovah's Witnesses, and don't we admire their zeal and perseverance?

For minorities, recognition requires visibility, visibility depends on power of attraction, and that, in turn, requires consistency of belief and behavior and the potential sympathy it creates. These things cannot be experienced if a group does not exist as a living entity. To be invisible is not to exist. All of these factors in some way depend upon, and are illustrated by, the capacity of a group to act and do something useful. Moscovici lists five forms of action of an active minority that contribute to the way a group sees itself and the way others see it:

- The capacity to focus on actions that influence others,
- Contacts with people outside with a view to their conversion,
- Preference for contacts with those who are furthest away and even opposed to the group,

---

52. Troeltsch, *Social Teaching*, 1:100ff.; Harnack, *Mission*, 367ff.
53. Moscovici, *Psychologie des minorités actives*, 133ff., 218f., 224, 231ff., etc.

- The ability to compare with others and learn from them, particularly in solving problems, and
- Accepting oppositional dialogue as a way of fostering confidence and sharpening one's metal.[54]

When we look at these suggestions, it is surprising how they intersect with Jesus' minority-oriented teaching and what might be called New Testament evangelistic principles, practiced in other generations and by some evangelistically oriented groups today.[55] Christian groups of all kinds, recognizing the usefulness of their minority status, would profit by reflecting on this analysis and developing tactics through which they might benefit from the present situation. Many such groups could experience an effective renewal and develop a new mission as a result of seizing possibilities that are there.

Conclusion

As a Reformed minority, we perhaps feel that history has passed us by. The magnificent project of our forefathers floundered on the rocks of humanism,[56] before Christianity as a whole was flattened by the steamroller of modernism and now, in ultramodern Europe, is dominated by materialism and "liquid fear";[57] so much is on offer that we can't get a hearing. We feel alienated from the global situation and tend either to draw into ever-decreasing circles with internal group agendas to make us feel secure, or get mired in divisive and time-absorbing conflicts over subjects that are nonissues for the society around us.[58] What can we to do when the tide is going out? Let us take heart from how James I. Packer describes the achievements of the Puritans:

54. Moscovici, *Psychologie des minorités actives*, 225ff. Cf. Moscovici, Mugny, and Van Avermaet, eds., *Perspectives on Minority Influence*, chaps. 4–5.

55. Green, *Evangelism in the Early Church*, chaps. 1–2.

56. Reinhold Niebuhr, *The Nature and Destiny of Man*, vol. 2 (London: Nisbet, 1943), chap. 6.

57. Zygmunt Bauman, *Liquid Fear* (Cambridge: Polity, 2006).

58. John R. W. Stott, *Issues Facing Christians Today* (Basingstoke: Marshalls, 1984), chap. 4 on alienation.

The Puritans lost, more or less, every public battle that they fought. Those who stayed in England did not change the church of England as they hoped to do, nor did they revive more than a minority of its adherents, and eventually they were driven out by calculated pressure on their consciences. Those who crossed the Atlantic failed to establish new Jerusalem in New England. . . . But the moral and spiritual victories that the Puritans won by keeping sweet, peaceful, patient, obedient, and hopeful under sustained and seemingly intolerable pressures and frustrations gave them a place of high honour in the believers' hall of fame, where Hebrews 11 is the first gallery.[59]

The important thing is that they *did something*: they fought spiritual battles, and they did so with a certain attitude of mind. This leads us to ask what we, as a Reformed minority, can do today and how we can do it.

The situation in Europe provides an opportunity for a unique missional contribution on the part of the Reformed minority. Of the Christian churches in general, it is said that despite their dramatic decline, "they will continue to exist in some skeletal form with increasing commitment from decreasing numbers of adherents."[60] It is recognized that Protestantism in particular is regrouping in three broad streams—namely sociological, ecumenical, and evangelical Protestantism—as a result of the churches drawing closer together and because of diverse reactions to modernity. One recent commentator concludes that sociological Protestantism will continue to melt away, benefiting other religions (Buddhism, New Age Movement), do-it-yourself religion, or atheistic indifference. Establishment-centered, ecumenical Protestantism will survive on its momentum from the past and brokered compromises. Finally, there is the growth of neo-evangelical, often charismatic, groups that are becoming more

59. James I. Packer, *Among God's Giants: Aspects of Puritan Christianity* (Eastbourne: Kingsway, 1991), 25.

60. Callum Brown, *The Death of Christian Britain: Understanding Secularisation, 1800–2000* (London: Routledge, 2001), 197.

prominent, although what the relationship between these groups and the traditional, mainline churches will be, remains to be seen.[61]

What does a Reformed minority have to offer in the context of this new Europe and the developing church situation? There is a "minus" in the Reformed tradition that is not encouraging; it would be dishonest to pretend that it is not there. Reformed theology has tended to have the best product, but the worst sales technique, and it is too often pushed by intellectually arrogant representatives. Reformed Christians are not even a minority as such, but a fragmented movement too often taken up with introspective issues rather than extroverted missional action. There is a warning here from what we have seen above: for a minority to grow, it must exist, it must be identifiable, and it must have attractiveness that propels its message forward.

To conclude on a more upbeat note, the "plus" in the Reformed heritage lies in the depths of its doctrinal mine—the infinite, personal God who acts and speaks, the doctrine of Scripture, salvation as grace, personal atonement, a realistic and human view of sanctification, and the integration of faith and life. Here is the reason for certainty and conviction to give away, packaged as true truth for life. These perspectives embrace history and culture and stimulate a dynamic worldview with ethical and social implications that propel community mission. The Reformed faith has done well and can do better as a holistic program of Christian discipling and training for the role of an active and unembarrassed minority "in Christ."

The Reformed faith, "Christian faith come into its own," is a lifesaver for souls drifting in the hypermodern void on a "sea of heartbreak, lost love an' loneliness."[62] It provides a firm foundation for seekers who are anxious to find some reason for living beyond the ersatz-isms spawned by autonomous unbelief, which were, after all, behind the catastrophe so graphically described above by Winston Churchill.

---

61. Sinclair, "La minorité protestante en Europe," in *Minorités religieuses dans l'espace européen*, ed. Bastian and Messner, 209–25.

62. The first expression in this sentence is from Princeton theologian Benjamin B. Warfield; the second is from the song "Sea of Heartbreak," by Paul Hampton and David Hal and recorded by Don Gibson in 1961.

13

Covenantal Apologetics and Mission

Guilherme Braun

Abstract

The divine covenant is all-encompassing; it includes the coherence existing in the cosmos. It is ultimately based on the love between the three persons of the Trinity, revealed to God's people in the gospel of Jesus Christ, through the Holy Spirit and to the glory of God. Reformational philosophers have developed a vision, driven by the biblical narrative of creation, fall, and redemption, which aims to do justice to the all-encompassing scope of the divine covenant. The centrality of the gospel is proclaimed in relation to the sovereignty of God as creator and sustainer of every facet of created reality. This is rooted in the Reformed worldview and leads to a deepened understanding of human freedom and responsibility, the multiplicity of human modes of being and acting in the world, thereby providing powerful insights for contemporary Reformed apologetics.

The Cosmos and God's Covenantal Word-Revelation

The *constitution* of the world is consistent with the covenant settled eternally between the three persons of the Trinity. The *nature* of the covenant is all-encompassing and inclusive of all the coherence that exists in the cosmos. The *basis* for the covenant is the love between the three persons of the Trinity, revealed in the gospel of Jesus Christ, through the Holy Spirit and to the glory of God.

293

Furthermore, the word of God has been preached to the whole human race since Adam. This word-revelation is all-embracing, implying a threefold relationship: man's relation to God (origin), man's relation to himself and other created entities in nonhuman cosmic relationships (coherence in diversity), and man's relation to the totality of his horizon of historical experience. This implies his responsibility with regard to created law-spheres and also his participation in the unfolding of God's plan for the world.

As Reformed believers, we believe in the unity of the covenant, since the word of God (the word of the covenant) has been preached to the whole human race. In other words, the incarnation of Christ and the preaching of the gospel link up with the same word of God preached to Adam. Even the fall into sin doesn't imply a breach. What happened with the word of God after the fall was that it obtained the character of a word of grace.[1] Human hearts that had been directed to the true origin, the triune God, became directed to idols, representing nothing other than the absolutization of something created.

God's covenantal order for creation remained after the fall, and man's religious nature also remained intact, regardless of the fact that the human heart had been uprooted from its true origin, and faith had become directed toward idols. Faith as a function is part of every person's constitution. While in Christians it takes the word of God into account, in non-Christians it is directed to idols. Idolatry involves the absolutization of a law-sphere of creation, such as greed (economical), wrong priorities (social), manipulation (ethical), legalism (jural), sentimentalism (sensitive), pseudo-harmony/drugs (aesthetical), etc.

Consequently, it is important to keep in mind that God's covenantal order for creation remains intact after the fall. Therefore, it is the calling of the church of Christ to proclaim the revelation of the sovereign God in the mediator, and that creation's destiny, including man, is to be fully restored in Jesus Christ, through the Holy Spirit, and to the honor of God.

---

1. Dirk H. Th. Vollenhoven, "The Foundations of Calvinist Thought," lecture delivered in 1934 at Düsseldorf, Germany.

As Reformed believers, we confess that "the supreme destination of the human being is to live in the covenant with the heavenly Father as his child."[2] Therefore, we proclaim that it is only by surrender to God in Jesus Christ and through the Holy Spirit that people become truly free. No contradiction exists between God's glory and human happiness. Nothing in life is as powerful and full of purpose as when man's covenantal relationship with the triune God is restored. This presentation of the Reformed covenantal vision provides the basis for deepened transcendental perspectives on the covenant.

Transcendental Perspectives on the Covenant

It has been said that true human freedom is possible only where man's covenantal relationship with the triune God is restored. This is certainly correct with respect to individual salvation. But if we understand the rich diversity and coherence of God's world, including human existence, we should include different cosmic relationships. Therefore, I shall offer some basic transcendental insights from Reformational philosophy in order to sketch a vision embedded in the Reformed covenantal tradition. This may help to better understand true human freedom as wholehearted service of God and to fulfill the cultural mandate by being faithful to God's word-revelation. A full sense of revelation includes Scripture as the inspired word of God, Christ as the incarnate Word of God, and the revelation of creation. This implies that we can live in true obedience to God's all-encompassing covenant only if we stand in a right relationship with God and his threefold word-revelation—Scripture, Christ, and creational revelation.

One of the main features of Reformational philosophy is its transcendental approach, which *inter alia* aims at uncovering the *supra-theoretical presuppositions* at the heart of every worldview.[3] Those

2. Vollenhoven, "Foundations of Calvinist Thought," 14.

3. Herman Dooyeweerd, "Cornelius Van Til and the Transcendental Critique of Theoretical Thought," in *Jerusalem and Athens: Critical Discussions on the Theology and Apologetics of Cornelius Van Til*, ed. E. Robert Geehan (Nutley, NJ: Presbyterian and Reformed, 1975), 74–89.

transcendental ideas, or supra-theoretical presuppositions, are: (1) the idea of time, (2) coherence in diversity, and (3) the idea of origin.[4] In order to make these three transcendentals more accessible, Jeremy Ive's transposition and Trinitarian explanation will be used.[5]

First, the idea of origin can be taken as *individuality* in ultimate dependence upon the triune God. Secondly, the idea of coherence in diversity refers to relationality, implying the radical diversity and coherence of every cosmic relationship. And thirdly, the horizon of human experience embraces the totality of the diverse aspects of reality, in other words, the self in time.

Temporal existence implies all sorts of subject-subject and subject-object relationships, as well as specific ways in which each entity functions in the different law-spheres created by God, such as space, movement, the physical, the biotic, and the sensitive. Human beings also function within normative law-spheres such as the cultural-formative, logical, lingual, social, aesthetical, economic, ethical, jural, and pistic spheres. Besides encompassing all aspects of reality, time also comprises the unfolding of God's plan, which involves both the uniqueness and purposefulness of each cosmic event. Everything that happens within creation, including the lives of creatures, happens according to God's plan and his order for cosmic time.

How can the three transcendentals be explained in terms of the Christian belief in the triune God? In covenantal terms, this is done by stressing that:

- The absolute origin of creation and individuality refers to the work of God the Father.
- The radical coherence in diversity (relationality) refers to the work of the Son in upholding the entire cosmos (Heb. 1:3). This implies that Christ's incarnation and work of redemption

4. Herman Dooyeweerd, *In the Twilight of Western Thought* (Grand Rapids: Paideia, 1960), 36–37.

5. Jeremy G. A. Ive, "A Critically Comparative Kuyperian Analysis and a Trinitarian, 'Perichoretic' Reconstruction of the Reformational Philosophies of Dirk H. Th. Vollenhoven and Herman Dooyeweerd" (PhD thesis, King's College London, 2012), 185–89.

restore the coherence of intersubjective relationships. As mediator, Christ reconciles us with God, with one another, and with creation as a whole, the cosmos as creation.

- The idea of time, as participation in God's providence and the purposeful unfolding of events, refers to the transformational work of the Holy Spirit in applying Christ's redemption to human hearts.

Thus, human beings are referred to the Father as absolute origin, and to the Son as Redeemer, bringing about the re-creation of the world. According to this global covenantal view, individual salvation is only the beginning of the new creation. As members of the body of Christ, believers are called to participate in God's mission and the restoration of his world.

Transcendental Perspectives on Human Freedom

How can human freedom be described in terms of this transcendental and Trinitarian framework? Several aspects should be noted:

Individuality—According to man's original design as created in the image of God, human mastery is the essence of human freedom. Already prior to the fall, man received the cultural mandate and the commandment to go and master creation.[6]

Relationality—God has given human beings many and varied abilities, functions, and talents: organic, sensitive, formative, analytical, artistic, economic, moral, pistic, etc. As part of God's creation, human beings function in all dimensions of reality, correlative to the different law-spheres that constitute the divine order of creation. Therefore, because God created the world with a rich and coherent diversity of laws and law-spheres, human freedom is not limited to one or even several aspects of reality. In its full meaning, human freedom refers to man as a whole.[7]

---

6. Hendrik G. Stoker, "The Essence of Human Freedom," in *Uit, deur en tot God is alle dinge: Werke van Prof. Dr. H. G. Stoker* (Potchefstroom, 2007), 2.

7. Stoker, "Essence of Human Freedom," 1.

Self and Time—The coherence and diversity of creation also point to human destiny on earth. Being created in the image of God and designed to master creation also imply that man is called to participate in God's mission, in the purposeful unfolding of world events.

Because of sin, authentic human freedom is not naturally a characteristic of human beings. True freedom is obtained by those who receive God's grace in Jesus Christ, through the missional work of the church. They are restored in their covenantal relationship with God and therefore in the realms of:

- *Individuality*: they learn to live in conformity with the covenant order and according to divine commandments, being dependent upon the triune God.
- *Relationality*: they respect the diverse law-spheres' order of creation.
- *Temporality*: they constructively participate in their cultural context, loving God and their neighbor with all their hearts, discovering and actualizing the potentialities of creation, bringing about restoration of broken relationships.

This describes what a holistic Reformed covenantal vision implies. Christ came to the world to redeem the entire cosmos, and consequently all areas of life are to be redeemed. To preach the true gospel is the same as to preach genuine human freedom, which is only possible by death and resurrection, repentance and regeneration, and the restoration of man's obedience to God's all-embracing covenant.

True human freedom implies wholehearted service of God, in Jesus Christ and through the Holy Spirit. This takes into its scope all of life, as well as God's creation order. Consequently, the structures of the cosmos as creation are also seen to be God's revelation. The apologetic task of the church, both present and future, is to proclaim this global covenantal vision and with it, true human freedom. How can this be accomplished?

Covenantal Apologetics and Contemporary Culture

Consider the fact that not everyone is called to be a scientist. This implies that theoretical scientific thinking is not always the best *apologetic point of entry*. Having received different talents and callings, people develop abilities and interests differently. As God has a specific plan for each person, there are different ways of living out our apologetic calling in the world. However, human beings do share the same creation order, and living in community, at least to some extent, they share the same culture.

By embracing the whole of life, the covenantal vision not only provides a way of *seeing* the world in its coherence in diversity, as dependent upon God, but also furthers understanding of *how* to participate in our cultural context in a way that promotes true human freedom as wholehearted service of God. According to the covenantal vision, our participation in cultural life as Christians can be truly missional. Christian apologetics should be part of our everyday lives, and this calling involves more than presenting theoretical arguments. It implies man's destiny to be truly free in Jesus Christ.

Man's calling to *master* creation is manifold and involves various responsibilities. For instance:

- In a cultural-formative sense, by developing and using technical know-how in order to open up new creational possibilities,
- Economically, in the development of abilities and in the management of means and time,
- Aesthetically, by creating and sustaining harmony in every relationship of existence,
- Socially, by giving priority to the right relationships at the right time,
- In the jural sense, by seeking justice in every relationship,
- Ethically, by loving God with all one's heart and one's neighbor as oneself (Mark 12:31), and
- Pistically, by living in a covenantal faith relationship with God in Jesus Christ, through the Holy Spirit, confessing sin and

seeking to obey God's commandments, and listening to God's Word in every specific situation.

To listen to God's word-revelation implies more than reading, believing, and obeying Scripture. It also implies the good order of creation, which is revealed as part of God's plan. Since God's revelation of creation implies a radical diversity and coherence, as human beings we are called to open our hearts and listen. To believe Scripture and to obey God's commandments in our lives is certainly a central aspect of Christian life, but the scope of apologetics and missions must encompass the whole of life, including participation in our cultural context and obedience to God with regard to the different law-spheres of creation.

Consequently, to live as a Christian in God's world implies sharing in the same culture with non-Christians, as God calls us to participate *as Christians* in our cultural context. Accordingly, every human being is subject to the laws and order of creation, established by God. Therefore, the difference between Christians and non-Christians is not of a "structural" nature, because every human being functions within the same aspects of reality. The difference is "directional": the human heart is the main difference. As Christians, we fundamentally do the same things as non-Christians, but we do them *differently*. This "structure and direction" distinction is crucial if we wish to participate in culture *as Christians*, integrating missions and apologetics into everyday life.[8]

Covenantal Perspectives on Technology and Popular Culture

God has given man cultural-formative abilities and talents, so that he may discover and use the potential of creation and open up new possibilities. But the human heart may be misdirected in a religious sense. This is the case with people who trust in science and technology

8. Daniël F. M. Strauss, *Being Human in God's World* (Bloemfontein, SA: University Press, 1998), 10.

with regard to questions relating to the origin of the cosmos and human existence. They don't realize that modern science was brought forth by modern technology. Through modern technology, man has been developing technical modes of revealing creation, using cultural-formative instruments, which in essence are nothing other than human perspectives on created reality.[9] Therefore, those modes of viewing can never encompass the whole of life, for human perspectives are limited, as are technological and scientific viewpoints.[10] That being the case, how is it possible that there are people who believe that science provides answers to the questions of origin?

Misdirected faith in science goes hand in hand with misdirected faith in the arts. They are interrelated, because in essence both are human modes of revealing creation (*poesis*), ways of bringing forth the potentialities of creation, including human possibilities, which find expression in the arts.

It makes sense nowadays to look at popular culture and its artistic expressions in order to understand where religious impulses find expression. One example can be given. Popular culture has become widely accessible through technology and mass media, and due to this accessibility the *narratives of popular culture* play an important role in the lives of millions of people. Take, for instance, a movie and the different human-technology relationships involved in it. Besides relating to a movie in (1) a hermeneutical (lingual) manner, trying to understand the story line, (2) people also relate to the movie in an intersubjective way, as the movie imitates human possibilities and real persons play "possible" characters—and the viewers have a psychological encounter with people in the movie. (3) Consequently, there is also what can be called a specification relationship, because individuals open themselves up to the persons and situations they "meet" in the movie and such activities actualize the human self.

As man is still in the making, those encounters provide us not

9. Martin Heidegger, *Die Technik und die Kehre* (Pfullingen: Guenther Neske, 1962), 20.

10. Don Ihde, *Technology and the Lifeworld: From Garden to Earth* (Bloomington, IN: Indiana University Press, 1990), 35–50.

only with narratives, but also with ways of encountering other people and actualizing the self in temporal existence. In terms of human perception, technological viewpoints (such as a movie) may indeed reach deep levels of interaction with our being. This can be taken further in order to illustrate the religious function of the narratives of popular culture. Those people and situations which are often imaginatively portrayed in movies not only provide virtual possibilities to actualize the self and to encounter other people, but also present narratives that allow viewers to step aside and religiously transcend the miseries of their own temporal existence. As poetic revelation, movies offer inspiration and guidance for those who open up their hearts.

The religious implications are evident. Indeed, just as technology can be seen as part of the revelation of creation, as a bringing forth of potential that God has placed in creation, popular arts via technology can also be seen as a kind of revelation of creation from a human perspective. Thus, humans reveal themselves and the world from different angles, to themselves and to others, sharing viewpoints with one another and before God. By illustrating ways in which the arts and technology intersect with one another, as modes of revealing creation, including humanity, I have underlined the fact that even in the most apparently secularized places, people still rely on pseudo-revelation in order to find meaning, coherence, and purpose in temporal existence. Be it technology and science or popular culture and poetic expression as a revelation of creation, the fact is that the religious impulse of the human heart never ceases to manifest itself in God's world. As Augustine pointed out, the human heart remains restless until it finds rest in Jesus Christ.

We are invited to fully participate in our cultural context and to present the Christian alternative, praying and hoping that God will open people's hearts through the work of the Holy Spirit. This may happen in various ways, for God created man with many functions, abilities, interests, and callings. After all, the best arguments for the Christian faith are still testimonies of people whose lives have been transformed by coming to Christ and having their hearts redirected to the true origin of creation, the triune God. Turning from idols, they have not only learned to respect and enjoy the radically diverse and coherent creation order, but have also found meaning and coherence in the intersubjective relationships of everyday life.

By receiving forgiveness in Jesus Christ and being reconnected to the true origin, the covenantal relationship with God is restored. This is not just so that we may go to heaven when we die, but also that we may participate in God's mission and live *as Christians* in our cultural context, praying to our Lord, "Thy kingdom come, thy will be done."

Conclusion

This article provided some philosophical perspectives on the nature and scope of the covenant. The chosen point of entry was the domain of covenantal apologetics as it relates to missions and human freedom in everyday experience. Following this trajectory, insights were suggested to enrich the covenantal vision promoted in this book. These philosophical-transcendental viewpoints are to be seen as presupposing the transcendent covenantal vision presented in other contributions. Several features of this contribution can be meaningfully related to the diverse themes presented, such as the eternal and Trinitarian origin of the covenant as a basic presupposition of any covenantal-Christian approach, the covenantal shape of Scripture and gospel-centered preaching, and the power of the covenantal vision to inspire a gospel culture capable of responding to the postmodern challenges of globalization, multiculturalism, and technology and to be transformative in an all-embracing sense.

Inspired by Reformational philosophy's nonreductive outlook, the proposed vision is also postrationalistic. It affirms that God, as absolute origin, is the ultimate reality and indispensable presupposition for the possibility of understanding created reality and the cosmos as creation. Consequently, this vision is driven by the biblical narrative of creation, fall, and redemption, and rejects scientism as an absolutization of theoretical reason, by emphasizing that every worldview is based on pre-theoretical narrative presuppositions.

By drawing on Reformational philosophy's multi-aspectual view of temporal reality, the Reformed-philosophical view of the covenant offers insights for the elaboration of covenantal ethics with an emphasis on the fear of the Lord, godliness, and holiness. It implies that ethics must embrace all aspects of reality and a nonreductive view of basic cosmic relationships. Thus, in order to live with eschatological hope in the tension between the decisive already fulfilled and the not yet completed, between present and future, covenant keepers are called to actively participate in God's mission to the nations. This most certainly implies economic and financial contributions to the missional church, which should take place within the order of the covenant.

Moreover, by elaborating the philosophical vision of the covenant in relation to contemporary apologetics, missions, and human freedom, it has been a concern to emphasize the centrality of the gospel as well as the sovereignty of God as the creator and sustainer of every facet of created reality. That said, the understanding of the nature of true human freedom, the multi-aspectuality of created reality in light of specific themes (i.e., technology, popular arts, everyday life, missions), provides insights that serve as valuable tools for apologetic usage in the battlefield of spiritual warfare, against anti-Christian doctrines and worldviews.

Being oriented to an all-embracing vision of creation, this approach also intends to inspire postcolonial missional strategies by respecting the individuality and the normativity of distinct cultural contexts, so that the church may become a blessing for all peoples by the transformative power of the gospel.

Finally, the proposed philosophical approach to human freedom and missions speaks the language of pluralistic, post-Christian postmodernity. By linking covenantal thinking to the narratives of popular culture and technology as forms of poetic revelation, concrete points of entry for covenantal apologetics are indicated, representing possible strategies to be adopted by the people of God as they face contemporary challenges with confidence. God is also using this age and stage in world history to finalize his covenant.

Epilogue

Kent Hughes

Missions has always been a big part of my pastoral ministry. I grew up in a missions-minded church where I served both as a youth pastor and as a pastor to university students and saw many go on to be commissioned as career missionaries. My church sent me out to plant a mission church. And, ultimately, I was called to pastor College Church in Wheaton, which had a century-long history of sending missionaries. I served there for twenty-seven years, and had the remarkable experience of seeing the annual missions budget grow from $180,000 to some $3 million. I say this so that you may understand why I have read this book with such interest, enlightenment, and appreciation.

The Potchefstroom conference assembled an international convocation of a dozen distinguished Reformed theologians with the understanding that the theology of the covenant is the source and well of world mission. Their thirteen essays draw from, and open the richness of, the covenant of redemption and the resulting scriptural covenants as they apply across culture. The effect is a bracing certitude as to the ground and ineluctable power of the gospel.

This afterword is threefold. First, there are some personal reflections and takeaways from these challenging essays that have been especially helpful and elevating to my own commitment to world mission.

Secondly, I have included a heartening historical retrospect on the extraordinary missional impact of covenant theology (so carefully articulated in the chapters of this book) upon the Princeton of Archibald Alexander and Charles Hodge—when an astonishing stream of missionaries took the gospel to the ends of the earth.

Finally, there is a meditation on the apostle Peter's charge to the covenant community to don the mantle of the *munus triplex*, the triple office of prophet, priest, and king, so as to declare the excellencies of Christ in this dark world.

Missional Takeaways

My reflections and takeaways will not necessarily be those of another reader due to our diverse backgrounds and understandings.

The *Pactum Salutis*

For me, the dazzling exposition of the *pactum salutis* (the pretemporal, intra-Trinitarian covenant of redemption) has been most salutary and helpful. Aside from the fact that its theological adumbrations date back to the Reformation, and that it was clearly articulated in the seventeenth century,[1] the fact that the *pactum salutis* was embraced and stoutly defended by Charles Hodge and the Princeton divines is highly significant in the light of the unparalleled flow of missionaries that came from Princeton.[2] Geerhardus Vos's assertion that an understanding of the pretemporal covenant between the persons of the Trinity provides a "center of gravity" for Reformed thinking should be taken to heart by all who wish to think biblically about missions.[3] Here, Davi Gomes's description of the *pactum salutis* is carefully worded so as to impart a missional vision, which it certainly does:

> The covenant of redemption (*pactum salutis*) refers to the "event" outside time and space, sometimes called a "counsel of peace," in which Father, Son and Holy Spirit, in an overflow of love in the Godhead, agreed upon and committed to create a people as an

---

1. Chaps. 1, 4.
2. Charles Hodge, *Systematic Theology* (London: James Clarke, 1960), 2:354–61.
3. Chap. 8.

object of love and grace, so that they would be brought into a familial relationship with God himself. This is expressed in God's own promise: "I will put my law within them, and I will write it on their hearts. And I will be their God, and they shall be my people" (Jer. 31:33). This intra-Trinitarian covenant is, for Reformed theology, the starting point in the metanarrative of human history. God himself purposes to be the sender, the sent, and the enabler in a mission of redemptive purpose, in order to establish, outside his own being, unique objects of his grace and glory![4]

This is where mission begins! The *pactum salutis* would be followed by the covenant of works, or creation (Gen. 2:15), which, because of Adam's sin, would invite the covenant of grace (Gen. 3:9, 16), which would then be followed by a missional train of epochal covenants: the Abrahamic (Gen. 12), the Mosaic (Ex. 19), the Davidic (2 Sam. 7), and the consummate new covenant (Jer. 31). Everything in the covenantal metanarrative of Scripture radiates Christ and mission. As Peter Lillback writes: "The continuity of the covenant in classic Reformed covenantal thought argues that the biblical covenants that comprise the covenant of grace are a unity that develop in a progressive, organic manner. This means that they are the same in substance; that is, they always point to Christ."[5] The source and origin of world missions is the *pactum salutis*, God's own covenant with himself.

How personally energizing it has been to see its radiating facets throughout the chapters of this book!

The Covenantal Structure of the Great Commission

My second takeaway is the covenantal structure of the Great Commission in Matthew 28:18–20, and how it communicates the force of the missional call to God's new covenant people. Here Flip Buys demonstrates how the structure of the covenants in Genesis 12, 15, and 17, Exodus 20, and Daniel 7 shape the contours of the covenantal structure of Matthew 28. And more, the Great Commission is

4. Chap. 1.
5. Chap. 3.

infused with three enthronement motifs that are present in the coronation of the Son of Man by the Ancient of Days in Daniel 7:13–14.
Therefore, Matthew 28 is the command of the enthroned Lord. And
when the covenantal structure of the Great Commission is clearly
observed, together with its coronation emphasis, it becomes clear that
Jesus, as the cosmic sovereign of the universe, is commanding his elect
to commit to world mission.

Mission to the nations, then, is central to covenant obedience.
Covenant obedience demands carrying out Christ's expansive command: "All authority in heaven and on earth has been given to me.
Go therefore and make disciples of all nations, baptizing them in the
name of the Father and of the Son and of the Holy Spirit, teaching
them to observe all that I have commanded you. And behold, I am
with you always, to the end of the age" (Matt. 28:18–20). Notice
the demanding and heartening "alls" of Jesus: All authority... all
nations... all that I have commanded you... always to the end of the
age."[6] Buys concludes, "Mission is therefore an imperative, founded
on the covenantal lordship of Christ our King. Its task is to produce
self-replicating communities of covenantal obedience to Christ among
the nations. Churches that are not involved in missions are covenant
breakers."[7] It is a jarring declaration that will rattle the doors of some
churches that are comfortable in their "Reformed" conventions.

It is imperative for every church in every age and clime to understand the Great Commission as the crowning covenant directive to
God's elect.

The Missional Imperative Alters All of Life

My third takeaway was generated by a penetrating quotation from
Christopher Wright in the opening chapter of this book:

> Now such an understanding of the mission of God as the very
> heartbeat of all reality, all creation, all history and all that yet lies
> ahead of us generates a distinctive worldview that is radically and

6. Chaps. 4–5.
7. Chap. 4.

transformingly God-centered. . . . This worldview, constituted by putting the mission of God at the very center of all existence, is disturbingly subversive and it uncomfortably relativizes one's own place in the great scheme of things.[8]

Indeed, giving center place to the mission of God is disturbingly and wonderfully subversive to our values and commitments, because it allows us to see them in the light of redemptive history and, hopefully, to align them with the divine mission. The commonplaces of Christian living will take on new fire and dynamism.

Giving. Materialism will give way to generosity in a way analogous to what happened in the impoverished churches of Macedonia when they gave to help Paul bring relief to the impoverished church in Jerusalem, so that, as Paul testified, "in a severe test of affliction, their abundance of joy and their extreme poverty have overflowed in a wealth of generosity on their part. For they gave according to their means, as I can testify, and beyond their means, of their own accord, begging us earnestly for the favor of taking part in the relief of the saints" (2 Cor. 8:2–4). My own pastoral experience is that when mission is central to the body of Christ, God's people will overflow with generosity that is, at times, astonishing. And when this happens, the spiritual life of God's people is elevated.[9]

Prayer. The missionary heart of the apostle Paul treasured the souls of believers and nonbelievers alike, as we see in the personal greetings to the church in Rome (Rom. 16), where he lists thirty-three names (almost all Gentiles), extending greetings seventeen times among them. And some twenty-four of the names were in Rome at the time, yet Paul had never set foot in Rome! Evidently, he had crossed their paths in his missionary journeys and kept track of where they were. And how did he do it? Well, there is no doubt that he had a Rolodex between his ears, but also a tracking list (a prayer list) tucked among the meager belongings that he carried with him.

---

8. Chap. 1, referencing Christopher J. H. Wright, *The Mission of God: Unlocking the Bible's Grand Narrative* (Nottingham: Inter-Varsity Press, 2006), 533–34.
9. Cf. chap. 9.

Those who have mission at the center of their existence pray by name, not only for their missionaries and their families, but also for the souls of the lost, and for towns and cities and countries and people groups, and "against the rulers, against the authorities, against the cosmic powers over this present darkness, against the spiritual forces of evil in the heavenly places" (Eph. 6:12). And yes, they have a list.

Scripture. When mission is central in a person's life, the Scriptures will be read, not asking, "How do they apply to my life?" but asking, "How must I conform my life to them?" in order to take the gospel to the ends of the earth. Moreover, if a person's reading of Scripture is informed by an understanding of the *pactum salutis* as the pre-temporal, intra-Trinitarian covenant (based on the love between the Father, the Son, and the Holy Spirit to send the Son to redeem his people), that person will read Scripture with increasing wonder and awe as a revelation of Jesus Christ and as a gospel tract that must be proclaimed to a lost world.

A Bracing Missions Retrospect

In 1821, Charles Hodge, as a newly appointed professor at Princeton Seminary, wrote to his brother, describing the effect upon him of the preaching of the distinguished missionary William Ward, a colleague of William Carey in Serampore:

> I never felt the importance and grandeur of missionary labors as I did last evening. I could not help looking around on the congregation and asking myself, "what are these people living for?" granting that each should attain his most elevated object, what would it all amount to? Then looking at these men in India, giving the Bible to so many millions, which I know can never be in vain, I see them opening a perennial fountain, which, they dead for ages, will still afford eternal life to millions.[10]

10. David B. Calhoun, *Princeton Seminary*, vol. 1, *Faith and Learning, 1812–1868* (Edinburgh: Banner of Truth, 1996), 140.

If we wonder at the deep effect upon the great theologian, we must understand that Hodge's missionary heart had been birthed in the fertile soil of Reformed theology in his home through the Westminster Shorter Catechism and in the church by his venerable pastor, Ashbel Green (later president of Princeton College). Ultimately, his burden for missions was nurtured at Princeton Seminary, where, at its founding ten years before, the General Assembly added a paragraph to the "Plan of the Seminary," voicing a driving purpose for the school, namely "to found a nursery for missionaries to the heathen."[11]

Princeton's great founders, Archibald Alexander and Samuel Miller, never flagged in their commitment to missions, and Charles Hodge gave precise, formative expression to the intra-Trinitarian covenant of redemption, which is the ground for salvation and world mission.[12] Thus Princeton Seminary became a great force in the nineteenth century, both theologically and practically, for world missions.

Early on, a "Concert for Prayer" was held on the first Monday evening of the month, which concluded with a missionary address by a professor, student, or guest. Dr. Alexander characteristically "poured out stores of information" on foreign missions.[13] A "Brotherhood" was formed of those especially devoted to labor on the foreign field. Their meetings were kept secret—"for the purpose of doing good, and more effectually reaching every member of the seminary"—which they did.[14] In 1814, the students formed the "Society of Inquiry on Missions and the General State of Religion," which continued meeting on the first day of the month for forty-five years.[15] Prayer and conversation about missions were gloriously *de jure* in the halls of Princeton and in the homes of the faculty, as evidenced by Hodge's own children, ten-year-old Archibald and his sister Mary Elizabeth, when they authored a letter to "Dear Heathen" and gave it to a recent seminary graduate who would soon set sail for Ceylon. The letter

11. Calhoun, 139.
12. Hodge, *Systematic Theology*, 2:358–61.
13. Calhoun, *Princeton Seminary*, 141.
14. Calhoun, *Princeton Seminary*, 143.
15. Calhoun, *Princeton Seminary*, 144–45.

concluded: "My sister and myself have, by small self-denials, procured two dollars which are enclosed in this letter to buy tracts and Bibles to teach you. Archibald Alexander Hodge and Mary Eliz. Hodge, Friends of the Heathen."[16] Princeton's ethos encouraged and equipped a stream of missionaries that would become a veritable flood during the decades that followed.

In August 1831, the professors and students of Princeton set aside a day of prayer and fasting for six students who were ready to depart for their missionary calls. The following year, the first of the group, Joseph Barr, was ordained by the Presbytery of Philadelphia and prepared to set sail for Africa, but was stricken with cholera and died while awaiting departure. The effect was galvanizing on the Princeton community as Dr. Samuel Miller, who had suffered the loss of his nineteen-year-old son just days before, preached at Barr's memorial service, challenging the students to regard his death as a personal call to missions.[17]

During the mid-1830s and early 1840s, Barr's colleagues set sail. John Morrison, Joseph Owen, and John Freeman went to India. Peter Dougherty took the gospel to the Native Americans of Grand Traverse Bay. Others took up the steps of their fallen comrade to Africa, where they too soon perished. David White and his wife died in 1837, within days of reaching Cape Palmas, in present-day Liberia. Oren Cranfield and Jonathan Alward arrived in Cape Palmas in 1841. Alward lived only a few days after his arrival and was buried next to the graves of the Whites. Cranfield died of malaria a year later. Robert Sawyer followed the fallen Princetonians to the "Dark Continent" at the end of 1841 and died after two years of ministry.[18] The sacrifices made by these pioneer missionaries did not quell the fires of mission, but strengthened the resolve of others. Robert Hamill Nassau wrote in his journal, "Many of my acquaintances protested to me. And one said, 'What a fool you are, Nassau, to go to Africa to die.'" Nassau wryly added, "I quietly determined not to

16. Calhoun, *Princeton Seminary*, 192–93.
17. Calhoun, *Princeton Seminary*, 172.
18. Calhoun, *Princeton Seminary*, 209.

die." After finishing his studies at Princeton, Nassau studied medicine at the University of Pennsylvania and then sailed for Africa, where he ministered for forty years.[19]

The 1850s were graced by the visit and extraordinary preaching of Alexander Duff, the first overseas missionary of the Church of Scotland, with more than thirty years of experience, having gone to India with his bride in 1829. When Duff visited America in 1854, he gave a celebrated much-preached sermon, which Hughes Oliphant Old calls "one of the most significant sermons ever preached."[20] It was entitled "Missions, the Chief End of the Christian Church" and was an exposition of Psalm 67:1–2, "God be merciful unto us, and bless us; and cause his face to shine upon us. That thy way may be known upon the earth, thy saving health among all nations." The sermon was preached in the Broadway Tabernacle of New York City to over two hundred clergymen and many others, and it lasted two hours. The message was so powerful that James W. Alexander, the son of Archibald Alexander and pastor of Fifth Avenue Presbyterian, was heard to say when Duff concluded, "Shut up now this tabernacle. Let no man dare to speak here after that."[21]

The effect of this was an increased emphasis on evangelism and missions. The class that entered the seminary in the fall of 1855 was unusually large. The following year, there were indications of the Spirit's work in greater attendance at prayer meetings and seriousness among the students. In 1857, Jeremiah Lamphier, a member of Dr. Alexander's New York congregation, began a midday prayer meeting in the third-story lecture room of the church, which became the famous Fulton Street Prayer Meeting—leading to a national revival of prayer. The next year, ninety-five students entered the seminary, the largest number in the nineteenth century. And from Princeton there continued an even greater stream of graduates to serve the church around the world.[22]

19. Calhoun, *Princeton Seminary*, 408.

20. Hughes Oliphant Old, *The Reading and Preaching of the Scriptures*, vol. 6 (Grand Rapids: Eerdmans, 2007), 697.

21. Calhoun, *Princeton Seminary*, 367.

22. Calhoun, *Princeton Seminary*, 370–71.

According to David Calhoun, "One out of every three students leaving the seminary during its first fifty years went out to preach the gospel 'on missionary ground.' Almost six hundred served for at least some time in 'destitute places' in America. Thirty-seven went to the American Indians. Seventeen became missionaries to the slaves. One hundred and twenty-seven men went to foreign mission fields—from Turkey to the Sandwich Islands, from Brazil to Afghanistan, from West Africa to Northern China."[23]

Among the notables who took up the Great Commission—"the last command," as the Princetonians called it—was William Thomson, who went to Beirut in 1832, where he lived during violent political vicissitudes and periodic evacuations. He helped found the Syrian Protestant College, which eventually became the American University of Beirut. In 1859, he authored the immensely popular *The Land and the Book*, which, during the next forty years, was outsold only by Harriet Beecher Stowe's *Uncle Tom's Cabin*.

John Nevius went to China in 1854, where he served for over forty years establishing missions and schools, traveling extensively, and writing on various missions-related subjects. He is perhaps most famous for a two-month visit in 1890 to Korea, where he taught the new missionaries his "Nevius Plan," a strategy for developing self-supporting churches that was subsequently adopted and led to the astonishing growth of the Korean church.[24]

Ashbel Green Simonton, who had been challenged to embark on foreign missions by a sermon by Charles Hodge, went to Brazil in 1859. In the eight remaining years of his brief life, he established the first Presbyterian church, as well as the first presbytery and the first seminary. Simonton succumbed to yellow fever in December 1867, leaving this message for his congregation in Rio de Janeiro: "God will raise up someone in my place. He will do his own work with his own instruments. We can only lean on the everlasting arm and be quiet."[25]

And then there are notables who made the supreme sacrifice to

23. Calhoun, *Princeton Seminary*, 406.
24. See chap. 9.
25. Calhoun, *Princeton Seminary*, 408.

take Christ to the lost world, whose names can be seen today set in bronze, that reads like this:

Of these the world was not worthy
WALTER MACON LOWRIE
class of 1840,
thrown overboard by pirates in the China Sea, 1847
JOHN EDGAR FREEMAN
class of 1838,
ROBERT McMULLEN
class of 1853,
who, with their wives, were shot by the order
of Nanasahib, 1857, at Cawnpore, India
LEVI JANVIER
class of 1840,
stabbed by a Sikh fanatic at Lodiana, India, 1864
ISADOR LOWENTHAL
class of 1854,
shot accidentally or by design at Peshawur, India, 1864
JOHN ROGERS PEALE
class of 1905,
killed with his wife by a mob at Lien Chow, China, 1905
FAITHFUL UNTO DEATH[26]

The center of gravity of Reformed theology is the pretemporal, intra-Trinitarian covenant of redemption, the very ground for salvation and world mission. Because the old Princetonians understood that covenant theology is the source of world mission, they gladly took up Christ's commission to "Go and make disciples of all nations." Indeed, some "sailed through bloody seas" to take the gospel to the ends of the earth.

To be Reformed was, and is, to have a missionary heart.

---

26. David B. Calhoun, *Princeton Seminary*, vol. 2: *The Majestic Testimony, 1869–1929* (Edinburgh: Banner of Truth, 1996), 23.

The Triple Office and the Mission
of Christ and the Church

This book was introduced by noting that John Calvin coined the elegant Latin term *munus triplex*, signifying Christ's triple office of prophet, priest, and king, which Christ fulfilled in his theanthropic person as the incarnate Son of God. As divine, he was, at the same time, prophet (the Word), priest (the infinite atoning sacrifice and intercessor), and king (the king of glory). As human, he was the rejected prophet, the sacrificed priest, and the crucified king. This threefold office of Christ was prophesied clearly in the Old Testament and gloriously worked out in the New, as Christ fulfilled his mission of redemption.

As to Christ's office of prophet, Moses prophesied, "The LORD your God will raise up for you a prophet like me from among you, from your brothers—it is to him you shall listen" (Deut. 18:15). And indeed, Christ, the second Moses, spoke all that God commanded him (v. 18; cf. John 4:25; 8:28; 12:49–50).

As to his office of priest, Christ's priesthood was dramatically foreshadowed when Melchizedek, king of Salem, brought offerings of bread and wine to Abraham (Gen. 14:17–20), and then was given memorable prophetic expression in "You are a priest forever after the order of Melchizedek" (Ps. 110:4). The writer of Hebrews demonstrated at length that Jesus had come as an eternal high priest after the order of Melchizedek (Heb. 6:19–8:11).

As to Christ's office as king, the Lord swore to King David a sure oath that an everlasting king and kingdom would come from his body, saying, "And your house and your kingdom shall be made sure forever before me. Your throne shall be established forever" (2 Sam. 7:16; cf. 12:12; Gen. 49:10; Num. 24:17; Isa. 9:6–7; Ezek. 34:23–24; Mic. 5:2). When the Christ came, wise men sought the "king of the Jews" (Matt. 2:2), and he was crucified as "the King of the Jews" (John 19:18–22). When he comes to judge the earth, we will see that "on his robe and on his thigh he has a name written, King of kings and Lord of lords" (Rev. 19:16).

On this side of the cross and the resurrection, the church has been charged to take up the mission of Christ by donning the mantle of the *munus triplex*, the threefold office of prophet, priest, and king. The charge is phrased in exalted terms that connote the exaltation and privilege of the church's call to world mission. It should be read slowly in order to grasp the magnitude and dimensions of the call: "But you are a chosen race, a royal priesthood, a holy nation, a people for God's own possession, that you may proclaim the excellencies of him who called you out of darkness into his glorious light" (1 Peter 2:9).

The call to the incarnate Christ's threefold ministry is charged with enabling power because we, as God's "chosen race," are in union with him. The exalted Christ remains our prophet, priest, and king, and he delights to enable us to live out the *munus triplex*. Taken corporately, this means that as the church, we are to be about mission locally and across the world. I will discuss mission pastorally (for that is what I am) in the order of the triple office.

The prophetic office. The end result of Peter's call is "that you may proclaim the excellencies of him who called you out of darkness into his glorious light." The call is to prophesy/preach—and this is where the church to be missional must publicly excel both in the church and out into the world. The reading and preaching of the Word must be central to gathered worship. And the preaching must proclaim his "excellencies." In a word, preaching must lift up Christ, which demands a redemptive-historical hermeneutic rooted in the *pactum salutis* and the Christ-centered axis that runs through the covenants in the history, narratives, poetry, and apocalyptic of both testaments. And if preaching is "to proclaim the excellencies of him who called you," then it must be excellent! It must come from the lips of a preacher who has prayerfully mined the riches of the sacred text and invited its truth to harrow his own heart before he dares to preach Christ. Preaching Christ is centripetal, and souls will be drawn to him. It is also centrifugal and missional. As the missional logic of the Scriptures penetrates the hearts of God's people, it will enlarge their hearts to reach out to the lost in their communities and across the world with the glories of the gospel:

> For "everyone who calls on the name of the Lord will be saved."
> How then will they call on him in whom they have not believed?

And how are they to believe in him of whom they have never heard? And how are they to hear without someone preaching? And how are they to preach unless they are sent? As it is written, "How beautiful are the feet of those who preach the good news!" (Rom. 10:13–15)

The priestly office. Peter's call begins by announcing, "But you are a chosen race, a royal priesthood." So we must understand that we have been appointed by God to a priestly ministry to offer up sacrifices of prayer and praise. Here, the primary reference is to the outward missional thrust of one's private prayer life in respect to proclaiming the excellencies of the redeeming work of Christ. Christ commends praying in secret, with plain speech (cf. Matt. 6:5–7). This said, speaking from a pastoral perspective, well-prepared congregational prayers have an immense effect on the prayer life of children and adults alike, as they learn to adore God, confess sin, give thanks, make petition, intercede, ask for illumination of the Word, and pray for missions. As a rule, pastoral/congregational prayers ought to include missional elements: for local ministries in the community, the poor and disenfranchised, the outreach ministries of the church, the evangelization of the peoples where the church's missionaries serve, and the missionaries themselves.

Since public prayer is formative and elevating for a gathered congregation, it is imperative that those who lead do so from the overflow of well-kept, prepared hearts. Seven "musts" can enhance our royal priesthood:

1. We who lead in prayer must have a deep, regular, private communion with God.
2. The emotion that we express in public prayer must be consonant with the feeling that we express in private prayer—we must be real.
3. Apart from personal, family, and confidential matters, our private prayer burdens must inform our public prayer burdens.
4. We must be utterly engaged in our prayers, so that God, not our "audience," fills our horizon.

5. We must ask God to first work in our hearts those things that we would like worked in the hearts of our people.
6. We must be "prayed up" and be prepared when we stand before God's people to lead in prayer.
7. Our hearts must be missional. If they are, over time the hearts of our people will reflect ours.

Private and public exercise of our royal priesthood is essential to the life of a missional church and world evangelization.

The kingly office of the *munus triplex* is implicit in Peter's use of "royal" (*basilios*) as descriptive of the office of priesthood and evocative of both the reign of Christ and our reign with him. The apostle Paul states first in Ephesians that the God of our Lord Jesus Christ "raised him from the dead and seated him at his right hand in the heavenly places, far above all rule and authority and power and dominion, and above every name that is named" (Eph. 1:20–21). Then a few lines later, Paul astonishingly adds that God "made us alive together with Christ . . . and raised us up with him and seated us with him in the heavenly places in Christ Jesus" (Eph. 2:5–6). We, as the redeemed, are presently "raised up and seated" in heaven with the King of kings and Lord of lords! We will "reign forever and ever" (Rev. 22:5) and participate in judging the world (1 Cor. 6:2–3).

Here, in this world, our kingly office is displayed by joyful submission to Christ's sovereign rule in all of life. For us, the Scriptures are sovereign, and inasmuch as we live in accordance with them, we reign under the successive regimes of this fallen world.

The exercise of the kingly office by the leaders of church can never be the exercise of regnant authority, but rather the faithful preaching of the Word, the joyous administration of the sacraments, the living out of the divine order for the home and the church, and the humble exercise of church discipline. The church lives as a missional congregation, "a holy nation, a people for his own possession, that you may proclaim the excellencies of him who called you out of darkness into his marvelous light"—so that the Gentiles "may see your good deeds and glorify God on the day of visitation" (1 Peter 2:9, 12).

The kingly office, lived out, will actualize covenant obedience to the crowning command of the King of the universe: "Go therefore and make disciples of all nations."

These three offices were the province of the first Adam. As a prophet, he possessed a true knowledge of God and spoke truthfully about him and all of creation and life. He was a priest because he communed freely and openly with God in prayer and the "sacrifice" of praise (cf. Heb. 13:15). As a king, he exercised dominion over all creation (Gen. 1:26–28). With the fall, all three offices were cut short. There were recrudescences of the three offices in Israel as godly men assumed these roles, only to fall to false prophets, dishonest priests, and ungodly kings. Yet there were prophecies of one who would come to fulfill the triple office. When Christ came, he came as the second Adam, the perfect prophet, priest, and king, and through these three offices he redeemed his people.

Christ bequeathed his three offices to the covenant community, so that she would proclaim his "excellencies" to the world. The power of the *munus triplex* is evident when the offices of prophet, priest, and king are brought together—so that they enhance one another in a graced bouquet—wafting the aroma of Christ to a lost world.

Select Bibliography on
Mission and Covenant

Aiken, P. "Should Reformed Believers Engage in Spiritual Warfare?" *Puritan Reformed Journal* 7.1 (2015): 245–255.

Allen, R. *Missionary Methods: St. Paul's or Ours?* London: World Dominion Press, 1956.

Bakke, R. *The Urban Christian.* Downers Grove, IL: IVP Academic, 1987.

———. "Urbanization and Evangelism: A Global View." *Word and World* 19.3 (1999): 225–35.

Bavinck, J. H. *An Introduction to the Science of Missions.* Philadelphia: Presbyterian and Reformed, 1960.

Berthoud, P. "The Covenant and the Social Message of Amos." *European Journal of Theology* 14.2 (2005): 99–109.

Blauw, J. *The Missionary Nature of the Church.* New York: McGraw-Hill, 1962.

Blocher, H. *In the Beginning: The Opening Chapters of Genesis.* Leicester: Inter-Varsity Press, 1984.

Boot, J. *The Mission of God: A Manifesto of Hope.* St. Catherines, ON: Freedom Press, 2014.

Bosch, D. J. A. *Spirituality of the Road.* Eugene, OR: Wipf and Stock, 2001.

———. *Transforming Mission: Paradigm Shifts in Theology of Mission.* Maryknoll, NY: Orbis Books, 1991.

———. *Witness to the World: The Christian Mission in Theological Perspective.* Eugene, OR: Wipf and Stock, 2001.

Bredenhof, W. *To Win Our Neighbors for Christ: The Missiology of the Three Forms of Unity.* Grand Rapids: Reformation Heritage Books, 2015.

Conn, H. M. *Eternal Word and Changing Worlds: Theology, Anthropology, and Mission in Trialogue.* Phillipsburg, NJ: P&R Publishing, 2002.

———, ed. *Planting and Growing Urban Churches: From Dream to Reality.* Grand Rapids: Baker Books, 1997.

———, ed. *Theological Perspectives on Church Growth.* Nutley, NJ: Presbyterian and Reformed, 1976.

Conn, H. M., and M. Ortiz. *Urban Ministry: The Kingdom, the City and the People of God.* Downers Grove, IL: InterVarsity Press, 2001.

Conn, H. M., M. Ortiz, and S. S. Baker. *The Urban Face of Mission: Ministering the Gospel in a Diverse and Changing World.* Phillipsburg, NJ: P&R Publishing, 2002.

Cronshaw, D. "Re-envisioning Theological Education and Missional Spirituality." *The Journal of Adult Theological Education* 9.1 (2012): 9–27.

De Ridder, R. R. *The Dispersion of the People of God: The Covenant Basis of Matthew 28:18–20 against the Background of Jewish, Pre-Christian Proselyting and Diaspora, and the Apostleship of Jesus Christ.* Kampen: Kok, 1971.

De Vuijst, J. *Oud en nieuw verbond in de Brief aan de Hebreën.* Kampen: Kok, 1964.

Dowsett, R. "Dry Bones in the West." In *Global Missiology for the 21st Century: The Iguassu Dialogue,* edited by W. D. Taylor, 447–62. Grand Rapids: Baker Academic 2001.

Dumbrell, W. J. *Covenant and Creation: A Theology of Old Testament Covenants.* Carlisle: Paternoster, 1984.

Eitel, K. E., ed. *Missions in Contexts of Violence.* Pasadena, CA: William Carey Library, 2008.

Engelsviken, T. "Missio Dei: The Understanding and Misunderstanding of a Theological Concept in European Churches and Missiology." *International Review of Mission* 92 (2003): 481–97.

Fesko, J. V. *The Trinity and the Covenant of Redemption*. Fearn, UK: Christian Focus, 2016.

Foster, S. J. "The Missiology of Old Testament Covenant." *International Bulletin of Missionary Research* 34.4 (2010): 205–8.

Frost, M. *Exiles: Living Missionally in a Post-Christian Culture*. Peabody, MA: Hendrickson, 2006.

Goheen, M. W. *A Light to the Nations: The Missional Church and the Biblical Story*. Grand Rapids: Baker, 2011.

Goodall, N., ed. *Missions under the Cross*. London: Edinburgh House Press, 1953.

Green, M. *Evangelism in the Early Church*. London: Hodder and Stoughton, 1974.

———. *Evangelism through the Local Church: A Comprehensive Guide to All Aspects of Evangelism*. Nashville: Nelson, 1992.

Guder, D. L., ed. *The Missional Church*. Grand Rapids: Eerdmans, 1998.

Gunton, C. *Christ and Creation*. Carlisle: Paternoster, 1992.

Haykin, M. A. G., and C. J. Robinson Sr. *To the Ends of the Earth: Calvin's Missional Vision and Legacy*. Wheaton, IL: Crossway, 2014.

Hedlund, R. E. *The Mission of the Church in the World*. Grand Rapids: Baker Book House, 1985.

Hesselgrave, D. J. *Planting Churches Cross-Culturally: A Guide for Home and Foreign Missions*. Grand Rapids: Baker Book House, 1980.

Hillers, D. R. *Covenant: The History of a Biblical Idea*. Baltimore: Johns Hopkins University Press, 1969.

Hjalmarson, L., and R. Helland. *Missional Spirituality: Embodying God's Love from the Inside Out*. Downers Grove, IL: IVP Books, 2011.

Hodges, M. L. *The Indigenous Church: A Complete Handbook on How to Grow Young Churches*. Springfield, MI: Gospel Publishing House, 1976.

Horton, M. *Introducing Covenant Theology*. Grand Rapids: Baker, 2006.

Hunsberger, G. R. *Bearing the Witness of the Spirit: Lesslie Newbigin's Theology of Cultural Plurality*. Grand Rapids: Eerdmans, 1998.

———. "Birthing Mission Faithfulness." *International Review of Christian Mission* 92 (2006): 145–53.

Jenkins, P. *The Next Christendom: The Coming of Global Christianity*. Oxford: Oxford University Press, 2002.

Karlberg, M. W. *Covenant Theology in Reformed Perspective*. Eugene, OR: Wipf and Stock, 2000.

———. "The Original State of Adam: Tensions within Reformed Theology." *Evangelical Quarterly* 59:4 (1987): 291–309.

Kline, M. G. *Kingdom Prologue: Genesis Foundations for a Covenantal Worldview*. Eugene, OR: Wipf and Stock, 2006.

———. *The Structure of Biblical Authority*. Grand Rapids: Eerdmans, 1975.

———. *The Treaty of the Great King*. Grand Rapids: Eerdmans, 1972.

Krabill, J. R., W. Sawatsky, and C. E. Van Engen, eds. *Evangelical, Ecumenical, and Anabaptist Missiologies in Conversation*. Maryknoll, NY: Orbis Books, 2006.

Kramer, H. *The Christian Message in a Non-Christian World*. New York: Harper & Bros., 1938.

Kuiper, R. B. *God-Centered Evangelism: A Presentation of the Scriptural Theology of Evangelism*. Grand Rapids: Baker Book House, 1961.

Legrand, L. *The Bible on Culture*. Maryknoll, NY: Orbis Books, 2000.

Lillback, P. A. *The Binding of God: Calvin's Role in the Development of Covenant Theology*. Grand Rapids: Baker, 2001.

———. "Calvin's Interpretation of the History of Salvation: The Continuity and Discontinuity of the Covenant." In *A Theological Guide to Calvin's Institutes: Essays and Analysis*, edited by D. W. Hall and P. A. Lillback, 168–204. Phillipsburg, NJ: P&R Publishing, 2008.

———. "Ursinus' Development of the Covenant of Creation: A Debt to Melanchthon or Calvin?" *Westminster Theological Journal* 43.2 (Spring 1981): 246–88.

Linthicum, R. C. *Building a People of Power: Equipping Churches to Transform Their Communities*. Waynesboro, GA: World Vision, 2005.

————. *City of God, City of Satan: A Biblical Theology of the Urban Church*. Grand Rapids: Zondervan, 1991.

Logan, S. T., ed. *Reformed Means Missional: Following Jesus into the World*. Greensboro, NC: New Growth Press, 2013.

Ma, W. "Theological and Missional Formation in the Context of 'New Christianity.'" *Ecumenical Review* 66.1 (2014): 53–64.

McCarthy, D. J. "Covenant in the Old Testament: The Present State of Inquiry." *Catholic Biblical Quarterly* 27 (1956): 217–40.

————. *Treaty and Covenant: A Study in Form in Ancient Oriental Documents and in the Old Testament*. Rome: Pontifical Institute, 1963.

McGavran, D. A.. *Ethnic Realities and the Church: Lessons from India*. Pasadena, CA: Carey, 1979.

————. *Understanding Church Growth*. Grand Rapids: Eerdmans, 1980.

Mendenhall, G. E. "Ancient Israel and Biblical Law." *The Biblical Archaeologist* 17.a (1954): 26–46.

————. "Covenant Forms in Israelite Tradition." *The Biblical Archaeologist* 17.b (1954): 50–76.

Minnear, P. *Images of the Church in the New Testament*. Philadelphia: Westminster, 1960.

Monsma, M. *Household Evangelism*. Grand Rapids: Board of Evangelism of the Christian Reformed Churches, 1948.

Müller, K. *Missionstheologie*. Berlin: D. Reimer, 1985.

Murray, S. *Church after Christendom*. Carlisle: Paternoster, 2004.

————. *Church Planting: Laying Foundations*. Carlisle: Paternoster, 1998.

————. *Post-Christendom: Church Mission in a Strange New World*. Carlisle: Paternoster, 1998.

Neui, Paul de. "Christian Communitas in the Missio Dei: Living Faithfully in the Tension between Cultural Osmosis and Alienation." *Common Ground Journal* 9.2 (2012): 48–67.

Nevius, J. L. *Methods of Mission Work*. 2nd ed. New York: Foreign Mission Library, 1895.

————. *The Planting and Development of Missionary Churches*. 3rd ed. New York: Foreign Mission Library, 1899.

Newbiggin, L. *Foolishness to the Greeks: Gospel and Western Culture.* Grand Rapids: Eerdmans; London: SPCK, 1986.

———. *The Gospel in a Pluralist Society.* London: SPCK; Grand Rapids: Eerdmans; Geneva: WCC, 1989.

———. *The Household of God: Lectures on the Nature of the Church.* London: SCM, 1953.

———. *Open Secret: An Introduction to the Theology of Mission.* London: SPCK; Grand Rapids: Eerdmans, 1978.

———. *Trinitarian Doctrine for Today's Mission.* London: Edinburgh House Press, 1963.

———. *Truth to Tell: The Gospel as Public Truth.* London: SPCK, 1991.

Niles, D. T. *Upon the Earth: The Mission of God and the Missionary Enterprise of the Churches.* New York: McGraw-Hill, 1962.

Oliphint, K. S. *Covenantal Apologetics: Principles and Practice in Defense of Our Faith.* Wheaton, IL: Crossway, 2013.

Osterhaven, M. E. "Calvin on the Covenant." In *Readings in Calvin's Theology,* edited by Donald K. McKim. Grand Rapids: Baker, 1984.

Piper, J. *Let the Nations Be Glad! The Supremacy of God in Missions.* Grand Rapids: Baker Books, 1993.

Rhodes, S. A. *Where the Nations Meet: The Church in a Multicultural World.* Downers Grove, IL: InterVarsity Press, 1998.

Ridderbos, H. N. *The Coming of the Kingdom.* Philadelphia: Presbyterian and Reformed, 1962.

Robertson, O. P. *The Christ of the Covenants.* Phillipsburg, NJ: Presbyterian and Reformed, 1980.

Roels, S. J., ed. *Reformed Mission in an Age of World Christianity.* Grand Rapids: Calvin College Press, 2011.

Rubingh, E. "Mission in an Urban World." *Evangelical Review of Theology* 11.4 (1987): 369–79.

Schirrmacher, T. *World Mission: Heart of Christianity.* Hamburg: Reformatorischer Verlag Besse, 2008.

Shepherd, N. "The Covenant Context for Evangelism." In *The New Testament Student and Theology,* edited by J. H. Skilton, 51–75. Nutley, NJ: Presbyterian and Reformed, 1976.

Smith, D. W. *Seeking a City with Foundations: Theology for an Urban World*. Nottingham: InterVarsity Press, 2011.

Stott, J. R. *Christian Mission in the Modern World*. Downers Grove, IL: InterVarsity Press, 1975.

———. *Issues Facing Christians Today*. Basingstoke: Marshalls, 1984.

Tiessen, T. L. "The Salvation of the Unevangelized in the Light of God's Covenants." *Evangelical Review of Theology* 36.2 (2012): 231–49.

Van der Waal, C. *Het Nieuwe Testament: Boek van het verbond*. Goes: Oosterbaan & Le Cointre, 1978.

Van der Walt, B. J. *When African and Western Cultures Meet: From Confrontation to Appreciation*. Potchefstroom: Institute for Contemporary Christianity in Africa, 2006.

Van Engen, C. *God's Missionary People: Rethinking the Purpose of the Local Church*. Grand Rapids: Baker Book House, 1993.

Van Gelder, C. "From Corporate Church to Missional Church: The Challenge Facing Congregations Today." *Review and Expositor* 101.3 (2006): 425–50.

Vicedom, G. F. *Missio Dei*. Munich: Chr. Kaiser, 1958.

Vogels, W. *God's Universal Covenant: A Biblical Study*. Ottawa: University of Ottawa Press, 1986.

Vos, G. "The Doctrine of the Covenant in Reformed Theology." In *Redemptive History and Biblical Interpretation: The Shorter Writings of Geerhardus Vos*, edited by R. B. Gaffin, Jr. Phillipsburg, NJ: Presbyterian and Reformed, 1980.

Walls, A. *The Cross-Cultural Process in Christian History*. Maryknoll, NY: Orbis, 2002.

Ward, R. S. *God and Adam: Reformed Theology and the Creation Covenant*. Wantima, Aus.: New Melbourne Press, 2003.

Wells, P. "Eschatology." *Reformed Theological Journal* 24.1 (2008): 59–75.

———. "Story, Eschatology and the Agnus Victor." In *Strangers and Pilgrims on the Earth: Essays in Honour of Abraham van de Beek*, edited by Eduardus Van der Borght and Paul van Geest, 343–56. Leiden: Brill, 2011.

Wielenga, R., and A. König. "Zending: waarom? Verbond als ant-
    woord." *Die Skriflig* 33.2 (1999): 255–71.
Wright, C. J. H. *Knowing Jesus through the Old Testament.* Downers
    Grove, IL: InterVarsity Press, 1992.
———. *The Mission of God: Unlocking the Bible's Grand Narrative.*
    Downer Grove, IL: IVP Academic, 2006.

Contributors

Pierre Berthoud is president of the Faculté Jean Calvin in Aix-en-Provence, France, and president of the Federation of European Evangelical Theologians.

Guilherme Braun is a postdoctoral fellow at the University of Pretoria, South Africa, and a postulant for the ministry of the Igreja Anglicana Reformada do Brasil (IARB).

P. J. (Flip) Buys is research professor of missions at North-West University in Potchefstroom, South Africa, and international director of the World Reformed Fellowship.

Ignatius Wilhelm (Naas) Ferreira is senior lecturer of missiology in the Faculty of Theology at North-West University in Potchefstroom, South Africa.

Davi Charles Gomes is chancellor of Mackenzie Presbyterian University, pastor of the Igreja Presbiteriana Paulistana in São Paulo, Brazil, and a board member of the World Reformed Fellowship.

R. Kent Hughes retired in 2019 as professor of practical theology at Westminster Theological Seminary in Philadelphia, Pennsylvania, USA, and was for many years senior pastor of College Church in Wheaton, Illinois, USA.

Benyamin F. Intan is president of International Reformed Evangelical Seminary in Jakarta, Indonesia, a member of the Council of the World Reformed Fellowship, and a senior editor of *Unio cum Christo* (an international journal of Reformed theology and life).

In Whan Kim is president/vice chancellor at Swaziland Christian University in Mbabane, Swaziland, and a board member of the World Reformed Fellowship.

Peter A. Lillback is president and professor of historical theology and church history at Westminster Theological Seminary in Philadelphia, Pennsylvania, USA, and a senior editor of *Unio cum Christo* (an international journal of Reformed theology and life).

Rob Norris is teaching pastor of Fourth Presbyterian Church in Bethesda, Maryland, USA.

Henk Stoker is professor of apologetics and ethics in the Faculty of Theology at North-West University and vice-rector at the Theological School of the Reformed Churches in Potchefstroom, South Africa, and a member of the Council of the World Reformed Fellowship.

Paul Wells lives in Liverpool, UK, and is professeur émérite of the Faculté Jean Calvin in Aix-en-Provence, France, extraordinary professor at North-West University in Potchefstroom, South Africa, and editor in chief of *Unio cum Christo* (an international journal of Reformed theology and life).

Index of Scripture

Index of Subjects and Names